School-Community Interaction

Richard W. Saxe
The University of Toledo

Introduction By
Robert J. Havighurst
The University of Chicago

McCutchan Publishing Corporation
2526 Grove Street
Berkeley, California 94704

Printed in the United States of America

Library of Congress Catalogue Card
Number—74-13595
ISBN—0-8211-1853-8

TO ROALD F. CAMPBELL

contents

foreword

Suppose an educator at the height of his career had dozed off one evening in the spring of the year 1925, and then, after a long and unexpected slumber, had awakened fifty years later, in 1975. What would surprise this modern Rip Van Winkle most, as he attempted to resume his role of school principal or superintendent of schools? Probably the most surprising and even disturbing experience would be the demands made upon him to relate his school or school system to the community.

As of 1925, the school system had certain responsibilities and functions on which there was general agreement, both in the community and in the school system. The elementary school was for all children. The high school was selective. Some pupils were not good "school material" and would therefore drop out of school when they reached the legal school-leaving age. They could go to work, or serve an apprenticeship in the home until they were ready to take on adult responsibilities. If a young person does not fit into the school patterns, he or she must find another way to grow up.

In this situation, the school administrator was essentially a *director of instruction.* He or she operated within the system to make it work smoothly. The school principal worked with the teachers to find the best ways of using their skills, interests, and qualities of personality. The superintendent worked with the principals in much the same way. Administrators faced inward within an institution that had a fairly well understood and accepted place in the community. The educational system was generally accepted and ignored by the local press, except for the usual notices of the beginning and end of the school year, and the high school athletic program.

To be sure, there was controversy in a few big-city school systems, generally fomented by teachers, who were beginning to organize on behalf of their economic interests. Also, the industrial and business leaders were coming into conflict with the trade unions over the place of vocational training in the school system. Occasionally these events would push the schools into local political controversies.

Now, in 1975, the school system is constantly in the spotlight of public attention and controversy. The large cities lose middle-class residents who move to the suburbs to get what they define as better schooling for their children. All communities, regardless of size, keep practically all of their young people in school until age seventeen. More than three-quarters of young people graduate from high schools. The schools are involved in almost every issue that affects the social health of the community.

Various changes in situations and events have cumulated since 1950 to make the school system more important than it was thought to be in 1925, and also more vulnerable to forces outside of the system that impinge upon it:

The drive for racial integration of students and teachers.

Migration of black and Spanish-American working-class population into the large cities.

High rates of unemployment among youth between the ages of fourteen and nineteen.

The movement for compensatory education, to raise the school performance of children from low-income homes.

Increasing per-pupil costs of education.

Publication of test data for individual schools within a school district.

Tendency to hold the schools responsible for low academic performance of children from low-income homes.

Attacks on conventional schooling by writers who advocate "open schools" or "deschooling."

Rise of the community school movement.

Rise of the "community control of the schools" movement.

The increased militancy of teachers' organizations in asserting their rights as experts to teach according to their experience and wisdom.

CHANGING ROLE OF THE ADMINISTRATOR

An educator of the "old school" is tempted in this situation to say to the public, "You are expecting entirely too much from the school system. You do not understand the importance of the family background of children, in relation to what they can and will learn from the school. You expect the schools to make up for all the evils and weaknesses of modern urban society. We educators can do in three hours a day with average children what we are trained to do—we can teach the basic mental skills and the knowledge about the world of human beings and natural forces that young people need to prepare for college or for work. Why don't you let us do this, and create some other kind of institution to baby-sit for children and youth, to cope with the incorrigibles who disrupt our classrooms, and to induct young people into the labor force?"

Of course, this would not work. The society maintains a child- and youth-serving institution, and adds on one responsibility after another as these emerge. Conceivably, the responsibilities may be so varied that they should be subdivided into several different programs, including a three-hour cognitive development school as a separate one, with separate staff and buildings. Unless something like this comes about, the educational administrator must achieve a new role —that of *expert in school-community relations.*

There are three administrative positions that require a focus on school-community relations. They are: school principal, district superintendent, and general superintendent.

The school principal relates the school to the local community of parents and other citizens. This is something the classroom teacher cannot do, since the teacher works with a relatively small and changing group of pupils and parents, and is not likely to see past this particular group. The principal represents the school in the local community, meets and knows the various interest groups, and provides continuity over a period of years. The principal may have to arbitrate a conflict between one or more teachers and a group of parents. Ideally, however, the principal foresees and avoids such conflicts.

The district superintendent has a larger and generally more diverse community, with fifteen or twenty schools at least, and some variety of ethnic and socioeconomic composition. Ethnic and political pressure groups tend to complain to the district superintendent if they do not approve the situation in a particular school. Furthermore, the district superintendent is the middle-man between the central school administration and the individual school principals. In this role, he may be able to put some flexibility into the policies and rules established by the central authority.

The general superintendent establishes the public relations policy and program, dealing with the press, television, and citywide pressure groups. His role requires him to work effectively with other local government agencies, with the organizations of teachers and principals, and with other employees within the school system.

IMPACT OF COMMUNITY FORCES ON THE SCHOOL SYSTEM

Since about 1960 there have been two major forces working from the outside community on the school system that force the school administrator to become a community relations expert. One is the push for *decentralization* of authority and decision making. Rightly or wrongly, it is widely believed that school systems generally are encumbered by too much bureaucratic red tape and by a centralization of authority in the school administration, which do not serve the local community well. Therefore, it is argued that the central administration in all large school districts should be reduced in power, and more power to make important decisions should go out into district offices and individual schools. Tied with this is the drive to get local citizen participation into the decision making at the district and local school levels.

Decentralization has been pushed by state legislatures, as in the cases of New York City and Detroit, where the large city system has been divided into semi-autonomous districts of smaller size. More often, the central authority (the board of education) delegates some of its authority to districts and to local schools, combined with provision for the election or appointment of community advisory councils. The powers of the advisory councils are often unclear, and remain to be worked out on the basis of experience. For example, does the advisory council have the power to remove a school principal from office or to discharge and appoint teachers?

Here the other force comes into play: namely, the drive for *cultural pluralism,* which means, in effect, that various ethnic and racial groups should be fully served by particular schools. Chicano-oriented schools in a Mexican-American community; Greek-oriented schools in a Greek-American community; Chinese-oriented schools in a Chinese-American community; black-oriented schools in a black community.

Where groups of parents and citizens, organized on these ethnic bases, move into local school advisory councils, there are bound to be demands for removal of principals and teachers who are not of a particular ethnic group, and for ethnic studies in the curriculum; and a school that has more than one ethnic group is likely to become a center of controversy. Or, there may be rival political factions within a given ethnic group.

These forces for cultural pluralism require the most skillful kinds of arbitration and mediation by the local school principal or district superintendent.

These comments on school-community relations and the work of the school administrator may have overstressed the complexity and the difficulty of the contemporary situation. In fact, parents want the best education they can get for their children, and citizens want the best school system. They need leadership from school administrators, and this leadership needs to be skillful, patient, and well-informed about the complex American society of today and tomorrow.

Robert J. Havighurst

Professor of Education and
Human Development
The University of Chicago

preface

There is controversy and even sometimes acrimonious conflict about the proper relationship of schools to their communities. The extent of this controversy and conflict is unprecedented in American public education. It has reached the point that some individuals or groups would abandon schools in favor of other means of education. Others would preserve schools but under different forms of governance that would permit them to have more influence on what the schools do. Hardly anyone votes in approval of the status quo.

It seems that all of these positions are in agreement on one major objective: *the schools must be made to be more responsive.* Obviously, agreement is quickly lost if we begin to specify in what ways the schools shall be responsive, to whom, and at what levels of size (national, regional, state, district, local). Pressures for reform are brought at all levels. Sometimes school administrators find themselves in the middle of conflicting demands from a local constituency and representatives of a larger jurisdiction (e.g., local school community versus district; city district versus metropolitan region).

Educators are poorly prepared emotionally and professionally for the pressures that accompany the changing relationships of schoolmen and their clients. Emotionally they feel betrayed and hurt that their actions and even their intentions are being questioned. Traditionally they have been perceived as the standard bearers of American values. Of course, educators have been attacked from time to time by critics of both the political right and the political left. Invariably, however, "right" (i.e., the educator's point of view) would prevail and most of the public would maintain or reaffirm its confidence in the schools. The phenomenon of the school administrator or teacher being openly and vigorously rejected by his community is new to us and is one that still defies a solution.

Professionally, school administrators have received little guidance and even less support from their line superiors in the educational hierarchy as well as from their mentors in colleges and universities. In effect, they have been thrown unprepared into situations where tried and true methods were almost certain to lead to disaster. As some administrators suffered the early effects of changing expectations, others watched anxiously and counted the months until they could accept an early retirement if the pressures should strike their district. Much has been learned by administrators involved in the struggle for new relationships and there are several case studies of school-community conflict. Unfortunately, detailing the specifics in such conflicts does not prevent the same sequence of events from occurring over and over again like some predictable Greek tragedy.

Perhaps nothing can be done to prepare for change of this magnitude—the forces may be so strong that no strategy can avert tragic consequences for some school administrators. It is to be hoped that this is not the case and the situation has not deteriorated to the extent that it is impossible for administrators to affect the way in which events occur or even to influence the outcome.

We take the latter position—that it is possible for educators to make a difference—and attempt in this book to help educators understand and deal more effectively with school-community interaction. This is an ambitious undertaking but necessary if we maintain that educational administration can be improved by study and analysis.

To enhance the understanding of educators, our study requires an explanation of the way changing conditions have caused some people to perceive well-intentioned educators as unfeeling representatives of a hostile Establishment. One's understanding of the conditions that contribute to the causes of problems should facilitate one's problem solving.

To augment the professional response to changing school-community interaction, we attempt to extract helpful principles and practices from research and actual experience in changing school-community relationships. The principles and practices need to be theoretically and empirically defensible.

We cannot anticipate a *Handbook of School-Community Relations* because the possibilities of situational variance are infinite. However, we should be able to help educators analyze their particular situations in terms of a broad perspective. The insight derived from theory and practice may then be used as a possible guide to administrative action.

The purpose of this book, then, is to describe changes in school-community interaction and to suggest appropriate responses by educators in general, and administrators in particular. We attempt this by attacking the problems of school-community interaction according to the strategy described in the Introduction.

acknowledgments

Many people have communicated with me about their perceptions of school-community interaction. Students in my community relations class read and evaluated each chapter as it was drafted. Colleagues in the department offered many suggestions. Parent partners and volunteers gave me their ideas. Teachers and school administrators were especially helpful in emphasizing the differences between districts and between schools. Newspaper reporters and public relations specialists shared their knowledge. Expert typists deciphered my painful hieroglyphics and homemade shorthand. All of these able people and others not mentioned gave freely of their time and talent because they cared about school-community interaction.

Their good help is gratefully acknowledged. If the results of this effort should be lacking in some respects, the fault is with me, not with those who helped provide the substance for this communication.

The dedication acknowledges a prior and continuing debt to my teacher, Roald F. Campbell.

introduction

We shall maintain that the schools are at a critical period in their history. The organization and many of the methods and procedures grew up to cope with problems of another era. The problems have changed. The schools have not changed sufficiently. There has been an obvious absence of ongoing attempts to improve schools other than by piecemeal, small scale efforts. Much of the energy of educators has been drained off in seeking ways to keep the traditional structure functioning. Pressures from many sources are continuing to force change in schools. Basic to all actions in a time of questioning and faltering confidence is the relationship of schools to their communities, micro- and macro-. This relationship is urgently needed to maintain support and to guide the efforts of educators to bring schools in line with changing conditions. This is a reciprocal relationship that we have termed *school-community relations.*

School-community relations are adversely affected by an organizational phenomenon—bureaucracy—and by psychological factors of educators—attitudes, opinions, interests. Because these define major barriers to favorable community relations, we shall consider each in some detail. This examination will help define problems of community relations.

Attempts to overcome the barriers of bureaucracy and educators' resistance to citizen participation have caused some parents to create groups of like-minded persons to support their mutual cause. Others have sought the help of existing groups that function to secure the goals of one or another special interest. Pressure groups and interest groups of all types will be considered, especially as they operate to influence or attempt to influence public education.

Individuals and pressure groups seek to secure power to influence decision makers. There are several ways of attempting to identify the powerful persons or groups in a community. Ways of gathering these data will be reviewed.

We will then consider several specific areas of community relations beginning with ways of assessing the needs and desires of a community. This will be followed by suggestions of how to discover and apply local community resources to educational problems. Some of the resources will be material, others human. The human resources will cause us to discover what new roles are being created to bring others into active partnership in improving education and, concurrently, community relations.

The ways in which educators communicate with (better, attempt to communicate with) communities will be examined. These will include the practices usually described as "public relations" as well as others that fall within the realm of "community relations" as we shall define the term.

Reactions of the schools to current pressures have been slow in taking shape. Some of these will be studied, especially decentralization and community control. Finally, we consider new ways of involving communities and citizens in the business of their schools without destroying essential prerogatives of educators.

Ideally the book will be read in the same order as the chapters are presented. However, it is possible for each chapter to stand alone so that it may be taken up according to the interests of various readers. Since each chapter does deal with a different aspect of school-community interaction, there is a separate body of literature for each topical area, with a list of suggested readings at the end of each chapter.

Some readers will use this book with a group interested in school-community interaction. They may wish to supplement or validate the central ideas of each chapter by performing some of the suggested activities listed at the ends of chapters. Those listed are merely suggestive of countless ways of testing the author's concepts against the real, specific school-community interaction in the several areas available for study by readers.

Where we have a bias—and we have many—it is identified. One of these biases is that there will not be *an answer* for problems of school-community interaction. There may be *answers*. Answers that suffice for today's problems may be worthless tomorrow. Hence, we commend the continuing study of school-community interaction to educators everywhere.

chapter one

Community Relations: Semantics

> "When I use a word," Humpty Dumpty said, in rather a scornful tone, "it means just what I choose it to mean—neither more nor less."
>
> "The question is," said Alice, "whether you *can* make words mean so many different things."
>
> "The question is," said Humpty Dumpty, "which is to be master—that's all."
>
> Lewis Carroll
> *Alice Through the Looking Glass*

Few aspects of educational administration are defined in so many ways and used with so much ambiguity as *community relations.* Indeed, like words in Alice's Wonderland, *community relations* means what the user wishes it to mean. Unfortunately, only the user and a few of like mind may acknowledge any particular meaning. This lack of a common meaning often leads to misunderstanding and inhibits effective communication. So, we need to begin by considering some of the usages of *community relations.*

PUBLIC RELATIONS DEFINED

Many writers use the terms *community relations* and *public relations* as though they were interchangeable. In fact, some attempts to define community relations immediately become considerations of *public relations* (Hubbell 1970). This would be all right for Humpty Dumpty and, as we shall maintain, sometimes it is all right for Alice and the rest of us as well. That is, in a sense, what is public relations at one level of an educational institution may be much like community relations at another level. This will take some explaining. If, for the moment, we mean by *community relations* all the communication that goes on between schools and their communities and by *public relations* we mean just those deliberate efforts by schools to influence the community's opinion, it is possible to make the case. At local school levels, relationships will predominantly fall in the general meaning taken for *community relations.* The community (and here readers should expect later difficulties with this term) is readily accessible. At the school district level, the community becomes more ephemeral, becomes the city, and the means of reaching it are more likely to be by *public relations*—news releases, television, radio, annual reports.

In this way, because the community of the city school administrator is so large and diverse, emphasis is given to ways of informing and persuading this broad community by means of public relations measures. Here we have made an important distinction. *Public relations* has become only one phase of the broader task of *community relations.* As such, a meaning for public relations will be more easily delineated. Public relations will deal with practices initiated by educators and designed to influence the public; such things as news releases, displays, photography and audiovisual presentations, publications, speeches, and the like. Kindred (1957) provides a definition that, although quite general, includes the essential elements of public relations. School public relations "is a process of communication between the school and community for the purpose of increasing citizen understanding of educational needs and practices and encouraging intelligent citizen interest and cooperation in the work of improving the school" (p. 16).

There is a nationwide organization, the National School Public Relations Association, that enrolls persons concerned with *public relations* as defined above; it is an affiliate of the National Education Association.*

Public relations originating with the schools and seeking to serve their purposes has been almost invariably favorable in its messages about schools. The notable exception is the bond issue campaign

---

* 1201 Sixteenth Street, N.W., Washington, D.C. 20036.

when shortcomings (usually physical) must be acknowledged to justify the requests for greatly increased resources. There is strong evidence of a growing trend to present unfavorable as well as favorable information in public relations releases. Recently the *Chicago Tribune* (10/21/73) featured an article headed: "The Board of Education Admits Much Is Wrong." Despite this trend toward reporting the bad news as well as the good, there is a legacy of disbelief that will certainly linger for a long time. Followers of public relations releases have learned that much has been left unsaid and only the most favorable data are shared with the public.

It is necessary to call attention to another usage of *public relations,* denoting, more often orally than in writing, a general level of public support at a given time. The question of "the superintendent's PR" does not refer to the practices he uses to inform and influence citizens, but to an assessment of the degree of support or opposition for him–to his popularity index.

One way of dealing with this usage of public relations would be to cite data drawn from a survey, data such as those used in the annual Gallup polls. In 1973 Gallup asked: "In recent years has your over-all attitude toward the *public* schools in your community become more favorable or less favorable?" The answers from the national sample were: more favorable, 32 percent; less favorable, 36 percent; no change/no opinion, 32 percent. Gallup then breaks the sample down by groups to show that the attitudes of parents with children in public schools are more favorable than those of parents with children in private schools and that the attitudes of persons with no children in school are becoming less favorable. He also finds, surprisingly, that slightly more professional educators are finding the schools less favorable (41 percent) than more favorable (39 percent) (Gallup 1973). We will need to recall this finding later. For now, our purpose is simply to note the existence of this second, less common, meaning for public relations–an index of over-all acceptance.

Perhaps enough has been said to make clear our usage of public relations. It is one aspect of community relations. That a linguistic analysis could lead one to another conclusion is quite likely, for, after all, which is the greater, "public" or "community"? Nevertheless, we are dealing with the prevailing usage and, like Humpty Dumpty, the words *public relations* mean what we choose them to mean.

MEANING OF SCHOOL-COMMUNITY RELATIONS

Our meaning of *community relations* may be somewhat more inclusive than other meanings. *Community relations will include all the interactions between any element of the school and any element of the community.*

What we really wish to focus on is the participation of citizens in affairs of mutual concern to school people and the community. This participation will run the gamut from the annual open house to community control, from show and tell to paid community aides. The term *community* itself will generally refer to any and all elements of the society (neighborhood, district, town, city) involved with the school for any purpose. When we depart from this global definition of community, we will attempt to be more specific. Generally this will be necessary when discussing what can be characterized as the parent group, that is, those citizens whose children are enrolled in the school or district concerned.

Clearly, this interpretation of community relations includes all activities that fall under public relations as previously defined and much more. Gordon McCloskey, whose careful study has long been the standard work for educators interested in community and/or public relations, seems to agree with the approach we have taken toward the meanings of *community relations* and *public relations*. In a discussion of what name to give to a committee, McCloskey states that:

> "Community Relations Committee" connotes civic unity and cooperative enterprise. Unfortunately, "Public Relations Committee" may connote a high-pressure effort to "sell" an unwanted service. The term "Publicity Committee" overemphasizes one aspect of a sound communication program and may cause some people to believe that educators' purposes are similar to those of irresponsible press agents. [1967, p. 298]

McCloskey is alluding to the negative connotation of public relations, a connotation that has become fairly widespread owing to frequent misuse of the term. *Public relations* was used by one of the principals in the Watergate incident to denote a hostile propaganda barrage: "Mr. Colson referred to the networks as 'the other side' and told Mr. Haldeman, 'I think it is time for us to generate a PR (public relations) campaign against the Democrats and CBS' " (*Toledo Blade* 11/2/73).

Despite such unfortunate associations with public relations, we intend to use the term as previously defined. It is but one phase, and a perfectly acceptable phase, of community relations. Perhaps someday the term will need to be redefined if the misuse continues. Something similar occurred with the word *propaganda* and we had finally to abandon the value-free use of that word for we knew readers would assume that the intent of propaganda is to distort or mislead.

A problem with our definition of community relations is its all-inclusiveness. That is, if the curriculum, as communicated to citizens by pupils, is a matter of concern, that concern becomes community relations. If the cost and the supplier of gym suits or band uniforms become matters that gain the attention of citizens, we are dealing with community relations as well as with the other obvious tasks of finance and pupil personnel. Almost anything that may cross the invisible boundary between school and community (in either direction) is potentially a community relations phenomenon. When interpreted in this fashion, it is extremely difficult to point to anything that may not, under some circumstances, be considered as having to do with community relations. That is exactly what we wish to suggest by the meaning given to *community relations.* Almost nothing happens in a school that is not or cannot become the community's business. Little happens in the community that cannot become the school's business.

If this seems a radical approach to take, it is probably because so many of us (educators) accept the protective wall of anonymity, shored up by apathy and inability to participate, that we associate with parents in giant urban school districts. If we were teaching or administering in small towns or villages, we would not be amazed at the magnitude of the task of community relations as we have defined the term. In small towns we would acknowledge that that is the way it *is.* Whether or not we would acknowledge that that is the way it is *supposed to be,* is an issue that is better postponed until chapter 3, where we can give extended attention to the attitudes of educators—professionals—about community—lay—relations.

Students of community relations recently seem, by implication at least, to give additional support to the broad view of community relations adopted here. For example, Johansen, in his systems approach (1973), shows the essential overlap of the school district and potential subsystems. His flow chart of communication further supports our position that events in one system (the community) *can* become important data for the other system (the school).

Richard Gorton indirectly supports a broad interpretation of community relations in his discussion of a graphic illustration of "Individuals and Groups Which May Hold Expectations for the School's Role." Gorton identifies nineteen generic groups (e.g., taxpayers' associations) that "may possess expectations for the role of the school in regard to any specific or problem" (1972, p. 23).

PROPRIETY OF PROMOTING COMMUNITY RELATIONS

Regardless of how it is defined, there is even an element of controversy about whether it is proper for educators to become involved in attempts to do something about community relations. Obviously, if our preferred meaning of community relations has been accepted, there can be no argument about whether educators choose to participate in attempts to influence community relations. They *are* influencing community relations whenever they do anything in their roles as teachers and administrators. For those favoring other interpretations of the term—especially interpretations that take on more the nature of public relations—there is a valid concern for the propriety of participating in activities deliberately designed to influence community relations.

A recent publication expressed perfectly the ambiguity about deliberate efforts of educators to influence community relations: "School administrators act as though it is not only possible but right to influence public opinion and behavior in the interest of a school's purposes, but they often *talk* and write as though such actions were wrong" (Committee for Informed Detroit Schools n.d.).

The real danger of ambitious efforts to influence public attitudes, aside from a possible waste of resources, is that the process might be confused with the substance, that is, to mount an extensive public information campaign as though the campaign itself could make a difference—regardless of what was actually happening in the schools! It is patently absurd to expect the public relations campaign to improve the schools. Other actions that become the substance of the public relations communications thrust can make the schools better, not public relations. A lawyer addressing a seminar on school-community relations put it this way: "What needs to be changed is not communications, public *appreciation* of what happens on campus, or image, or rapport with the community. What needs to be changed is *what takes place on campus*!" (Weltmer 1973, p. 6)

In view of the particular focus of community relations identified —citizens' participation in school matters—there is ready justification for the propriety of studying and working on community relations. At one time all citizens had a say in the determination of school policy and practice by means of a gathering such as the revered New England town meeting. Even when the growth of towns and cities made this impossible, large boards and large operating committees of boards were devised to attempt to keep the public in close touch with its schools. It was not until after 1800 that the governance of education ceased to be lumped with all other municipal governmental functions. (Campbell [1971, p. 112] puts the date of school government's differentiation from general government at 1827.)

Even when professional superintendents and trained staffs were employed, the unending need of the people to get reliable information about their schools continued. This can best be seen in the rise and proliferation of school surveys (see, for example, American Association of School Administrators 1964; Sears 1925; and Caswell 1929). Today decentralization and community control support our thesis of the people's need and right to be involved with their schools. Tomorrow there may be accountability of various types, free schools, and alternative educational institutions. Whatever develops, it is in the American tradition for people to be informed about their schools and to participate in some ways in the determination of educational policy.

If further justification of the need for citizens' participation in school matters is needed, it can be found in Cremin's *The Genius of American Education* (1965). After describing the strained relationship between educators and citizens, Cremin points out that "the profession is obligated, both in its own interest and in the interest of the service it performs, to assist the public in developing an ever more sophisticated body of opinion about education" (p. 110).

THE WISDOM OF PROMOTION

Even if it is agreed that it is quite proper for administrators to study and engage in community relations, it still may not necessarily be wise to do so. For, as we shall soon see, community relations is literally a two-way street. To implement a program of community relations as conceived in these pages will mean to open the schools in new ways to the participation and influence of citizens—who are not educators.

We intend to examine the traditional attitudes of educators in detail and to provide evidence to support our conclusions. However, to anticipate that argument, it can be asserted here that schoolmen almost instinctively "know" that opening up the school system leads inevitably to increased contacts with citizens, to additional demands, to criticism; in short, opening up leads to trouble. For most schoolmen the ideal climate heretofore would have been one characterized by an apathy tempered by feelings of mild support for the schools. Why then is it prudent to seek a change that must certainly add to demands on the time and talent of educators?

The most compelling argument in support of changing school-community relations is to decrease the vulnerability of schools to a destructive assault by a small, but determined, faction. It is difficult for administrators, even for school boards, to protect the schools from organized attacks.

Militant groups—whether from the right or the left—have found it easy to disrupt schools, take over board meetings and intimidate individuals. Readers who are not already battle scarred veterans of such confrontations, even conflicts, will profit greatly by reading the second half of Tom Wolfe's wicked little book, *Radical Chic and Mau-Mauing the Flak Catchers* (1971). Too often school administrators and board members have to serve as flak catchers, a new and not very happy role.

The point here is that educators would do well to adopt a policy of open school-community relations and engage in practices that enable the bona fide school-community constituency to be aware and involved in the issues so that they, as well as the highly motivated, often skilled faction members, may appropriately influence the outcome. If uninvolved, the broad based constituency is virtually disenfranchised by default when forced to make concessions by a noisy, articulate, organized minority. It is not sufficient for administrators and board members to have a sense of the prevailing majority opinion on controversial policies, practices, and people. A "sense of something" is a poor persuader and a thin shield in a heated confrontation. It will not, by itself, prevail even if it is an accurate assessment of the majority's opinion. Community relations must involve concerned citizens as well as teachers and administrative leaders. It is to be hoped, and would seem logical, that the existence of a body of involved citizens would legitimate school governance and, more important, help educators survive the first vigorous assault by those of another mind.

In the same vein, it seems clear that there is a modern imperative to involve more citizens in school affairs. For reasons known to all of us, there is a crisis in the legitimacy and authority of all of our national institutions: government, school, church, even family. Young people are not alone in questioning the legitimacy of educational programs and even of their duty to support the public schools by their tax monies. Free schools, alternative schools, defeated bond issues and levies are all symptoms of discontent. This lack of confidence in institutions is complicated by the pervasive social problem of mass society: a feeling of powerlessness, of anomie.

Reasoning this way, one feels that institutions, including and especially the schools, need to regain the trust and support once so freely, almost unquestioningly, given. This kind of trust can only be renewed if schools can become more responsive and if people are involved in important ways with matters that concern them. In this way the over-all community may support the schools again as new, mutually advantageous relationships are established. A new sharing and responsiveness can be initiated by opening up school-community relations.

SUMMARY

In this discussion we have noted that problems of meaning confound efforts to discuss community relations. The term *public relations* will be used to refer to that phase of community relations that consists of deliberate efforts by the schools to influence community opinion. *Community relations* refers to all interactions between any element of the school and any element of the community. A particular focus for our purposes will be placed upon the participation of citizens in school affairs.

Elements peculiar to American history and democratic ideology support efforts of educators to affect community relations. It seems both wise and proper to promote good school-community relations.

Recent events mandate a more open approach to community relations if schools are to regain public confidence.

SUGGESTED ACTIVITIES

1. Find out who are the persons given primary responsibility for public relations and community relations in a school district.

2. Ask a superintendent and a principal to rank the tasks of administration (that is, curriculum and instruction, finance and business management, pupil personnel, physical facilities, school-community relations, staff personnel) in order of importance. Predict in advance which one will rank school-community relations higher. Ask then which task the administrator feels most competent to deal with, and which least competent to deal with.

3. From your experience describe briefly an episode or action that you would classify as predominantly a community relations activity. Do the same for public relations.

SUGGESTED READINGS

American Association of School Administrators. *Educational Administration in a Changing Community.* Thirty-Seventh Yearbook. Washington, D.C.: 1959. Chapters 1 and 2.

Jackson, Kathleen O'Brien. *The Politics of School-Community Relations.* Research Analysis Series, number 2. Eugene, Oregon: ERIC Clearinghouse on Educational Management, 1971.

Jones, James J. *School Public Relations.* New York: Center for Applied Research in Education, 1966.

Kindred, Leslie W. *How To Tell the School Story.* Englewood Cliffs, N.J.: Prentice-Hall, 1960. Chapters 10 and 11.

McCloskey, Gordon. *Education and Public Understanding.* 2d ed. New York: Harper & Row, 1967. Chapters 1 and 2.

Rosenberg, Max. "Community Relations—Approaches Educators Use." *The Education Digest* 39, no. 5 (January 1974): 42-44.

Sumption, Merle R., and Engstrom, Yvonne. *School-Community Relations.* New York: McGraw-Hill, 1966. Chapter 1.

REFERENCES

American Association of School Administrators. *Management Surveys for Schools Their Uses and Abuses.* Washington, D.C.: 1964.

Campbell, Roald F.; Bridges, Edwin M.; Corbally, John E.; Nystrand, Raphael O; and Ramseyer, John. *Introduction to Educational Administration.* 4th ed. Boston: Allyn and Bacon, 1971.

Caswell, Hollis. *City School Surveys.* New York: Teachers College, Columbia University, 1929.

Committee for Informed Detroit Schools. "Keep Informed Detroit Schools." Detroit: n.d.

Cremin, Lawrence A. *The Genius of American Education.* New York: Vintage Books, 1965.

Gallup, George H. "Fifth Annual Gallup Poll of Public Attitudes Toward Education." *Phi Delta Kappan* 55, no. 1 (September 1973): 38-51.

Gorton, Richard A. *Conflict, Controversy, and Crisis in School Administration and Supervision: Issues, Cases, and Concepts for the '70's.* Dubuque, Iowa: William C. Brown, 1972.

Hubbell, Ned. "What Is School Community Relations?" *Seminar on School-Community Relations.* ERIC no. ED 044 820. Muncie, Indiana: Indiana Public School Study Council, 1970.

Johansen, John. "Serving the Client System." In *A Systems Approach to Educational Administration,* edited by Robert C. Maxson and Walter E. Sistrunk, pp. 238-255. Dubuque, Iowa: William C. Brown, 1973.

Kindred, Leslie W. *School Public Relations.* Englewood Cliffs, N.J.: Prentice-Hall, 1957.

McCloskey, Gordon. *Education and Public Understanding.* New York: Harper & Row, 1967.

Sears, Jesse B. *The School Survey.* Boston: Houghton Mifflin, 1925.

Toledo Blade 11/2/73. "Memos Reveal White House Plotted Attack on Networks."

Weltmer, Charles L. "A Citizen's Viewpoint on School-Community Relations." In *Citizens, Businessmen, and Educators: The Elements to Better School-Community Relations,* a conference reported by W. Arthur Darling, p. 6. Dayton, Ohio: Institute for the Development of Educational Activities, 1973.

Wolfe, Tom. *Radical Chic and Mau-Mauing the Flak Catchers.* New York: Basic Books, 1971.

chapter two

School District Organization, Bureaucracy & Schools

For forms of government let fools contest;
What'er is best administer'd is best.

Alexander Pope
Essay on Man

In this chapter we shall maintain that schools as presently constituted take on some aspects of bureaucracy. Contrary to the trend apparent in much writing about education, we do not perceive bureaucracy to be at the root of all current problems. The bureaucratic organization at its best or worst cannot be held responsible for some of the incredibly myopic actions of a few members of the educational hierarchy. Despite this perhaps unexpected kind word for what has become a traditional whipping boy, we shall imply that bureaucracy *at its best* is no longer able to respond to current needs in school-community relations. In its typical form it has proved a barrier to effective school-community relations.

BACKGROUND

At first, mothers or relatives or no one taught our children, then there was the dame school. We are told that in colonial days education in New England was characterized by the broad participation of citizens in policy formation. The notion of the town meeting, which dealt with education as with other governmental functions, comes to mind. As towns became more populous and schooling more complex, certain persons accepted particular responsibility for the governance of education. This development, accompanied by the appearance of professional school administrators, eventually grew into the familiar model of the school district. This is usually represented schematically as shown in figure 2-1. The hierarchical arrangement, with its several

FIGURE 2-1. THE TYPICAL MODEL OF A SCHOOL DISTRICT (SIMPLIFIED)

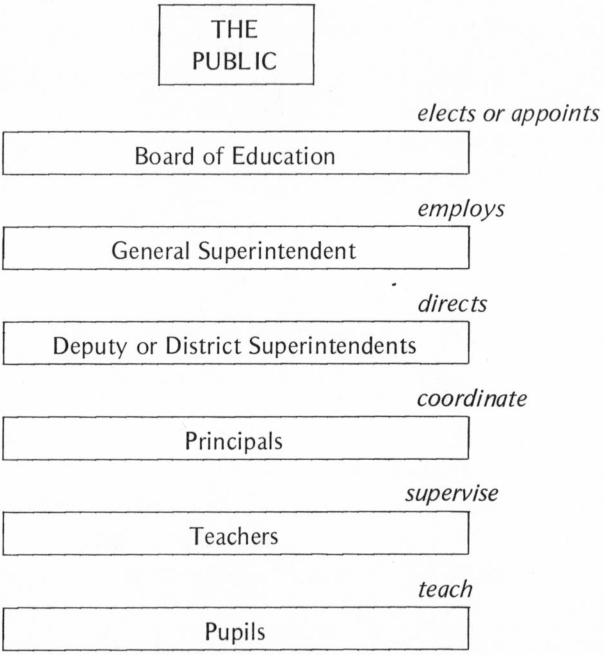

layers and implicit chain of command, is a harbinger of problems associated with bureaucracy. Concurrently with the growth of cities and the beginning of specialization by educators there was an industrial revolution. And there was Max Weber, who is generally given the dubious distinction of founding the concept of the ideal bureaucracy. Bureaucracy is a way of organizing the administration of an enterprise to coordinate the various specialized activities needed to accomplish the goal of the enterprise. Bureaucracies are characterized by:

A high degree of specialization.

Hierarchical authority structure with limited command and responsibility.

Impersonality of relationships among organizational members.

Recruitment of officials on the basis of ability and technical knowledge.

Differentiation of private and official income.

Files and official jurisdictional areas, regularly ordered by rules, policies, regulations, bylaws.

Administration based on written documents.

Administration by stable and comprehensive general policies.*

Because of the problems of growth and the existence in society of ways of dealing with bigness and specialization, the schools followed along and adapted bureaucratic organizational practices. Callahan (1962) and Cremin (1961) describe this relationship of schools to society (the larger community). F. W. Taylor, the founder of the scientific management movement, is acknowledged as having almost as important an influence on education—through society—as Weber. A philosopher and reformer, Mary Parker Follett (see Metcalf and Urwick, eds. 1940), aided by the empirical research of Elton Mayo (see Mayo 1933), launched a counter force to the mechanistic and inhuman approach to education that was growing out of forces fed by Weber (bureaucracy) and Taylor (efficient management). The resulting wave of democratic human relations in education seems to have restrained the Taylor influence but not to have had much impact on the movement toward a better bureaucracy in schools. (For the thrust of the democratic human relations reaction to scientific management, see Koopman et al. 1943.) About 1900 bureaucracy seems to have become a corrective for school reform groups wanting

* For detailed discussions of bureaucracy, see Mouzelis (1967), p. 39; Weber (1958), ch. 8, especially p. 214; and Lane, Corwin, and Monahan (1966), ch. 7.

to abolish the corruption and abuse of patronage associated with ward politics in the sprawling cities. Bureaucracy became the schoolman's attempt to raise the quality of education and to be fair to all students.

It seems then that bureaucracy in schools came about with the best of intentions. It has become so commonplace that some find it almost impossible to conceive of alternatives. Professor Steven Miller of Loyola University in Chicago put it this way: "The paradox is that we cannot function in today's world without burocracy [*sic*]. The educational establishment has to be administered by someone whether we like it or not" (*Chicago Tribune* 10/29/71, sec. 1, p. 20). It is interesting to see how people will organize groups of people to accomplish any task (e.g., the annual charity collection). Almost invariably they break the task down into groups and establish some kind of hierarchy.

Despite our acknowledging Weber as the father of bureaucracy, it is possible to see elements of bureaucracy in antiquity. One of my favorite illustrations is found in the Toledo Art Museum. There, together with a sarcophagus, are the items found enclosed in the Egyptian burial tombs. Among these are small clay figures called "ushebtis." These are to be the servants of the dead in the next world. The intriguing aspect to students of administration is that for every ten ushebtis there is a supervisor or steward in charge.

Evidence of a hierarchy and supervisor can even be found in the Bible where we find the suggestion that third level supervision should have two subordinates; second level, five; and first level, ten. "Thou shalt provide . . . rulers of hundreds, rulers of fifties, and rulers of tens" (Exod. 18:22).

So, bureaucracy is endemic and international. And, almost invariably, it seems associated with stupidity and frustration. We read of Ram Chundar, an Indian in New Delhi denied a passport to attend the funeral of his wife in New Orleans (she died while visiting there with their three children) because: "Now she is dead, what useful purpose will be served by you going there and wasting foreign exchange?" (Hawkins 1970)

In South Viet Nam, fifteen thousand bureaucrats have been ordered out of their offices into a revolutionary new retraining program, which, it is presumed, will teach them to cut red tape. "The program includes eventual decentralization of the government's administrative tangle and, possibly, making it easier to dismiss senior burocrats [*sic*]." The counterbureaucratic campaign seems in order when we learn that presently it takes eighteen months to register a motor bike (*Chicago Tribune* 12/2/73, sec. 2, p. 16).

In a chapter titled, "Red Tape and Registers," a British writer, Gerald Haigh, comments on the sanctity of the attendance register kept in red ink:

> No mistakes were permitted. If you marked present some child who was absent, the only way of putting the matter right was to go out and fetch the absentee in from his sick bed or hospital ward. The risk of epidemics or complications was less to be feared than the wrath of the Head who saw scratching out and alterations in the register. [1972, p. 59]

As we can see from the last quotation there is also a tendency, almost a need, to poke fun at bureaucracy and bureaucrats. All administrators must have read one or another of the books about Parkinson's Laws (Parkinson 1957). Teachers have taken special delight in the administrators in Bel Kaufman's staircases (1964) or Peter's various levels of incompetence (Peter and Hull 1969). This writer has also lampooned the absurdities of bureaucracy as misconceived by American educators (Saxe 1970). Not a month goes by without an addition to the growing body of works critical of bureaucracy—and now see Martin (1973). Yet, it proliferates.

Some of the antipathy toward bureaucracy is a misplaced hostility directed at administrators rather than at the concept of bureaucracy. One of the first thoughts of a citizen bent on economy is to cut out all that waste downtown. "Think of what it would do for the pupil-teacher ratio if all the non-teaching personnel were set to work teaching." When bureaucracy was blamed for the high cost of education in Chicago, Hope Justus, a reporter for the *Chicago Tribune,* gathered the financial information necessary to determine the accuracy of the charge. It was believed that there was no money for teachers because the system was "overburdened with highly paid administrators." Justus found that the 222 members of headquarters staff together accounted for only 0.6 percent of the school budget. And so it went with other accusations of the ill effects of bureaucracy (*Chicago Tribune* 1/19/73).

Although the charge of "too many chiefs and not enough Indians" can sometimes be refuted, other attributes of bureaucracy do seem ill suited to education. To the degree that these attributes exist, it is possible to hypothesize that they may be especially harmful to school-community relations. Bureaucracies are supposed to be impersonal; sometimes schools should not be impersonal. Depersonalization for schools is questionable. The standardization of products is a worthy goal provided one does not talk of pupils and teachers as products. Hierarchy of command is not compatible with professional autonomy. Conformity was once a goal of those who thought that schools should be melting pots. It continues to be part of the bureaucratic model. Some wonder to what extent the inculcation of conformity should be part of the mission of the school. Perhaps the important question we are raising is: To what extent are conformity, depersonalization, and other such functions necessary characteristics of bureaucracy?

PROBLEMS OF TYPICAL SCHOOL DISTRICT ORGANIZATION

Since our purpose here is not to consider modifications of the bureaucratic model but to point out ways in which bureaucratically organized schools are barriers to good school-community relations, considerations of other models must be put off until the final section of the book. It is necessary now to review the typical model of school organization presented in figure 2-1.

In school systems functioning according to figure 2-1, the citizen was to be represented by the elected or appointed board of education. In theory the individual participation of the town meeting model was replaced, in the typical model, by delegates or representatives. Of course the citizen, particularly the parent of a school pupil, also had direct relationships with administrators and teachers at the local school building level. These relationships were circumscribed by the concept of professionalism and the tenets of bureaucracy, which, accompanying the typical model, structure the roles of educators and citizens. The educator is the professional responsible to other professionals who are ultimately responsible to the representative board. The citizen does not meet the professional at the building level to discuss objectives. These are determined at the top of the organizational chart.

In effect, there is nothing in the model to guide or explain the role of citizens at the building level. There is a general dictum that school administrators should "have good public relations." Sometimes the term "community relations" may be used. In either case it may be interpreted to mean only that the building administrators should prevent anything that would lead to attention that might be unfavorable or even embarrassing to the superordinate school administrators. This is an extremely negative view of the matter, but I believe it is a fair statement of the case and indicates the absence of a working model or conceptual design to guide administrators and the public.

At any rate, there is this general notion that local administrators should cultivate cordial rather than hostile relationships with citizens. This condition is, however, effectively neutralized by elements of the bureaucratic professional model. Educators deal with parents from a position of superior knowledge and status and they are, as bureaucrats, supposed to be unemotional and detached. A superior bureaucrat is not ideally suited to establishing rapport.

Another negative aspect of the local school-community relations climate is caused by the administrator's need to protect pupils and to preserve a safe environment for learning. This is evidenced by placards such as those reproduced in figures 2-2 and 2-3. Even though the wording in such signs could be improved upon, the intended message remains: Keep Out! Administrators in giant urban schools have even found it necessary to station uniformed guards to enforce the message of the signs. Mechanisms such as this help preserve a learning environment of sorts (an island, an oasis?). They also create a schism between school and community. They intimidate citizens and discourage visitors. Figure 2-4 shows one principal's attempt to soften the tone of the message, which he embellished with a drawing of a cartoon character, as well.

If the attitude of the public schools toward parents is merely restrictive, it is well-nigh prohibitive to other citizens. Clearly they do not belong and the burden is theirs to show cause why they should pause on school premises. This is quite proper for, according to the typical model, there is no valid role for any adult other than a parent or an employee in the school environment. The *public* is shown once, and only once, at the top of the figure where it is placed to select a representative school board.

Adding to the difficulty of the administrator's task at the building level is the teachers' seldom-voiced but quite real fear of parents. This is related to elements of professionalism, i.e., the professional cannot be questioned by the client in matters professional. But,

FIGURE 2-2 VISITORS SIGN—OHIO

ALL VISITORS
MUST REPORT TO THE PRINCIPAL'S OFFICE

VISITORS—STATE STATUTE 2917.21.1 OF THE OHIO CODE PROHIBITS THE TRESPASSING ON SCHOOL PROPERTY. THIS REGULATION PERTAINS TO THE BUILDING AND GROUNDS.

FIGURE 2-3 VISITORS SIGN—CHICAGO

Welcome

Parents and other visitors on school business are always welcome in the Chicago Public Schools. Please go directly to the office of the principal.

JAMES F. REDMOND
General Superintendent of Schools

Note: "A person commits disorderly conduct when he knowingly: (1) Does any act in such unreasonable manner as to alarm or disturb another and to provoke a breach of the peace; . . . A person convicted of a violation . . . shall be fined not to exceed $500 . . ."

Criminal Code of Illinois
Ch. 38, Par. 26-1 (Ill. Rev. Stat. 1967)

FIGURE 2-4 HOMEMADE VISITORS SIGN

Welcome—
We're glad you
came, but please report
to the office.

NOTE: The formal signs required by law were also displayed but there were fewer of them and they were smaller.

because education is often viewed as a pseudoprofession, the professional is not really protected from his clients by the intricate mysteries of his calling. Anyone can understand and discuss education. So, the teacher, not having a secure professional armor, is vulnerable to the parents of his assigned clients (Saxe 1969).

Teachers in this situation look to administrators to protect them from parents. And, because teaching is so far from being a science, the teacher expects precisely that the administrator will back him in all situations, whether he has acted wisely or unwisely, rightly or wrongly. The belief among teachers is that a united front must be presented to outsiders and that any criticism of the teacher that the administrator might have must be delayed until the confrontation is over and then given in strictest confidence. Such behavior by administrators will be perceived as loyal and good by teachers.

The attitude of teachers toward parents is illustrated by a recent headline: "New York Teachers to Walk Out if Parents Walk In" (*Educators Negotiating Service* 7/1/72). This refers to a new union policy that provides that "if a group attempts to enter a classroom, the teacher shall, first, notify the principal that, unless the intruders leave immediately, no teacher will be able to remain in the classroom." The policy could permit groups to observe teachers maintaining surveillance over pupils but not teaching them, the purpose being to prevent community boards or principals from allowing groups of parents to observe and evaluate.

Much more could be said about the built-in rigidity of the typical model, which, though it protects the school system from isolated attacks, fails to allow local school units to respond appropriately to changing situations. Concerns of individuals or groups that cannot be accommodated at the local level must be passed, like the ubiquitous bucks they are, up the hierarchy to the top. Or they may be shifted directly from the local school to the top. However, at the top they are quite properly perceived as local and perhaps peculiar to one or only a few individuals or schools. And the top must deal with the broad perspective.

Thus, we have a stalemate of sorts built into the typical model. Local problems are out of place at the top but the local level does not seem capable of taking the initiative to solve them. When such problems do reach the top (and there are countless ways in which they can be diverted on the tortuous route) they are usually routed back down through the levels of the organization chart for appropriate action. One cannot explain precisely how or even where it happens, but somewhere in this rerouting, there is invariably added an implication that each level is being censured (mildly or severely depending upon circumstances) for disturbing the equilibrium of the higher levels. Again this is dysfunctional in the typical model. The previously mentioned general policy to refrain from rocking the boat, to grease the squeaking wheel, or to oil the troubled waters implies that something must be done to remove the pressure (threat?) that has found its way to the top. However, the addition of explicit or implicit criticism of the levels intervening between the top and the point of pressure creates hostility toward the offending citizen who started the whole thing. This hostility, whether communicated overtly or covertly by the school administrator who deals with the citizen, creates tension and distrust that exacerbate the situation and nullify the intent of the general desire for "good" community relations.

There is a procedure that throws much light on this malfunction of the typical model. It is the procedure of "going over the head" of an individual at any level in the organizational chart. The model suggests (a better word might be *requires*) that communications proceed "through the channels." When levels are bypassed, the model has been circumvented and, quite naturally, this is somewhat embarrassing to all those who, by virtue of their positions in the organization, must preserve and use the model.

BUREAUCRACY MISPERCEIVED

We shall come back to the general problems of the citizens' access to schools when we examine decentralization, community control, and new models for citizen participation. For now, it should be noted that the prevailing model of district organization is similar to that suggested by figure 2-1. (For a complete description of the typical model of organization, see Griffiths et al. 1962, p. 21.) The other ways in which bureaucratic procedures are harmful to community relations will be discussed throughout the book. However, since our discussion has been mainly theoretical to this point, it is necessary to introduce a few specific instances to put this chapter in its proper perspective.

The first incident can be titled: "Thirty days have September, April, June, and November, except bureaucrats have only twenty-eight." The essence of the incident is a rule that pupils cannot be absent more than a specified number of days and still receive credit for the term. The seventh grade pupil in question underwent emergency surgery to repair an inguinal hernia and was out of school for three weeks. The school authorities were fully informed of all developments and his classmates picked up assignments that were completed and returned by the recuperating pupil. Upon the pupil's return to school, his parent was immediately and officially informed that the child would have to repeat the grade because his attendance record showed excessive absences.

We need not pause here to examine all of the ramifications of the incident. Readers merely need to know that there was no malice intended to the pupil or his parents. There was no previous pattern of problems to explain what seems to be a clear case of arbitrary action. The sole explanation lies in the existence of a rule and the unemotional, detached decision made when a bureaucrat applies the general rule to a particular case.

A second case involving absence from school adds a new dimension to one's understanding of the simplistic, dispassionate decision making of a bureaucrat. This incident may be captioned: "Insult and Injury." A freshman in high school suffered a serious fracture during wrestling practice while competing against a boy in a heavier weight class as a favor to the coach and to the other boy who needed an opponent. Upon his first day back at school (with his arm in a cast) after hospitalization and recuperation, the student was given a test by his algebra teacher. The ensuing low mark was duly recorded and weighed against him in the subsequent cumulative average grades he obtained throughout the year.

Without considering possible alternative procedures open to the algebra teacher, we need to understand the unemotional, fearlessness of this teacher-bureaucrat who did not hesitate to place the administration and his colleague, the wrestling coach, in serious jeopardy. Coach and administration were vulnerable for several reasons, most important for suggesting that the student compete out of his weight class. Even with the good will of the injured student and his parents, coach and administration would be fortunate to weather the incident unscathed by legal action or official sanction. The algebra teacher knew all that but he was giving a test that day and bureaucrats have to "call them as they see them." Again, it is necessary that readers believe that there is no reason to suppose that the algebra teacher harbored malice toward any of the parties potentially injured by his adherence to procedure.

SUMMARY

In this chapter we have demonstrated that the typical organization of school districts does not provide adequate means for citizens to participate. The absence of these means leads to situations in which citizens are rebuffed by schools and frustrated in their legitimate concerns.

Elements of bureaucracy are a part of the school organization model. Although intended to increase the quality of education and ensure fair treatment for all, the ritualistic observance of bureaucratic rules and procedures can lead to incidents that may cause irreparable harm to school-community relations. There are ways of living within this system and there are alternatives to the system. We shall consider both of these palliatives to the dismal situation we have portrayed in these pages.

SUGGESTED ACTIVITIES

1. Draw a schematic model (similar to figure 2-1) to represent the organization of a school or district with which you are familiar.

2. Visit a school or school district office building and see if you can find their version of a "Visitors Sign." Copy down the exact wording of the sign. Show it to some parents of school children and find out how they perceive it. Try to design a better wording for such a sign. Find out how parents perceive your version.

3. Visit any bureaucratically organized agency on a real, but simple, errand (the drivers license agency to obtain a booklet of rules of the road; a post office to inquire the price of one ounce of first class mail to Tanzania). Then visit the office of your local school or central office on a similar errand (to find out, for instance, what date kindergarten pupils may be enrolled; if Russian is offered as a foreign language in any high school). Com-

pare the two visits, including the physical arrangements and your treatment by the person responding to your query. In what ways were the two experiences similar? How might you improve on the response of the educational institution? What are the reasons behind your suggestions?

SUGGESTED READINGS

Anderson, James G. *Bureaucracy in Education.* Baltimore, Maryland: Johns Hopkins Press, 1968.

Brubaker, Dale L., and Nelson, Roland H., Jr. *Creative Survival in Educational Bureaucracies.* Berkeley, California: McCutchan, 1974.

Burnham, James. *The Managerial Revolution.* Bloomington, Indiana: Indiana University Press, 1941.

Callahan, Raymond E. *Education and the Cult of Efficiency.* Chicago: University of Chicago Press, 1962.

Meyers, Russell W. "Bureaucratic Theory and Schools." *Administrator's Notebook* 20, no. 5 (January 1972).

Page, Martin. *The Yam Factor.* Garden City, N.J.: Doubleday, 1972.

Royko, Mike. *Boss.* New York: E. P. Dutton, 1971.

Saxe, Richard W. *Schools Don't Change.* New York: Philosophical Library, 1967.

REFERENCES

Callahan, Raymond E. *Education and the Cult of Efficiency.* Chicago: University of Chicago Press, 1962.

Chicago Tribune, 10/29/71, sec. 1, p. 20. "Bureaucracy and Chicago Schools."

———, 1/19/73. "Bureaucracy Costs of City's Schools."

———, 12/2/73, sec. 2, p. 16. "Retraining South Viet Nam's Bureaucrats: Back to Boot Camp."

Cremin, Lawrence A. *Transformation of the School.* New York: Knopf, 1961.

Educators Negotiating Service, 1 July 1972, p. 193.

Griffiths, Daniel; Clark, David; Wynn, Richard; and Iannaccone, Laurence. *Organizing Schools for Effective Education.* Danville, Ill.: The Interstate, 1962.

Haigh, Gerald. *Beginning Teaching.* London: Pitman Education Library, 1972.

Hawkins, Frank N., Jr. "Bureaucracy Impeding Progress in India." *Pittsburgh Post-Gazette,* 18 November 1970.

Kaufman, Bel. *Up the Down Staircase.* Englewood Cliffs, N.J.: Prentice-Hall, 1964.

Koopman, G. Robert; Misner, Paul; and Miel, Alice. *Democracy in School Administration.* New York: Appleton-Century-Crofts, 1943.

Lane, Willard R.; Corwin, Ronald G.; and Monahan, William G. *Foundations of Educational Administration.* New York: Macmillan, 1966.

Martin, Thomas L., Jr. *Malice in Blunderland.* New York: McGraw-Hill, 1973.

Mayo, Elton. *The Human Problems of an Industrial Civilization.* Boston: Harvard Business School, 1933.

Metcalf, H., and Urwick, L., eds. *Dynamic Administration: The Collected Papers of Mary Parker Follett.* New York: Harper, 1940.

Mouzelis, Nicos P. *Organization and Bureaucracy: An Analysis of Modern Theories.* Chicago: Aldine, 1967.

Parkinson, C. Northcote. *Parkinson's Law.* Boston: Houghton Mifflin, 1957.

Peter, Dr. Laurence J., and Hull, Raymond. *The Peter Principle.* New York: William Morrow, 1969.

Saxe, Richard W. "An Unstudied Problem: Parent Visiting." *The Educational Forum* 33, no. 2 (January 1969): 241-245.

———. "Toward a Feary of Administration." *National Elementary Principal* 49 (April 1970): 26-30.

Weber, Max. *Essays in Sociology.* Translated by H. H. Gerth and C. Wright Mills. New York: Oxford University Press, 1958.

chapter three

Educators' Opinions of Community Relations

He who can, does. He who cannot teaches.

George Bernard Shaw

One of the no-longer-hidden problems of school-community relations is the attitude of educators toward the "lay" community. We shall maintain that educators in general view the participation of citizens with a mixture of resentment and apprehension, educational rhetoric to the contrary. The public, for its part, returns both of these attitudes in kind. It fears the professional and the persons who presume to assess the worthiness of its progeny. Moreover, there is deep in the American tradition a distrust of the academic, an anti-intellectualism, and there is always the opinion, well expressed by Shaw, whom we quoted. (His jibe has been extended to colleges of education as: "Those who can't teach, teach teachers." Here perversely we see that educators are castigated by those with anti-intellectual values at the same time as they are demeaned for their lack of intellect.) So, despite all the campaign oratory about "partners," the school-community relationship is in some respects a shotgun wedding.

PROFESSIONALISM AND THE VESTED INTERESTS OF TEACHERS

Teachers have good reason to be sensitive to citizens' intrusions into educational affairs. Only recently have teachers attained a position of relative power in educational decision making. They have a long history as menials. The collective memory of teachers goes back past Pete Dixon, Mr. Peepers, Miss Brooks, Miss Dove, and Ichabod Crane to a time when teacher-bondservants were offered at a lower price than craftsmen—often without buyers. At long last, teachers abandoned their passive, reacting stance and assumed a more acting, initiating posture. When they did this, they discovered what they should have known all along, that their adversaries were not the administrators but the citizens—parents of school children and others.

Even at this "sophisticated" age we find pervasive—although not completely successful—attempts to create a new rhetoric that proclaims a coalition of parents and teachers against their adversary the administrator. Arnstein, writing for the Association of Supervision and Curriculum Development, argues that "if any significant change is due to appear in education, it is not to be sought from boards of education or from school administrators. If it comes at all, it can come only from those who are most directly involved in the processes of education and most directly affected by those processes: the teachers, the students and the local parents" (1971, p. 25).

Much of the radical rhetoric, after denigrating everything that happens in schools, attempts to salvage something for the new free schools advocated by assuming that there is an alliance between parents and teachers. The events at Ocean Hill-Brownsville destroy this rhetoric with harsh empirical data. (See, for example, Carter 1971.)

If liberal reformers and would-be revolutionaries have not grasped the realities of the controversy about power distribution in educational governance, the organized teachers' leaders have. They know that community control would cost them hard-won privileges. (Several of Albert Shanker's weekly columns in the *New York Times* present the position of the American Federation of Teachers on community control and the participation of citizens; see, for instance, "Continuing Conflict in Brownsville," *New York Times* 18 November 1973.) When we leave the issue of power and self-interest, we find another obstacle in the concept of professionalism. Whether or not teaching is a profession can be argued elsewhere. The point here is that, to the extent that teaching is a profession, the professional and his professional reference groups determine good practice —not the clients. In view of their long history as poor but (probably) worthy public servants, teachers, not surprisingly, may wish to take advantage of whatever perquisites accompany professional status. The perquisites, we have said, can be argued about elsewhere but, for an early review of the issue, see Lieberman (1956) and then Brenton (1970). Among these perquisites is being allowed the status of experts.

Certainly leaders of minority groups have also understood the new adversary relationships to the organized teaching profession. We need to say more about this in discussions of community control and decentralization. Aside from this issue, we have some evidence that, especially in inner-city schools, parents and teachers do not want the same things for the community and for the pupils. In his study, Harry Gottesfeld (1969) found important differences of opinion between teachers and parents about community involvement and the need for strict discipline.

A statement by one inner-city parent will help to show the changing attitude of some persons toward teachers.

> Like I say, I live by the school but I don't send my children there. They go to a school where the teachers are a little older. I feel many of the teachers are just too young. They don't have enough experience of life to know how to treat children, and especially Black and Puerto Rican children. . . . Many of them just don't know about Black children or understand the community. I think they come to learn but they're supposed to be there to teach! [Mirthes 1972, p. 20]

The annual Gallup polls continually reflect differences in thinking between educators as a group and others who are not educators. (See, for example, Gallup 1973.) The growing pressure for accountability from all classes of school patrons is the clearest sign of the lack of harmony between the organized teaching profession and citizens. Here, again, teachers have a sound basis for their stand. They know, if others do not, that even at this late date, it is impossible to secure agreement about what is good teaching. Moreover, teachers recognize that they do not know definitively what is the best teaching as a surgeon knows his operation is correct or a lawyer that his brief is complete. They certainly know that their administrators do not know and they are not about to trust citizens to assess their teaching. They will not even trust one another to evaluate their teaching! But the pressures for accountability seem irresistible, so the issue is far from settled. Clearly, however, it is an issue that reveals the schism between teachers and citizens. Accountability was an issue in the lengthy Detroit teachers strike; see *New York Times* 10/7/73.

A speaker at a convention of the American Association of School Administrators criticized educators in general about their attitudes toward parents:

> You would think . . . that the evidence of the importance of the home to the success of children in school would lead administrators and teachers to relate more closely with parents. Instead you find teacher union contracts providing that a teacher may not be asked to confer with parents more than once a year. Some contracts rule out any obligation to call on parents. A principal no longer *can* suggest that teachers participate in PTA's because it's not in their contract. [Boutwell 1971, p. 5]

ADMINISTRATORS IN THE MIDDLE

The preceding quotation serves as a good introduction to a consideration of administrators' attitudes. The administrator is truly "the man in the middle." We are always wary of dealing in clichés because, at least in this chapter, one of our goals is to raise serious questions about some clichés in education, e.g., that parents and teachers are natural partners; the unity of purpose of parents and teachers; that all are concerned only with good of the child. Nevertheless, we describe the administrator as the "man in the middle" because he finds himself between a pair of legitimate demands: teachers demand professional authority to determine the methods of teaching, pupil relations, assessment, etc., and parents and the community demand the democratic right to affect the processes and participate in the governance of "their" schools. In this role he serves as an arbiter and sometimes as a negotiator. If he is not successful in his negotiations, he can be accused either of abusing professional privileges (of teachers) or denying legitimate educational concerns (of parents and community). Often in this apparent dilemma the administrator can, if he is trusted and has acquired a substantial bank of "idiosyncrasy credits," persuade one of the parties to the disagreement to make appropriate concessions. Idiosyncrasy credits are, according to Hollander (1964, p. 12), credits accumulated by a leader by his performing as a member of a group. These credits the leader may "spend" to innovate in attempting to meet the goals of the institution.

For example, faced with the likelihood of the parents' refusing to pay for additional work materials required by teachers and the likelihood that the teachers will insist (and threaten sanctions for noncompliance) that the materials (i.e., the parents' money) are essential, the administrator is in an unenviable position. His decision of what action to take will be an analysis of best practice and feasibility; "ideal" solutions seldom being tenable. Administrators must negotiate the best possible solution, the solution that, given present limitations, is the closest approximation of the ideal. Simon (1965, pp. xxv, xvi) coined a set of terms that nicely describe the nuances of finding the best feasible solution. A "maximizing" decision is one in which the best alternative is selected from among all the possibilities available. A "satisficing" decision is one that is satisfactory, one that, given all the ambiguities of the real world, will do. Needless to say, administrative men, according to Simon, must usually "satisfice" rather than maximize.

In order to secure the best possible solution, the administrator, using Hollander's idiosyncrasy credit notion, cashes in some of the credits he has earned by his previous behavior. In effect, if he asks the parents to honor the request to purchase additional materials, they may be persuaded to do so because of the administrator's credits. In effect, they are saying "OK, you have done several very good things for our children, so we will go along with you on this request for extra money." Conversely, if the administrator asks that the teachers withdraw their request for additional funds, they acquiesce because, they might reason: "OK, you have really helped us accomplish a lot of our objectives, so we owe you this one."

Analyzing the hypothetical issue in this way, we have the advantage of emphasizing the central role of the administrator. Neither side (teachers or parents) needs to have acknowledged the superiority of the other's position. The decision, if arrived at in this fashion, belongs to the administrator as well as to the other parties. Despite the fact that he has "earned" the right to influence the decision, he now has future credit vested in how the solution works out for all concerned. Finally, administrators with no credits in their bank may have to "borrow" influence with implicit or explicit good deeds in the future.

In order to make our point, we have deliberately ignored other ways of dealing with the issue. For one thing, the administrator could attempt to stay clear of the controversy. Or he might seek to avoid such disputes by convening a group to formulate a policy governing conditions and amounts of future assessments for additional funds. He might also rule according to his evaluation of the soundness of the plan regardless of whether it, in effect, alienated one party or another to the argument and so let the chips fall where they may. "Be sure you are right and then full steam ahead." Or he might determine which group is the more powerful and accede to its demands.

It is to be hoped, even as the administrator is spending idiosyncrasy credits to influence a solution, that he would go beyond "satisficing" and work toward a solution that would take on the characteristics of a Mary Parker Follett "integrating" decision—one that includes the desires of both parties and is, in fact, a gain for each. (Bertram Gross (1964) provides a succinct analysis of Mary Parker Follett's concepts.) Integrating decisions are contrasted with domination and compromise. In the example about the extra money, we have already alluded to a decision by domination. A compromise would be to reduce the amount of funds required by half. An integrating decision might find parents contributing services or material resources better than those to be purchased but at no additional cost.

Since our focus at the moment is on the attitudes of administrators toward community relations, this is not the place to deal with the strategy and tactics of creating and implementing new relationships. We have developed the theme of administrator as man in the middle—between teachers and the community. We consider now the administrator as being in the middle between teachers and students.

The administrator, whenever he is brought into a dispute by either a teacher or a student, is again in the position of an arbiter who becomes a participant in the decision, once it is made. Unless it is really a routine decision where the administrator's participation is more ceremonial than anything else, his actions will, in effect, make new policy, strengthen existing policies or change policies that affect community relations.

Suppose, for example, that a teacher decides to withhold the grade of a student who has completed all course requirements except for a homework assignment. A decision for the teacher is to confirm the professional autonomy of the teacher, but at the cost of seeming unconcerned with student interests. Supporting the student would indicate an appreciation for individual differences but might well alienate many teachers who would perceive it as an appalling lack of support for them. Perhaps the administrator could engineer another Follett integrating solution and use the dispute as a vehicle to work with the faculty to design alternative programs that provide for individual differences. Realistically ("satisficing"?) we cannot expect happy endings to all such controversies. (What would Solomon have done if both mothers had been prepared to relinquish the child rather than settle for half?) The administrator is, once again, in the middle.

Should additional examples of the student-teacher issue be needed, they are easily found. What about the student who cannot receive a grade in physical education until she "makes up" twenty showers?* Then there is the nasty problem of denying an educational experience (a pleasant field trip) to a student because his conduct suggests that he is a bad risk.†

If we consider an administrator at a middle level he is likely to find himself in the middle between the central administration (the superintendent, and the board) and teachers or any other group at the building level. The manner in which a principal conveys an unpopular directive to others has an important influence on the way it is received and implemented. Principals disseminating a contract, self-assessment teacher evaluation scheme (a procedure intended to improve teaching without causing anxiety among the teachers) were poorly prepared for the general panic and hostility generated by the scheme. They would be rare models of loyalty if they did not at least imply that the plan was none of their doing and, by putting the responsibility on their superiors, retain their rapport with the teachers.

One principal found himself in a position of conflict between central administration and parents about a systemwide directive to collect information from parents to support a request for additional federal money available to impacted areas. In his estimation the request was a needless invasion of privacy. He refused to comply and was, as a result, removed from his position for insubordination. The community demonstrated to protest his removal (Rankin 1972).

---

* The feminine pronoun is used here because the example was furnished by a young lady who believed the showers would "ruin her hair."

† Any educator knows the masculine pronoun is appropriate here, and not for reasons of style.

Another principal found himself between the central administration (the athletic commission), students, and the community. When sanctions were applied against the football team's supporters for fighting and vandalism after the game, the principal led community protests against the sanctions. Happily, this principal survived the controversy.* He was more fortunate than a superintendent who came between his board and teachers. The board had ordered the superintendent in Ridgefield, Connecticut, to discipline teachers for using controversial books. The superintendent was fired when he refused (*Chicago Tribune* 3/2/73). More will be said about the problem of divided allegiance when we consider decentralization and models of citizen participation.

The role of the superintendent as man in the middle is represented in figure 3-1. It shows the superintendent as a link between other

FIGURE 3-1 THE SUPERINTENDENT AS MAN IN THE MIDDLE

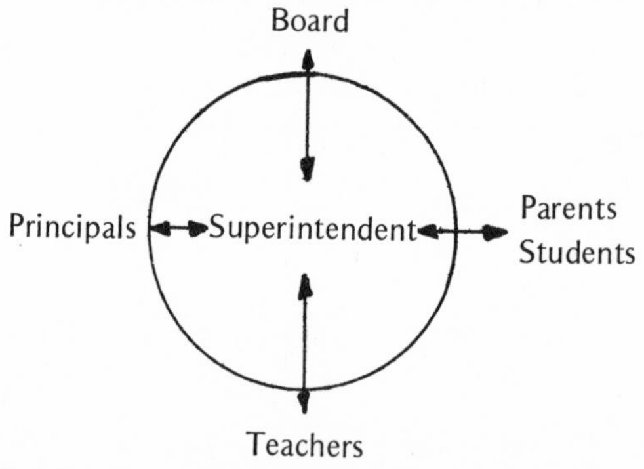

groups for some purposes. Of course, many of the groups and others that we could place on the circle can and do communicate directly with one another. However, when there is a dispute, it is the superintendent who is called upon to arrange a solution. The superintend-

* The disorders involved supporters of Scott High School and Central Catholic High School, both in Toledo, Ohio. Scott was placed on probation while no action was taken against Central Catholic. Due process was an issue in the controversy.

ent is generally placed in the central position for systemwide issues. However, he may be brought into the same role on appeal from a local situation.

In the local (school building) situation it is the principal who is in the middle as shown in figure 3-2. The relationships at the local level

FIGURE 3-2 THE PRINCIPAL AS MAN IN THE MIDDLE

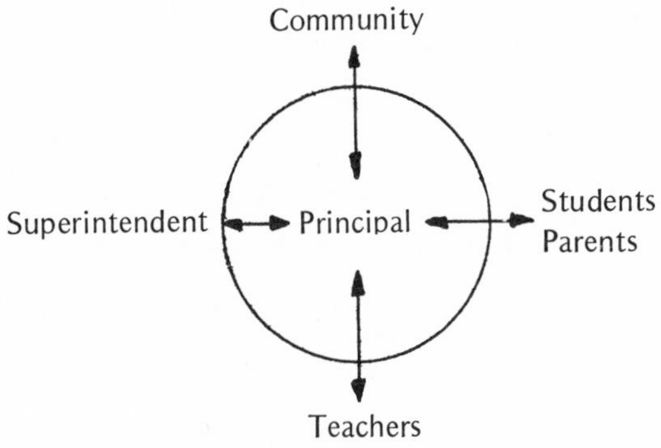

are, in many ways, analogous to the systemwide relationships. In some ways, the principal deals with the same groups, only on the local level, as the superintendent. If the community shown in figure 3-2 should be formalized and represented by a regularly constituted board of control, there would be a parallel to the systemwide board of education. There is, however, nothing analogous to the line relationship of principal as subordinate to superintendent to be found in the systemwide scheme and that explains the dilemmas of the principals in Chicago and Toledo who discovered that there were important differences between the local and the systemwide structures.

ADMINISTRATORS' ATTITUDES

Looking back on the role of administrator as man-in-the-middle, we find it not surprising that administrators in general have been less than vigorous in seeking ways to involve parents and community in school matters. Here we need to pause and clear up an apparent inconsistency between the professional literature, which has long urged greater participation of citizens, and our assertion that it is generally perceived as, at best, a mixed blessing. Probably most readers know that educational writers have for several years laid the blame for many of the problems of schools at the feet of the apathetic public. Parents were scolded for not supporting PTAs or attending annual or semiannual open houses. In some inner-city communities, educators viewed with dismay the "lack of interest" shown by parents. They wondered how the schools could be expected to reach children if the parents would not participate.

Note at once that there is no question of the sincerity of the schoolmen who lamented the lack of parent support. Support is the key word. What the rhetoric of the forties, fifties, and sixties was all about was for parents to support the schools on the educator's terms (i.e., come when I send for you, on my time, to discuss my agenda). Schoolmen then, as now, were not campaigning for parents to participate in what might be perceived as threatening, interfering behavior. So it seems not at all inconsistent that the same persons who deplored the lack of *one kind of participation by citizens* may be less then enthusiastic about what they perceive to be a *different kind of participation.*

Opinions of Experienced Administrators

In a survey of the opinions of principals of schools in big cities, there was clear indication that the principals believed that school-community relations were becoming more important to the success of their programs. Responses were received from principals in forty-four of fifty-six cities in the sample (a 79 percent return). Thirty-four of those responding to the open-ended invitation to react to the stimulus of "The Elementary Principalship Today" mentioned the increasing importance of their role in school-community relations (Saxe 1970).

The comments of these educators in giant city schools are most revealing. We shall let them speak for themselves by excerpting comments from their statements. From Richmond, Virginia, we learn that the principal must be informed of the latest developments in education.

> With parents, the principal must be a public relations expert. He must be prepared at all times to explain, defend, or compare all facets of the

> school program, from the reading program to the preparation of cafeteria food. In order to do this he must be knowledgeable of programs in other schools, districts, and states, as well as actions of the local school board. That parents are more concerned than ever about schools and education, is evidenced by the increasing number of books and articles dealing with the subjects. The principal knows immediately from his telephone calls and visits when such a publication has hit the news-stands. School board meetings that once could be held in the confines of a small conference room have had to move to large areas to accommodate crowds of concerned parents. [Nall, in Saxe 1970, p. 50]

A similar concern appears in the statement of a principal from Tampa, Florida.

> The public's interest in its schools has never been keener, which in itself is a very good thing. It has, however, had the added effect of pressuring today's elementary principal into the rather demanding role of public relations man, selling not only the educational program of his school, but also that of the county and state systems, in addition to defining the role of the teaching profession to an increasingly better educated public. He has to be knowledgeable political-wise in interpreting school financing and tax sources, budgets and school needs to the tax weary public. He becomes a motivator and advisor to parent groups, and an interpreter and administrator of school board policies and curriculum. A working knowledge of school board procedures involving routine business practices, as well as of local county and state policies and laws is a necessity. [Deen, in Saxe 1970, p. 52]

The emphasis in these two statements seems to be placed on the role of the principal as spokesman for his school and, perhaps, for public education in general. The same emphasis is echoed by a principal from Tucson, Arizona, but new elements of pressure groups and other agencies are added.

> In working with parents, the principal must often be a diplomat. He is frequently a "go-between" between parents and teachers. The principal must be able to explain school board policy, state law, selection of textbooks, the grading system, or any other question concerning schools, for the elementary principal is THE administrator to the parents of his school area. Working with the community as a whole has become increasingly more important in our changing society. Growing public interest in education has increased the principal's community involvement. Often the principal is asked to meet with pressure groups who demand change or are upset by it. The principal is also involved with welfare agencies, the police and other agencies in the community. [Vernon, in Saxe 1970, p. 50]

Principals in Washington, D.C. seem to have been involved in issues of decentralization and community control before some of the principal-respondents in other cities. Principal Winston E. Turner commented as follows.

> Traditionally one of the functions of the principal has been to effect a good working relationship between the school and community.

Today, however, there are new dimensions to this area. Every day one hears such questions as:

> Who shall control the schools?
>
> Shall the schools be decentralized?
>
> How shall principals and teachers be hired?
>
> Shall we extend the school day? The school year?
>
> How do we fuse the recreation program with the education program?
>
> What shall the code of dress be? Who will determine it? [In Saxe 1970, p. 58]

The first clear advocation of extensive participation by citizens comes from Sara Nichols, principal of Little Creek School in Norfork, Virginia.

> There is need to acquaint the public with information about the schools. Involving parents in the overall school program is our responsibility. Providing opportunities for parents to study and to discuss school problems, along with students and faculty, can serve as a supportive force in the search for ways to help pupils build a more durable society. Helping parents to understand that the curriculum to be effective must be relevant to the individual needs of children is a responsibility of the principal. We must make provisions for parent participation through study, visiting, and group or individual conferences to examine the curriculum. Parents can assist in reevaluating instruments and methods used in reporting pupil progress. They should be informed about recent innovations in the learning process, and helped to understand that children can be better motivated through varied and different methods of instruction. Through the common understanding of parents and educators, suggestions and innovations may be considered and tried out in a joint effort to improve instruction. With a better understanding of the needs of the school, we can hope for greater public support in making changes that will make the elementary program more functional for children.
>
> I believe the elementary principal is moving in the right direction and is accepting the challenge to work democratically in his school and community. These principles of democracy can move through the entire hierarchy of our profession; and as time moves on these same principles will lead toward a more unified profession. No principal loses any of his prestige or his security working in an environment of shared leadership. There is no place for the authoritarian principal who sits on an "ivory throne" and hands out mandates. [In Saxe 1970, p. 60]

Finally, the notion of the involvement of citizens is extended and developed in an anonymous reply. (Respondents were asked to indicate if they wished to remain anonymous.)

> Boards of education have made a number of attempts to provide for community participation in decision making within the existing legal structure. "Parent congresses" have been established. A parent congress is made up of representatives from parent organizations in each district school. The

congress is autonomous; but it does not have legal responsibility for the schools. The members meet regularly with school board officials and may question board policy and make recommendations for change in existing policies and practices. More active community participation has been encouraged through the allocation of special funds to each parent congress. Such funds may be spent only on the initiative of the congress. Within certain legal limits, the funds may be used for the educational benefit of children in the district. While elementary principals may be consulted by parent congress representatives on the expenditure of such funds, the decision belongs to the parent congress and is binding upon the principal. Thus, we find the principal in a somewhat different role with respect to parent groups. He would be implementing decisions made by the local community.

Community schools have also been established to provide service to the community. Financed largely by foundation grants, community schools involve the use of school facilities and instructional and administrative services for up to thirteen hours per day. Children and adults in the community participate in a variety of tuition-free educational and recreational programs, for the most part, during the late afternoon and evening hours. The choice of activities that are offered is made cooperatively by members of the local community who serve on a community school advisory board, by the neighborhood at large through interest survey responses, and by a community school coordinator and the principal. While the on-the-spot responsibility for a community school rests with the principal, the success of the school depends upon whether it provides the services the community wants. The need for sensitivity and responsiveness on the part of the community school coordinator and the principal becomes obvious. Such schools provide numerous positive opportunities for the coordinator and the principal to work closely with members of the community. [Anon., in Saxe 1970, p. 64]

Opinions of Beginning Administrators

The statements show that these experienced administrators are aware of the importance of community relations and that it is changing. Taken as a group, the principals seem to be best aware of the task of communicating the business of schools to others. More recently we were able to review the ideas of a group of fifty administrators just beginning their careers in several different capacities in one of the large cities studied. Some of these statements also emphasize the communicating, public-relations orientation of the principal to the community. (Since the statements were made in confidence we must preserve anonymity.)

I

As a school principal (elementary) my responsibilities to the community are to see that communication lines are always open to parents. In this way any problems that may occur can be handled in the open with as little ill feeling as possible. It is also my responsibility to provide a way for parents to become familiar with the subject matter, activities, and functions provided at the school their children attend.

It is my responsibility to be as helpful as possible to the community my school represents. Helpful in terms of PTA and Mothers' Club activities. Helpful when a parent calls to inform me that children have been walking on lawns. Helpful when a parent informs me that her child is being bothered by other students. The list could go on and on but it is the responsibility of a principal to see that all community matters are taken care of.

In dealing with community matters a principal should be a good listener, be polite, be honest, and above all show all people that he is truly interested in the well being of the community his school represents.

II

Time must be found by the principal to listen and to take part in various school activities. One such activity may well be the PTA meetings, which he should attend. This gives him an opportunity to present various school programs and policies to the parents; these may then be discussed.

The principal must allow the parents to visit the school on various occasions so that the parents may more fully understand the various programs which the school is offering. He must also be willing to talk to parents who may wish to discuss any aspect of their child's educational program.

An attempt must be made so that the community knows that the school is working with them and not in opposition to their needs and wishes. The principal needs to find time and visit with various community leaders and discuss various aspects of the relationship between the school and the community which it serves and represents.

III

One of the responsibilities of administration is public relations. Honesty is very important. Keep the public informed. Let the public inform you. These lines of communication must be continually kept open.

A few of the beginning administrators had a broader perception of their responsibilities to the community.

IV

Communities have personalities. After evaluating this personality, one should capitalize on leaders within the community to establish a communication line between school and community. Newspapers, radio and TV are vital assets to building a positive public relations for your district. PTAs can be used in a supervisory nature in establishing priorities perceived by community for school. Mothers' Clubs are valuable also in working toward the obtaining of needed physical tools for pupils and staff. In all of these areas, there has to be a clear understanding of goals held by all of the members, then everyone needs to work toward accomplishing of those goals.

V

The principal must be responsible to the community in which his school is located. For too long the schools have tried to "go it alone" by not working with community. I believe the principal should be trained in positive public relations by publicizing what the schools are doing. In addition to this, I believe the principal should involve the parents (and all other interested adults) in as many school functions as possible. If the principal were to identify the influentials within the community, and partially involve them in some of the decision making for that school, they would certainly serve as positive public relations agents for that school. Finally, the principal has a responsibility to the community to again provide the best educational program possible for that school.

Perhaps it should be noted that our quoting these statements is in no way an endorsement of their content. For example, in IV and V above, the approach of relating to the community through a network of influentials should be carefully considered. Misunderstood, this tactic could be of questionable value.

Finally, because the attitudes of these neophyte administrators are so strikingly similar, we present one more to serve as a prototype.

VI

I believe that my responsibilities to the community are of the utmost importance. For without community backing my job as principal would be an uphill battle. The community must be kept fully informed as to the school program and the reasons for any implementation of new programs.

There must be a complete type of open door communications between the community and the school. The public should feel free to come into the building at any time and observe the educational process that is taking place.

I am not advocating the school being run by a group of parents, but I am advocating a give and take between the parents and the school.

Opinions of Beginning Students of Administration

We have now seen the perceptions of veteran and beginning administrators concerning community relations. Another group—persons taking their first university course in educational administration—was asked about how they believed persons in the community feel about school administrators in general.* The pattern of replies indicates

* These data are regularly collected from students in my class, Introduction to Educational Administration.

that these students believe that communities know little about school administrators and that they are probably neutral in their feelings toward administrators. A few of these comments follow.

> I don't feel the general community knows that much about what an administrator is or what he does.
>
> The working community sees them as overpaid bureaucrats.
>
> Most people with opinions about administrators feel that they constantly ask for huge sums of money.
>
> It appears to me that the general community respects administrators. They comment—"Oh he is a principal!"
>
> Some dislike them because of personal grievances and some admire and respect them.
>
> I would say that people in the community don't know enough about the administrators to have an opinion. The involved members feel basically the same as teachers do.
>
> They are left out of the ball game. They are blind and uninformed about what is really happening in their schools.
>
> The community feels that most administrators try to do a good job.

Opinions of Multiunit School Principals

Data from one other large group of administrators are available. Because it is a new organizational plan that is associated with a new curriculum design, it seemed probable that there would be different kinds of community relations in multiunit (MUS) and individually guided education (IGE) schools. In the multiunit school, a unit leader, two or three teachers, an aide, and sometimes a secretary and a student teacher are grouped with between 100 and 150 students. IGE is a comprehensive design for individual instruction featuring new instructional materials. (For a complete description, see Dickson et al. 1973, chapter 4.)

A survey form was designed and revised after a pilot test of selected principals of multiunit schools in Toledo. It was then sent to principals of all multiunit schools in Wisconsin (Wisconsin because there are more multiunit schools—147—there and because multiunit schools were introduced there more extensively earlier than in any other state). Eighty-three percent of the principals (121) returned the survey data. (For a complete report, see Saxe 1974.)

The first question compared the involvement of the community in school matters in multiunit schools with that in the self-contained classroom organizational plan. Twenty-four principals reported that the community was, in their estimation, involved to the same extent in both types of organizations. All of the other respondents (ninety-three) reported that they estimated the community to be more involved in multiunit schools. No principal believed the community was less involved in multiunit schools. Four principals did not answer the question.

These data support our position that the relationship of the community to its schools changes when the multiunit organization is implemented. Principals believe that the community becomes more involved in school matters. We have no information about the nature or extent of the additional involvement. Conceivably, communities could be relating in exactly the same ways to the schools, only more frequently. Other findings, however, suggest that the nature of the community involvement as well as the extent is different in the multiunit schools.

The second question listed several possible ways in which parents might participate in MUS matters according to different types of issues. The types of participation were defined as follows:

None. There is no need to involve parents in decisions about this matter. Typically they will not be consulted about it.

Inform. Although the school makes this decision, it is considered proper and necessary to inform parents.

Ask Opinion. The preferences of parents are determined although the school makes the decision.

Participate by Delegate. Parents are represented by a delegate or a committee.

Personal Participation. The parent is an active participant in decision making about this.

Makes Decision. The parent has the prerogative (whether used or not) of making this decision.

Principals were asked to check the most appropriate term to describe parents' participation in their MUS for each of twelve common activities. The results for this question are shown in table 3-1.

The easiest way to interpret the table is by inspecting the entries across the row for each activity. Entries on the left report that parents have little participation in the activity. Entries to the right assign an increasingly important type of participation to parents. General inspection of the entire table gives the impression that parents are

TABLE 3-1. PARENT PARTICIPATION IN SCHOOL ACTIVITIES IN MULTIUNIT SCHOOLS

Activity	Number of Principals Reporting on the Types of Participation by Parents						
	None	Inform	Ask opinion or advice	Participate by delegate	Participates personally	Makes decision	Other
Curriculum content	5	50	20	11	2	1	2
School time schedule	15	43	20	6	1	0	0
Learning materials	11	47	14	10	4	3	
Special events	2	21	22	19	33	5	2
Homework policies	2	32	28	9	7	3	6
General disciplinary policies	6	46	22	6	6	2	2
Particular disciplinary action for own child	0	12	27	3	38	9	1
Field trips	0	36	20	12	17	4	1
Marking, reporting	2	21	34	19	9	6	2
New programs—Innovation	3	26	39	18	9	2	2
Personnel selection and assignment	51	30	4	1	0	0	0
Pupil placement	12	34	31	0	13	2	1
Column totals	109	398	281	114	139	37	19

not especially active in the schools concerned. We have no evidence of how principals would perceive participation in these same activities in a self-contained organization but, nevertheless, these data do not portray unusually active participation by parents.

The row by row inspection also reveals the predictable pattern. Parents are not importantly involved in activities seen (by educators) as being exclusively or predominantly rights and duties of the educators (e.g., personnel, curriculum, learning materials). Parents are most importantly involved in peripheral matters (e.g., field trips and special events) and, of course, in disciplining their own children. It must be noted in passing that the very activities reserved to educators in these schools are the same ones that, we shall discover, are most vigorously sought by advocates of community involvement (control).

It is not fair to read into this table any more than a description of the perceptions of MUS principals of the status quo in their several schools. It need not represent their idea of good practice or poor practice. We did not ask that question. Some principals did comment that they were dissatisfied with the nature and extent of the parents' participation and were seeking means to increase it. The point remains that, despite the report that there is more participation, table 3-1 does not seem to reveal a new trend in parent participation in multiunit schools. We shall introduce additional findings of this survey when we examine practices of communication.

OPINIONS OF ADMINISTRATORS IN OTHER COUNTRIES

The review of the opinions of American educators shows that they are only beginning to adjust to the new demands in community relations. To put this in a better perspective and to emphasize the enormity of the difficulties to be overcome, it will help to look at the same issue in other countries. We do this briefly for Russia and Britain.

The Soviet Union

An article in the *New York Times* noted that educators in the Soviet Union "have been urging greater interplay between home and school." The national minister of education, Mikhail A. Prokofyev, was urging greater involvement of parents in the teaching process as one of several innovations. A contributing problem was the feeling by parents, both of whom work, that cooperating in school chores by teaching at home was an added imposition. Moreover, some of the parents were distressed because "the new math is really beyond me" (Shabad 1972). Despite the vast cultural and ideological differences, there are familiar elements in the problems of community relations in the Soviet Union as reported in this article.

Great Britain

Attitudes of educators in Britain about community relations are easily determined. True, there is evidence of pressure for increased involvement of citizens, but the opposition of educators is determined and based on a long tradition. The *Daily Express* (London) reported on this issue in a column headed, "Heads Fight Parents' Power Plan" (1973). According to Bruce Kemble, the reporter, "The 1,900 strong Headmasters' Association showed that they have no intention of giving parents the right to question their competence."

One headmaster had proposed that parents should test the competence of faculties every five years and incompetents should resign or be retrained. The head of Leek High School replied, "I couldn't be retrained if parents sacked me. I was never trained in the first place" (ibid.).*

Only half of the heads had even PTAs at their schools. One headmaster commented: "I daren't set up a PTA. Parents already come to the school in floods with their complaints. They're an absolute menace." The heads also would have no part of involving students in the running of schools. Finally, one head assured his colleagues that, even if pupils and parents could become school governors, "it was still possible for heads to write into the small print . . . clauses preventing them from overruling the head" (ibid.).

In a somewhat more temperate vein, an editorial in *Trends in Education* deplored the "tradition of parental apathy and a tendency to avoid contact with authority in general and therefore with the school which their children attend" (1973, p. 4). According to the editorial most heads attempt to bring the parents of new students into school "at the earliest possible moment" by an interview, tour, display, or meeting with the staff. "Some would emphasize in talks

---

* This is not merely a facetious remark. Few, if any, school administrators in Britain receive any formal training in administration.

to parents and in written communications that the school is theirs and their children's, that its doors are always open and that suggestions are welcomed" (ibid.). One wonders how the editor would have been received by his colleagues at the meeting reported in the *Daily Express*!

It does seem as though our counterparts in Britain have the same ability as American educators to deplore public apathy at the same time as they take action to discourage public interest. The contradiction, as we have noted, is, to administrators, more apparent than real. They wish and seek vigorous public participation on their agendas on their terms. They resent and resist public interference on other agendas not of their choosing. As one British writer puts it: "There is on the whole too much mutual suspicion between parents and teachers, and too little cooperation in the task of educating the children. To some extent . . . this is inevitable, because school and home do make differing demands upon a child and to some extent will pull against each other" (Haigh 1972, p. 50).

SUMMARY

In this chapter we have attempted to remove the confusion caused by lofty preachments about home and school unity. Our purpose is to permit some progress toward a real alliance by describing the conflicts of interests. Among these are the professional interests of teachers. The position of administrators as arbiters between sometimes contending factions helps put community relations in perspective and also prepares us to understand the opinions of administrators about community relations. A review of these administrators' opinions shows signs of change in the prevailing perception of a narrow view of community relations as a matter of giving information and securing support. The review also shows that there is still much misunderstanding and resistance to improved community relations. A look at two foreign countries revealed that similar concerns are cropping up in nations as different as Britain and the Soviet Union.

SUGGESTED ACTIVITIES

1. Interview five or ten parents of school-age children. Find out the date of their most recent visit to the school attended by their children. Find out also the general purpose (i.e., open house, sports event, parent interview, etc.). Finally ask whether the visit was initiated by the parents or by the school. Present your data in tabular form and draw inferences. To what extent do you think your findings are typical or atypical?

2. To experience vicariously the dilemma of the administrator in a situation where a teacher has clearly acted unwisely try to place yourself in this situation:

   A second grade boy has spent the entire day behind the piano in the classroom because he persisted in disturbing other pupils by talking and distracting their attention in various ways. The parent has questioned the teacher about this procedure and now they seek to have you, as principal, resolve their differences. The parent "doesn't want her boy sitting behind the piano because he won't learn anything there." The teacher maintains that "he can sit with his class anytime so long as he observes the rights of other boys and girls to learn."

   Try to design a solution that will preserve the "face" of both parent and teacher. Consider whether you can:

   1. As an educational leader, support the "behind-the-piano" tactic.
   2. Seemingly remove from the teacher the means of controlling the learning situation in the classroom.

   After you have solved this relatively simple incident, prepare others based on your own experience. For example, the failing grade given apparently arbitrarily without supporting evidence or warning. Are there administrators who invariably support the parent's side of such controversies? The teacher's side? If so, would one have good public relations and the other good staff relations?

SUGGESTED READINGS

Doll, Russell C. "The Sociological Monkey on the Team Leader's Back." In *Perspectives on the Role of the Teacher Corps Team Leader,* edited by Richard Saxe, pp. 141-155. Toledo, Ohio: University of Toledo, 1971.

Goldman, Harvey. "The Principal and the School Community." *Theory Into Practice* 2, no. 1 (February 1972): 9-17.

McCloskey, Gordon. *Education and Public Understanding.* 2d ed. New York: Harper & Row, 1967. Chapters 8 and 9.

Rasp, Alfred; Munson, Robert; and Ensign, Gordon. "A New Design for Teacher Participation." *Theory Into Practice* 2, no. 1 (February 1972): 22-27.

REFERENCES

Arnstein, Donald. "Freedom and Bureaucracy in the Schools." In *Freedom, Bureaucracy and Schooling,* edited by F. Haubrich, pp. 3-29. Washington, D.C.: Association of Supervision and Curriculum Development, 1971.

Boutwell, William D. "Educators Try to Avoid the Public, Speaker Claims." *AASA Convention Reporter.* Washington, D.C.: American Association of School Administrators, 1971.

Brenton, Myron. *What's Happened to Teacher?* New York: Coward-McCann, 1970.

Carter, Barbara. *Pickets, Parents and Power.* New York: Citation Press, 1971.

Chicago Tribune, 3 February 1973. "Teacher Chief Fired in Book Controversy."

Dickson, George E.; Saxe, Richard W.; et al. *Partners for Educational Reform and Renewal.* Berkeley, Ca.: McCutchan, 1973.

Gallup, George H. "Fifth Annual Gallup Poll of Public Attitudes Toward Education." *Phi Delta Kappan* 55, no. 1 (September 1973): 38-51.

Gottesfeld, Harry. *Educational Issues of the Ghetto as Seen by Community People and Educators, Final Report.* United States Office of Education sponsored research, Ed 038 481. New York: Ferkauf Graduate School of Humanities and Social Science, 1969.

Gross, Bertram. "The Scientific Approach to Administration." In *Behavioral Science and Educational Administration,* edited by Daniel E. Griffiths, pp. 33-72. Chicago: National Society for the Study of Education, 1964.

Haigh, Gerald. *Beginning Teaching.* London: Pitman Educational Library, 1972.

Hollander, E. P. *Leaders, Groups, and Influence.* New York: Oxford University Press, 1964.

Kemble, Bruce. "Heads Fight Parents' Power Plan." *Daily Express* (London), 26 March 1973.

Lieberman, Myron. *Education as a Profession.* Englewood Cliffs, N.J.: Prentice-Hall, 1956.

Mirthes, C. "A Mother's View of Education." *Twin Parks School* 1, no. 1 (Summer 1972): 20-21.

New York Times, 10 July 1972. "Residents of Detroit Taking Five-Week Strike by Teachers in Their Stride—For the Time Being."

Rankin, William. "A Rebel with a Cause." *Chicago Principals Reporter* 62, no. 1 (Winter 1972): 20-22.

Saxe, Richard W., ed. *Perceptions on the Changing Role of the Urban Elementary School Principal: Report of a Survey*. Toledo, Ohio: University of Toledo, 1970.

———. "Multiunit Schools and their Communities." *Elementary School Journal* 74, no. 2 (November 1974): 103-111.

Shabad, Theodore. "New Soviet Ideas of Schools Aired." *New York Times*, 22 November 1972.

Shanker, Albert. "Continuing Conflict in Brownsville." *New York Times*, 18 November 1973, section E, p. 11.

Simon, Herbert A. *Administrative Behavior*. 2d ed. New York: The Free Press, 1965.

Trends in Education 31 (July 1973): 3-4.

chapter four

Pressure Groups

> Power abdicates only under stress of counter-power.
>
> Martin Buber

In this chapter we shall consider the relationship of special interest or pressure groups to school-community relations. Such groups include informally organized groups of citizens seeking to change something about a school as well as formally organized, powerful, national pressure groups. Some, perhaps most, will owe their existence to dissatisfaction with some aspect of education. Others will invariably support educators on certain issues. Many will only enter into educational disputes when their particular interest is involved; when their ox is being gored. All are potentially important to school administrators, who should be aware of their interests, tactics, and influence. They are a part of the local community as well as the city, state, region, and national communities. They are neither completely benevolent nor malevolent.

Our previous discussion has anticipated some aspects of the role of pressure groups. We noted that in the typical model a citizen might be rebuffed at the local school level. One of the things he could do next was to redirect his efforts at higher levels. Sometimes he might seek the support of existing or temporary, ad hoc groups to support him in his dealings with the bureaucratic, educational control structure. These actions involve the use of pressure groups or interest groups to augment the influence of individual parents or a small group of persons interested in an identical issue.

In this discussion of pressure groups we shall rely on a very generalized description, with the admonition to readers that our classification includes many different types of individuals and organizations within the same set of rubrics. It also fails to distinguish between a pressure group and an interest group that may or may not be acting as a pressure group.

A pressure group, within these pages, is any collection of individuals or any organization that presents demands or attempts in any way to affect policy formation or implementation. The Black Panthers are a pressure group.* The Catholic Church is a pressure group.† The American Legion is a pressure group.‡ The PTA is a pressure group. The Association of Physical Education Teachers is a pressure group.§ The American Federation of Teachers (AFT) and the National Association of Manufacturers (NAM) are pressure groups.

The parents in the 2700 block of Cheltenham Drive are not yet a pressure group. But, tomorrow, if they meet at Smiths' house and plan to unite in an effort to have the open classroom (or multiunit, or self-contained classroom, or anything, for that matter) adopted by the Old Orchard School, they are a pressure group. Chances are they will appoint a spokesman and give themselves a name (Concerned Parents Club) but, once they begin exercising or attempting to exercise influence together, they are a pressure group.

There is a handy directory of national organizations that maintain their headquarters or have an office in Washington, D.C. (Hawley 1969). It lists entries according to these headings:

Associations of Professionals.

Associations of Institutions.

---

* Panthers won six out of eighteen seats on the citizens' board of the Oakland model cities program, resources from which usually fund many inner-city school programs (*Toledo Blade* 8/25/72).

† We will note the role of some Jesuits in organizing communities for certain action tactics.

‡ The award of American Legion medals to outstanding elementary school graduates is traditional in many schools. The more extensive program of the Legion is mentioned by Campbell in *Introduction to Educational Administration* (1971), chapter 10.

§ Physical educators have the strongest lobby in California, according to Leroy F. Greene, state assemblyman and chairman of the Assembly Education Committee (1972).

Organizations Concerned with Curriculum.

Councils, Commissions, and Conference Boards.

Accrediting Agencies and Spokesmen for Professional Standards.

Media and Materials Groups.

There are ninety-seven entries in the directory, ranging from the Adult Education Association of the USA to the World Confederation of Organizations of Teaching Profession. These are all pressure groups.

Those who wish to study a more thorough treatment and more careful classification of pressure groups should see the work of Campbell and his colleagues: *The Organization and Control of American Schools,* 2d ed. (1970), chapters 12-14. Campbell first discusses School-Oriented Groups, such as the PTA, National School Boards Association, the National Committee for Support of the Public Schools, and The Council for Basic Education. Campbell also describes types of locally based groups.

SCHOOL-ORIENTED GROUPS

Undoubtedly, the best known school-oriented pressure group is the PTA. For years the PTA or an equivalent mothers' club (really a more descriptive term for most PTAs of the past) was the best supporter of school policies. The PTA was the best vehicle available for parents at the local level according to the organization of the typical model represented in figure 2.1. For most, participation through the PTA room mother, executive board, and monthly meeting was more ceremonial than real.

However, even the harmless, actively school supporting PTA was feared, resented, and resisted by teachers. Attendance at PTA meetings by teachers was in my case a great concession paid to me as principal for past and possible future good deeds. This attitude shows rather nicely the difficult position of administrators in the typical model. Teachers recognized that it was part of the *administrator's responsibility* to "have good community relations" and were willing to cooperate with an administrator whom they believed could protect them from the risks involved in relating to the community. Moreover, it was a tradeoff of the administrator's idiosyncrasy credits (see our discussion of Hollander's concept of idiosyncrasy credits in chapter 3). The teachers were willing to do something that they would otherwise be reluctant to do in return for some action of the principal that they had seen as being supportive of their best interests. Further indication that attendance was a quid pro quo was the absence of those teachers with whom the administrator was temporarily persona non grata.

At many PTA elections, I observed teachers voting as a bloc for candidates for office perceived as less threatening to the school sanctuary. Often, because in slum neighborhoods parents cannot or will not participate, the teachers' bloc vote was enough to carry the election. It seems that the implications of this are clear. The partnership between home and school is at best an uneasy alliance. Neither partner has complete trust in the other. Perhaps the situation is analogous, to some extent, of the place of administrators in the teachers' association. For a time administrators were accused of dominating proceedings. They were finally forced out on the grounds that they did not have common cause with the teachers who were members and might even be adversaries. Are the *P* and the *T* of the PTA partners or, as they seem to imply in so many ways, psychological adversaries?

As recently as July 1972, a politician analyzing lobbies at the state level (in California) assessed the influence of the PTA in these words: "The PTA has all the muscle of a piece of wet spaghetti. It has always been a fourth rate tool of the school system" (Greene 1972). Despite this uncomplimentary evaluation, there are signs that the PTA, along with the rest of society, is changing. With the loss of the traditional widespread acceptance of school practices, the PTA could not long survive with a policy of supporting schools and minding its own business (i.e., staying out of school business).

In September 1972, Elizabeth Mallory, national PTA president, described the new philosophy, "If it affects the life of the child, it's PTA business" (Lawrence 1972). Mrs. Mallory clearly rejected the old role of the PTA: "I think PTA members are beginning to see that what they need to be is a force working for the children rather than a fund-raising auxiliary." If anything, the move to a more aggressive role is a bit tardy for the PTA, which has lost 3 million members since 1963. Membership in 1972 was 8½ million members in 40,000 local units (ibid.).

Lillie Herndon, 1973 national president, accepted the new version of the PTA. In her first remarks as presiding officer she urged members:

> As we begin another year of work, I would like to ask each of you as a PTA member to determine the needs of children in your community. Set new goals based on these needs and then plan an action program designed to achieve, in greater measure than ever before, that which is desirable for every child. And as all of us—parents, teachers, and students—focus on every child in our work, PTA will surely grow in power and credibility. [1973]

The PTA used to take the word of the school authorities about the needs of children. Moreover, it would not have been considered proper for the old PTA to "plan" a program. Planning was a task for professionals.

That the PTA is, indeed, changing is the theme of an article by Paul Simon, then lieutenant governor of Illinois, now teaching at Harvard and Sangamon State universities. Simon (1972) attests to the power of PTA as a national and state force. At the same time as Simon was writing, the PTA in Ohio was vigorously campaigning for the defeat of an effort to repeal the state income tax (*Toledo Blade* 10/9/72; note also Walton 1974). The PTA, in coalition with other proschool forces, was successful in spite of the growing resistance of taxpayers in Ohio to support even minimal educational programs.

The PTA will not easily shed its old image. Erma Bombeck's column of 24 September 1972 is not yet nostalgia. Her final paragraph captures the friendly-comic image of PTA:

> I know that someday when I go to that big PTA in the sky, someone will remember that brave little mother who single-handedly gave birth to 80 cupcakes, who drove 15 kids with bubble-gum breath to a turkey farm, and who got knocked in the face with a Frisbee and who carries a black eye with her today.

Doubtless, the forces that are questioning the role of women in society are working with other pressures to support the new direction of the PTA. Some of us will regret the passing of the old version even though we must endorse the need to change.

Whatever its contributions, and they were many, the PTA of the 50s and 60s certainly was not a vehicle for parents to communicate freely with their schools. The PTA had no authority. It could not in any real sense make legitimate the operation of a school in a community. As an organization it seemed to be better suited to the needs and life style of middle-class school patrons than to lower-class patrons. It was supportive of the schools, harmless, respectful, and yet it was feared by teachers.

A problem with the typical model and the associated PTA is that provision is made only for very general participation. This is fine in theory because, at the general level, deliberations are not clouded by personal concerns. However, the parent of a school pupil is almost invariably motivated by a most particular, restricted interest in his own child.

Another group that is solely interested in public schools is the National Committee for Support of the Public Schools (NCSPS). This organization was founded in 1962 by Agnes Meyer, the philanthropist. For several years the committee operated mainly through annual conferences and nationally known consultants. Good publications were produced but the impact of the committee's activities was limited, see, for example, National Committee for Support of Public Schools 1970.

After the death of Mrs. Meyer, NCSPS became inactive due to a lack of funds. At this moment there are signs of a vigorous revival under new leadership provided by Carl L. Marburger, former Commissioner of Education for the state of New Jersey, William Rioux, President of the Merrill Palmer Institute in Detroit, and Stanley Salett, former Assistant Commissioner in New Jersey.

In November 1973, two hundred thousand questionnaires were distributed as a pilot survey for a later mailing of 1 million. Respondents were asked to indicate their interest in these issues: accountability, parents' and children's rights, school finance, reading, children's toys, taking on the bureaucracy, equal opportunity, certification and credentials, local citizens' groups, educational materials in the home, curriculum and teaching methods, nutrition, and special education. The future emphasis of the NCSPS will be based upon resulting data.

It seems that the new NCSPS expects to activate and support "a network of citizens' organizations to represent your interests in your school district, your city, your state." The Washington headquarters "will represent your interest—the public interest—in the power struggles that determine how money is spent, how policy is made, how children will be affected in every classroom." For individuals, NCSPS will provide the "best available information on educational issues, your rights and how to fight for them, plus guidance on educating children."*

It remains to be seen what form the new NCSPS will eventually assume. It could become the Common Cause or the Nader's Raiders of education. The objectives are, indeed, ambitious. The original version had little if any impact on schoolmen. If the new leadership lives up to only a part of its promise, NCSPS will soon become known to all school administrators.

"The Council for Basic Education (CBE) was incorporated in the District of Columbia on July 3, 1956, as a non-profit educational organization pledged to the encouragement and maintenance of high academic standards in American public schools" (Council for Basic Education 1960, p. 4). Most schoolmen quickly perceived CBE as a critic of education with a program of emphasis on fundamental intellectual disciplines and emphasis on social adjustment. It is my impression that time and events have tempered this judgment so that CBE is no longer seen as a hostile adversary but as a responsible critic of public education.

CBE operates mainly through publications, the monthly *Bulletin,* books, and occasional papers. There is no network of state or local units. Membership is now set at five dollars. A list of publications currently in stock and available at a nominal cost will give an excellent idea of the orientation of CBE.

What Every Intelligent Woman Should Know About Education.

Teacher Education: Who Holds the Power?

Five Views of the New Math.

The Role of History in Today's Schools.

Raising Standards in the Inner-City Schools.

The New English.

The Electronic Revolution in the Classroom: Promise or Threat?

---

* National Committee for Support of Public Schools, Promotional Letter, form IV, 1973. As evidence of the public relations sophistication of the newly reoganized NCSPS note that they pilot-tested four different versions of the letter to select the one that produced the best response. The organization has now changed its name to National Committee for Citizens in Education (NCCE). See *NCCE Report* 1, no. 1 (January 1974): 1.

What Are the Priorities for City Schools?

Merit Pay and Alternatives: Descriptions of Some Current Programs.

Phonics in Beginning Reading: A Guide for Teachers and Parents.

Inner-City Children Can Be Taught to Read.

The New Case for Latin and the Classics.

What Is Career Education?

There are also nine books currently available. Two of these are: *Who Controls American Education?* and *Reform in Education: England and the United States,* both by James D. Koerner. Mortimer Smith is the Executive Director and editor of the *Bulletin.*

Whether CBE affects local school-community relations is impossible to tell. Their emphasis on basics and hostility toward "progressive education" are not likely to bring them into current controversies unless it is as advocates of accountability. Because of the current cluster of radical critics (e.g., Illich and Remmer) who would do away with schools, CBE seems by comparison almost friendly and supportive. There are other groups with a continual interest in public schools but generally they do not operate as pressure groups at the local level. We turn now to other interest groups.

OTHER INTEREST GROUPS

In another chapter of *The Organization and Control of American Schools,* Campbell considers groups interested primarily in something other than education. These groups may support or oppose schools on any kind of issue: textbooks, teachers and administrators, finances, goals, anything. The groups include extremists of the right and left, Negro organizations, women's organizations, taxpayers' organizations, and the like. We have already mentioned the Black Panthers, who would be considered extremists of the left.

Extremist Groups

An extremist group of the right has recently been in regional news reports. Members of the Ku Klux Klan, complete with black hoods and robes purchased from the former grand dragon of the United Klans of America, who approved of the plan, tarred and feathered a high school principal. One of the convicted Klansmen testified that "a Washtenaw County unit of the Ku Klux Klan felt that Mr. Brownlee [the high school principal], who is white, was discriminating against white students at his Willow Run school. He said that the KKK unit felt Mr. Brownlee's treatment of black students was too liberal" (*Toledo Blade* 10/10/73).

While the Klan was busy reinforcing its image, another right-wing group was at work changing its image. The John Birch Society

> has learned something from recent history, and has turned its knowledge into public relations policy. . . . Basically the new policy consists of keeping out of the limelight, of not publicizing lurid charges against top government officials as it used to do back in President Eisenhower's last years in office. This got the society a lot of publicity, but it often had a negative effect. [LeBlanc 1972]

The Birch society has about eighty thousand members and is strongest in the western states. The society considers itself anticommunist, antiestablishment, and has "educational goals." It distributes Welch's bulletins, the magazines *American Opinion* and *Review of the News,* and provides books, films, and speakers.

In very many places school administrators are favored with pressure groups of the right and the left, sometimes simultaneously, sometimes in a chain reaction of stimulus and response. In Jackson, Michigan, a suburban high school principal was persuaded by a left-of-center group, Concerned Citizens Against the War, to schedule Jane Fonda to speak to three hundred students in an optional assembly program. The principal was, however, persuaded to cancel Miss Fonda's speech because of "strong external pressures" reputed to have been made by "a group of fundamentalist ministers and right-wing organizations" (*Toledo Blade* 9/12/72).

Racial and Ethnic Groups

When Campbell's second edition of *The Organization and Control of American Public Schools* was published in 1970, blacks were dominating the media and causing Campbell to give special emphasis to Negro organizations: NAACP, CORE, SCLC, SNCC. More recent events indicate that Spanish-speaking and native American groups are also vigorously seeking to improve educational opportunities for their members. Groups in these categories are especially active at local levels and will be considered again when we begin the study of decentralization and community control.

Such groups are often involved in efforts to place members of their racial or ethnic group in administrative or teaching positions. For example, American Indian militants seized and held the school administration building for twenty-one hours at the Fort Sill Indian School in Oklahoma. Their goal was to replace white school administrators with Indians. The superintendent and principal of the school were given administrative leave (*Toledo Blade* 10/4/72). We will see the same approach employed by other groups in their search for community control.

The more militant, paramilitary groups seem to be on the decline. The Brown Berets, an organization of Americans of Mexican descent, was apparently disbanded to "avoid factional violence." The prime minister of the Berets, when resigning, said that the decision to disband was prompted by "insurgency within the group, 'hippieism' and harassment of members by police" (*Toledo Blade* 11/3/72). The Berets at one time had about five thousand members in ninety chapters. The prime minister had served a jail term for an East Los Angeles school walkout and a street demonstration.

Sometimes the needs of groups in this category create complex problems for administrators as well as the courts. For instance, in Hawaii the Kamehameha school's admission policy—students of native Hawaiian ancestry only—is facing a legal challenge. The policy is clearly racially exclusive, and discriminatory, and probably unconstitutional. But, it does seem, especially to Hawaiians, a special case. The spokesman for seventy thousand Hawaiians of native ancestry said: "We cannot stand by and let people kill us." Other spokesmen note that "the memory of the past is practically all that [the native Hawaiian] has left of what was once only his" (*Toledo Blade* 8/4/72).

As if the Hawaiian dilemma were not perplexing enough, consider the problem of a Chicago public school, which had received fifty-seven thousand dollars of additional state funds for a new bilingual program. Now representatives of the Greek-speaking community say they want nothing to do with the program, which offers instruction in Greek and then in English. The parents prefer their children to learn English as soon as possible and then take instruction only in English (*Chicago Tribune* 11/1/73).

Women's Organizations

A vigorous new pressure bloc is in the making. Already campaigns are underway to remove learning materials that portray females in passive, subservient roles. Girls, too, can aspire to become pilots; boys can aspire to vocations formerly exclusively feminine. Some of this pressure is profeminist, some proandrogynousness. Older textbooks will soon be castigated like poor old Dick and Jane. Professional journals recently devoted entire issues to these concerns, see, for example, the entire issues of *Educational Leadership* (November 1973) and *Notre Dame Journal of Education* (Winter 1972). Courses and departments of studies of women's roles will be sought.

The League of Women Voters continues to support education at national, state, and local levels. The League is usually active in providing information about candidates for office and sponsoring meetings where candidates discuss issues. In Toledo the League has taken on the multiunit school project—a joint effort of public schools and universities—as a service activity. League volunteers staff the materials center and serve as aides. At present, thirty-four women are giving their services for one half day a week and the program is expanding; see Dickson, Saxe, et al. (1973), p. 265. The American Association of University Women (AAUW) continues programs similar to the League.

Whether long established organizations such as the League and AAUW will take up the fight against sexism in education remains to be seen. One assumes that they will. Of concern to administrators will be local groups of the National Organization of Women seeking immediate reforms in counseling and physical education, for instance, counseling in which girls are discouraged from pursuing prestigious "male" professions (e.g., law, medicine), and a vastly disproportionate budget for sports and physical education. It will not be enough to let the outstanding girl athlete compete in tennis, golf, or even swimming.

At a meeting on Options in Public Education held in Minneapolis in October 1973, there was a workshop on Sexism in Education by the Emma Willard Task Force. The following suggestions are taken from the brochure distributed at that meeting:

> Go beyond meeting minimum requirements of Federal civil rights legislation.
>
> Examine your own curriculum, textbooks, and materials for sexist stereotypes; eliminate them.
>
> Put pressure on publishing houses to publish nonsexist materials; boycott those who don't.
>
> Include books by and about women in your curriculum and library; this means chemistry and math books as well as social studies and literature.

Invite women speakers for school programs.

Stop tracking by sex; this includes college-bound programs as well as home economics, shop, and athletics.

Provide inservice staff training on sexism; apply what you learn.

Start a Women's Studies program, but don't "bury" the issue of sexism in this program alone; discussion of sexism should not be restricted to Women's Studies or to females.

Get rid of sexist language; try she/he, her/his, person, instead of he, his, man.

Your school staff provides role-models; hire male secretaries, cooks, librarians; hire female administrators, coaches, and maintenance personnel.

You yourself are a role-model for students; be sensitive to your own attitudes and behavior. [Emma Willard Task Force 1973]

Taxpayers' Organizations

Currently we can expect taxpayers' organizations to deter additional funding for education. This, surprisingly, is not always the case. Stephen Bailey's landmark publication, *Schoolmen and Politics* (1962), reported that taxpayers' organizations are often allies of public education, particularly for broad based taxes (viz., sales taxes), which transfer the tax burden to nonbusiness groups (pp. 39-40). A more typical instance of a taxpayers' organization is described by Browder (1970). Browder describes the origination of the Commuterville Taxpayers' Association, which began by attacking some board members, teachers' salaries, the "ridiculous school budget spiral, high salaried administrators, a 'secretive' board, and personnel proliferation" (p. 199).

"National Networks of Influence" are described by Campbell and his associates in a third chapter. Here a case study (Jamgochian 1964, reported by Campbell, p. 519) examines "the network of influence used by the U.S. Chamber of Commerce with respect to the Public School Assistance bill introduced into the Congress in 1961." In this same section (pp. 517-519), Campbell reviews a study of the American Legion made by William Gellerman to reveal the requirements of many interest groups to establish a position and build support for the position among member units.

Administrators seem well aware that some groups not primarily interested in education are nonetheless of major importance in regard to policy formation. For example, it is routine for schoolmen to belong to Lions, Kiwanis, and similar business-professional groups.

Many administrators still assiduously cultivate the good will of the business elite and the Chamber of Commerce. One such, when queried about the effect of his frequent absence from his administrative post on good will meetings, commented that this phase of his job was more important than curriculum development or the other inservice tasks he might be needed for (Cunningham 1972). In some situations he may well be quite right. However, the times are such that acceptance by the business elite is no longer sufficient political legitimation for the administrator. In fact, one wonders whether the obvious affiliation with one interest group—together with the absence of affiliation with those of different persuasions—is even good practice.

Campbell's attention to noneducation groups is supported by a growing body of research. Recently a researcher in Chicago found that

> the organizations which dominated school politics were not concerned primarily with education issues. They were small businessmen's leagues, property and homeowner's associations, and civic improvement groups that were generally unconcerned with drop-out rates, low achievement test scores, or the selection, training, assignment, and promotion of teachers and administrators. Instead, they were concerned with the effect of school policies on the ecology of the community—the migration of population and the aesthetic appearance of school buildings. [Weeres 1971, p. 2]

Another classification of pressure groups is found in *Decision Making and Schools for the 70's* (Pharis, Robison, and Walden 1970, pp. 11-27). Here groups are classified as legal or extralegal, formal or informal, and transitory or permanent. The authors point out that informal political influence is not necessarily bad. It should be neither overrated nor overlooked.

ATTITUDES ABOUT PRESSURE GROUPS

There is much ambiguity surrounding the role of pressure groups in education. It seems obvious that such groups play an important role in a democracy by providing another way for the individual to secure access to governing bodies and to make possible the communication of his needs to authorities. This is part of the same network of communication as are letters to newspapers or elected representatives. The difference is that the pressure group is readily available and has been created to represent the special interest concerned.

The ambiguity about pressure groups and education may be related in some ways to the now thoroughly debunked myth of the separation of education and politics.* The notion that education as a kind of public religion should be above partisan attempts at influence might have slowed the development of permanent organizations designed to lobby and engage in other pressure group tactics.

In support of this quaint notion that such groups are not seen as exactly proper in education, we note the denial of their influence on decision making as reported to us by Ohio legislators. In a survey completed in May 1969, we asked members of the Ohio legislature to indicate the sources of influence of importance to them in arriving at their positions on three different bills on education. The bills dealt with districting, finance, and curriculum. The results showed clearly that legislators wished to be perceived as being influenced by constituents, themselves (i.e., their own values and judgment), and—in a very low third place—the position of their political party (Saxe and Rosenberger 1970, p. 7).

The role of pressure groups, according to our legislator respondents, was negligible. One respondent was so offended at our even suggesting that he could be affected by other groups that he told us he would oppose increased support for a university where professors wasted their time on such nonsense. This particular respondent had never been a strong supporter of universities, so his threat was meaningless. Nevertheless, it is symptomatic of an important attitude that may be characteristic of many legislators.

In interpreting the survey it seemed to us that legislators were, in effect, telling us: "Look here now, we are our own men, not to be swayed by anyone, but *if we were* to listen to outside influences, the following might be among them." In the cluster mentioned were: the Ohio Education Association, the State Department of Education, the Republican Speaker of the House, the Buckeye Association of School Administrators, and the Ohio School Boards Association (ibid., p. 8). Note, first, that two of these, the Speaker and the State Department, cannot be considered, in themselves, pressure groups nor spokesmen for such groups.

---

* According to most of the recent professional literature on the topic of politics and education, education is, and ought to be, political. Our own research supports this; see Saxe (1969). An especially cogent discussion of the relationship between education and politics is found in Bailey (1967).

With the exception of the Speaker of the House, the group of organizations of some importance consists of members of Conant's educational establishment (1963, pp. 15-16). The group did not vary from bill to bill. We make no conclusions from this survey other than the clear finding that legislators possess an idealized image of themselves as independent decision makers, influenced only by their values and the needs of their constituents, and sometimes perhaps by the position of their parties.

It does not matter whether the image is accurate or not. What is significant, for those of us who may deal with legislators on educational matters, is knowing that the legislator needs to perceive himself in this way. Among organizations receiving minimal attention as sources of influence on the bills surveyed were: Retail Merchants Association, PTA, newspapers, Farm Bureau, and various individuals such as the governor and some committee chairmen.

To this point we have suggested that pressure groups are part of the process of educational governance and should be so considered by administrators. We also noted that state legislators, at least, acted as though it were not in keeping with their idealized concept of their role to be influenced by pressure groups. Nevertheless, we know that pressure groups are active at the state level as well as all other levels. There is ample documentation of the success of special interest groups at the state level in the enactment of laws requiring the attention to one interest or another in the required school curriculum. Attention to the evils of tobacco and alcohol comes to mind most readily. (See, for example, Marconnit 1966.)

FUTURE PROSPECTS

If the past is a guide for the future, we should expect to see current efforts to reform education represented by much pressure, many bills, and some laws. All of us at the time of this writing would probably predict that such pressures would most likely be exerted on behalf of ecology. We would be absolutely correct in this forecast. The New York Senate has voted to direct the State Education Department to "work up courses in survival arts and human arts." According to advocates of the bill, which passed easily, "survival arts are the skill and knowledge needed to live in a technological, congested society and include simple auto and home maintenance, solving and analyzing problems, ecological understanding, and to function effectively as a consumer" (Haggart 1972).

Also high on our list of predictions would be action to bring about accountability of some kind for all levels of schooling and all role groups of educators. This prediction, too, will soon be proven accurate. Several states are moving toward performance based certification of teachers. We mentioned briefly the role that accountability played in the 1973 Detroit teachers' strike. The pressures toward accountability are coming from diverse sources—taxpayers want their money's worth, fundamentalist educators want the skills achieved, minorities want their children properly equipped. Strong as these pressures are, the resistance from opposing pressure groups is formidable. If one were (probably unwisely) to venture a prediction, it would be that some forms of accountability would be mandated but without the stringent remedial capabilities sought by many advocates. That is, educators probably will not be liable to dismissal if their students do not reach agreed upon levels of mastery.

It seems likely that when the full impact of Watergate and associated events is felt, it too will result in a pressure on schools. There may be no new special pressure group created to "do something about" Watergate. It can be picked up as a concern of existing groups interested in education. We have already seen articles blaming the schools (progressive education) for the scandals. What could be more reasonable than to seek a solution by reforming the delinquents—the schools. Probably what will be sought will be a return to the "old values" by a renewed attention to moral education. (Never mind that the schools cannot accomplish this. That will not concern reformers needing a rediscovery of law and order.)

Many of the actions of pressure groups can be predicted precisely because of their announced special interest. For instance, we should expect patriotic organizations to reward patriotic virtues and to view with alarm actions perceived as unpatriotic. And the organizations will not disappoint us. We expect ethnic interest groups to favor the presentation of material complimentary to their groups and to oppose the teaching of anything that presents them in an unfavorable light. The downtown coaches' club will favor a new athletic facility and more night football games. They will oppose any curtailing of the number of games played and policies that prevent postseason bowl championships.

As an aside here we may note that the sports pressure groups are among the most enduring and predictable of all. However, even here there is evidence of change. Many of the privileged urban youth seem to have rejected interscholastic athletics as childish, if not inspired by the establishment. In this they are not completely wrong, according to administrators who testify that vandalism goes down, morale goes up, and school levies pass when the team has a winning season (Saxe 1970). In a dispute in Yellow Springs, Ohio, in which sports fans collided with advocates of culture, there were overtones of racial pressures.

> The football Bulldogs almost didn't make it to the scrimmage stage last spring when the school board rejected the club's offer to field a team. But the board reversed itself when petitions were circulated, and many persons in Yellow Springs view the switch as a gesture to the town's Negroes, who make up 25 percent of the population. Half the team is Negro. [Walton 1971]

Part of the problem is that many gifted musicians were needed for the football team and the orchestra conductor did not believe that his group could survive the competition for scarce resources. Moreover, "If football comes to Yellow Springs, can a marching band be far behind?" [Ibid.]

It should be noted, in testimony of the strength of sports groups, that the school teams are the last to be in danger of having their activities curtailed in the face of a threatened nationwide fuel shortage. Educational field trips may be cut and the school day lengthened, but the team's road schedule will be honored.*

Some topical pressures seem well-nigh irresistible, but time can change that. It was once tradition for all male students to be absent at the beginning of each hunting season. One superintendent notes that now "hunting is a dying tradition. Fewer students are requesting permission to get out of school opening day. We have misgivings about letting any go, but we'll follow the policy" (Wolfe 1972). Another superintendent required a hunting license and a note from parents. Yet another reports that the percentage of boys absent on opening day of the season is down from over 50 percent to less than 15 percent.

---

* When Los Angeles schools canceled field trips but continued to transport athletes to games, an irate Robert Snyder wrote to the editor of the *Toledo Blade* (12/1/73): "That strikes me as being rather typical of the mentality of too many school boards in this nation which allow educational opportunities to take a back seat to athletic events at any turning where resources are likely to be short."

The demise of hunting fever is mentioned to underscore the relationship of issues affecting education to attitudes and conditions in the larger society. At one time schoolmen would have been reluctant to confront this issue. The high school prom and the senior trip are not precisely examples of the effect of pressure groups but an administrator must be aware of their significance to others. There is a time for action, a time for discretion.

STRATEGIES AND TACTICS OF PRESSURE GROUPS

A happy aspect of permanent or semipermanent pressure groups is that the administrator knows their goals. True, this does not always make it possible to find a way of relating to such groups, particularly when there may be two or more with diametrically opposed platforms (sex education versus no sex education; integration versus segregation).

There are existing groups with a plan of action and resources to support widely held general goals that will advance the interest concerned. From time to time they may intervene in local affairs in response to special organizational programs or in response to a local appeal for assistance. In these cases there is often as great a problem between the representatives of the broadly based pressure group and their local supporters as there is between the educational institution and the pressure group. This often leads to some tragic and absurd effects on the local level.

This is an area of concern for administrators as well as for local members of nationally affiliated pressure groups. There is assumed an interest in a broadly conceived goal that may not always represent the particular concern of a given local unit. I have recently been urged by one pressure group of principals of which I am a member not to buy a certain brand of trousers (communication from the Chicago Principal's Association on behalf of William A. Lee, President, CFL, IUC). I know nothing of the merits of the controversy concerned, but it has little to do with my present concerns about the principalship. Some years ago the National Association of Secondary School Principals wished to ban *Life* magazine because it was seemingly dealing unfairly with American schools in a series of articles entitled "Crisis in Education." Here was a case of being invited to join in an ill-advised sanction determined unilaterally at some distant national headquarters. The point is that administrators may find themselves under attack tomorrow for some issue that, today, is of no local concern whatever. However, if the organization of the pressure group is in good order, local spokesmen may loyally report the new grievance. When this happens it is difficult not to liken the national pressure group's tactic to a physician who advocates a given surgical procedure, at which he excels, regardless of the actual ailment of his patient.

TACTICS

The tactics of pressure groups will vary greatly from violent demonstration to subtle influence. The nature of the organization has much to do with the activities considered appropriate. The PTA, for example, is constrained by its objectives as well as its tradition. The Students for a Democratic Society have a different, more active style of operation. Patriotic organizations may use all the communication media to ban a book that they perceive as subversive but they may not forcibly remove and destroy the volumes. It is part of their orientation to see that their cause is just under law. To secure their objective through secret or illegal means would make no sense at all. They must be open and extremely moral in their tactics.

Probably militant confrontation tactics have been most disturbing to administrators and board members. The rise and fall of one such group is revealing of the tactics and their effects. In 1971, two community organizers trained in Saul Alinsky's methods—a Jesuit priest and a Jesuit seminarian—started the Central Toledo Action Committee. CTAC was funded by the Toledo Diocese. Neighborhood groups were formed and encouraged to seek solutions to their problems through confrontations with city officials and landlords. Members of the CTAC groups picketed the homes of officials, disrupted meetings, and were accused of making disturbing phone calls. A judge announced that he was resigning from the housing court because he and his family were being harassed by the Jesuit organizers.

At the end of the first year of the program, the majority report of the Central City Ministry Department supported CTAC, saying of their tactics: "While others find them distasteful, they are no more pressure tactics, for all their visibility, than a phone call from a rich contributor to a politician." The minority report noted that "some tactics of themselves are offensive to many people. To this extent, the tactics tend to cloud the issues and cause adverse reactions among the general public" (*Toledo Blade* 11/1/72). Such tactics were termed totally unacceptable by the minority, who were outvoted by ten votes to two.

Early in the second year of operations, the city manager issued new rules "for city officials to follow in dealing with any citizen groups that specialize in the harangue and harass school of social concern." An editorial wondered whether, "having now got the attention of public officials, there is a need to indulge in the kind of boorish behavior ascribed to CTAC—including use of obscene language and signs, personal threats, harassing members of families of city officials in their own homes and distributing objectionable literature" (*Toledo Blade* 3/6/73, p. 20).

Near the end of the second year of operation, CTAC claimed credit for repairs to over 300 rental units and the destruction of 144 firetraps. With the support of organized labor, the city manager's ruling against picketing at the homes of officials was defeated by city council. The Reverend Redding, Director of Community Relations for the diocese, said he would not have done things in the same way as the Jesuit organizers but would not have accomplished one-tenth as much: "I wonder if my nice little hat-in-hand approach would have gotten us that far?" Father Redding acknowledged that an alleged stabbing by a "marginal" CTAC member was a serious setback (*Toledo Blade* 10/27/73).

At about the same time, it was reported that CTAC was seeking funding from other sources. Father Redding hoped that the organizers would continue and noted "that the fact that the diocesan funding will cease does not mean they leave" (*Toledo Blade* 8/20/73). A city commissioner of inspection (buildings) reported that he had been ready to resign because CTAC's "sixteen weekend marches on his home had disrupted his family life to the point of making his wife extremely nervous and having traumatic effects on his eight-year-old son . . . the worst thing was the fear tactic" (Lindeman 1973).

Finally, an editorial noted that CTAC, being disbanded, blamed its demise on inner-city residents who did not want its help. "Is it any wonder, then, that inner-city residents may well have come to feel that CTAC really had little to offer them in resolving their crucial concerns because it seemed so much more fascinated with its own continuous confrontations" (*Toledo Blade* 11/15/73, p. 16).

Whatever the truth is about CTAC, the episode has implications for educators. Abrasive tactics are likely to be used if they prove effective. Most educators will find them personally repugnant. Board members are not prepared for personal abuse. The process is intended to be intimidating. The organizers of CTAC never abandoned the confrontation tactic despite growing concern by their supporters as well as protests by their targets. These tactics were widely disseminated in connection with federally funded Community Action Programs. We shall discuss them again in connection with decentralization and community control.

Organizations without so sacred a goal as the survival of democracy, or morality, or religion, or getting rats out of bedrooms cannot be so direct and forceful. In our own research (Saxe 1965) we found that the giant Ford Foundation quickly learned this lesson—actually, the Fund for the Advancement of Education, created by Ford, was studied. After an unsuccessful direct attempt to reform teacher education in an entire state, the Foundation became more circumspect, realizing that it was important in the change strategy first to secure the cooperation of a prominent insider in the institution concerned. The institutions (universities) to be changed were selected because of their prestige and their geography. They were seen as centers of excellence in their several regions of the country. It was hoped that changes demonstrated in these "lighthouse" institutions would be quickly copied by others. The Foundation was to assist the influential insider, by its money and prestige, in implementing an innovation that included the Foundation's essential intentions. This relationship is different from the usual approach of a pressure group that is obviously wooing or forcing an educational institution. The Foundation at that time did indeed seek out certain institutions but it appeared that the university had sought the Foundation's assistance for its—the university's—program.

The National Association of Manufacturers (NAM) for a time had an open, direct liaison with the American Association of School Administrators. This is further evidence of the long-standing notion that it is quite proper for the school administrator to be allied with business leadership. Now the NAM will supply free materials presenting its viewpoints. Because of the wealth of material available, many districts have established screening committees to examine and approve free and inexpensive material. This tactic is clearly very indirect pressure, but it is an important one for established, well-financed special interest groups.

Not all groups are "supposed" to function as pressure groups and tactics appropriate for one group may be improper for other groups. Recently a "Children's March for Survival" in Washington, D.C. drew severe criticism because materials critical of the President were being distributed in local schools and because ten thousand pupils were recruited to participate in the march. "The upshot was 1,000 children got lost and were found crying in a mess of chicken bones, garbage, and discarded bagfuls of bread; fierce denunciation in the press and in Congress for exploitation of children, and no apparent points scored at the congressional power center" (Thimmesch 1972). Apparently this cause seemed so noble that the board and administrators departed from the tradition of avoiding any appearance of using pupils to secure an objective. This same lack of restraint and objectivity is sometimes evidenced in financial campaigns for bond issues.

An interesting exercise in pressure tactics occurred in California where various conservative organizations (American Taxpayer's Union, California Families United, Families for God and Country, Parents and Taxpayers, Inc., and the Citizens Committee of California) cooperated in marches to oppose progressive, permissive, and humanistic education. "From Sonoma to San Diego, small parental armies are marching on local school boards protesting sex education curricula, evolution being taught in the classroom, drugs being 'pushed' in the schoolyard, and a general lack of 'moral leadership' by teachers and administrators" (Sitomer 1970).

The conservative groups united in supporting a set of guidelines to instill concepts of "morality, truth, justice, and patriotism." These guidelines "offset and balance the immorality, antipatriotism, and destructive behavior being propagandized to young people in school today." The coalition of parental pressure groups did secure an agreement from the state board "to include references to Biblically derived teachings." They are now concentrating on sex education and evolution (ibid.).

Campbell's discussion of policy formation (1971, chapter 16) provides an excellent perspective on the role of pressure groups. Such groups align themselves with movements to change education that are generated by basic social forces. The pressure groups get on the bandwagon and attempt to direct the process of change in a direction that will advance their own goals. They use press, TV, political action, money, and influence to bring about their goals. They will direct their efforts at the most accessible targets.

It is difficult to move to another issue in community relations without offering educators some hope of being able to deal with the pressures we have described in these pages. However, since the problems and issues in school-community relations are intertwined, we will attempt to discuss solutions at one time to reduce repetition. To anticipate that argument, it should be clear that educators will wish to keep issues in the open and be sure that all interested in schools have access to the processes of policy formation.

SUMMARY

Pressure groups are a part of the process of policy formation and decision making in a democracy. There is some ambiguity about them that may be associated with the long-held misconception that politics and education must be kept apart. The tactics of pressure groups vary depending upon many things but particularly upon the "sacredness" of their cause. They operate in concert with other groups using widespread concern as their legitimating force for particular concerns that, they purport, will relate to the remedy of the basic social discontent. There are numerous pressure groups. Some rise and fall, others will always be with us.

SUGGESTED ACTIVITIES

1. Interview a superintendent and ask him to identify pressure groups. Try to find out which groups are active on which issues. Ask the superintendent whether the pressure groups affect policy formation.

2. Interview a board member, asking the same questions.

3. Interview a principal, asking the same questions.

4. Interview the leader (or educational chairman) of a pressure group. Ask how the group identifies issues in which it will

become active. Find out what tactics the group uses. Remember that the PTA and veterans' groups are pressure groups, as are business and professional associations.

5. Ask each member of your graduate class or each member of your school faculty to make a list of all the pressure groups to which he or she belongs. Have someone prepare a master list and make a frequency distribution of the memberships. Are the ones to which most of us belong generally the most powerful? If not, what explains the power of some groups?

6. Select an educational issue of current national or local importance. Identify groups that will support the issue and those that will probably oppose the issue. Possible issues: accountability, work or career education, new procedures to finance schools, federal involvement. On what basis were you able to predict the pressure groups and the stands they would take?

SUGGESTED READINGS

Bailey, Stephen K.; Frost, Richard T.; Wood, Robert C.; and Marsh, Paul E. *Schoolmen and Politics.* Syracuse, New York: Syracuse University Press, 1962.

Campbell, Roald F., et al. *The Organization and Control of American Schools,* 2d ed. Columbus, Ohio: Charles E. Merrill Publishing Co., 1970.

Campbell, Roald F., and Layton, Donald H. *Policy Making for American Education.* Chicago: Midwest Administration Center, 1969.

Campbell, Roald F., and Bunnell, Robert, eds. *Nationalizing Influences on Secondary Education.* Chicago: Midwest Administration Center, 1962.

"External Pressure Groups." *The Administrator* 4, no. 3 (Spring 1974). Entire issue.

Gittell, Marilyn. *Participants and Participation: A Study of School Policy in New York City.* New York: Center for Urban Education, 1966.

Gross, Neal. *Who Runs Our Schools?* New York: John Wiley and Sons, 1958.

Iannaccone, Laurence. *Politics in Education.* New York: Center for Applied Research in Education, 1967.

Kimbrough, Ralph B. *Political Power and Educational Decision-Making.* Chicago: Rand McNally, 1964.

Kirst, Michael W., ed. *The Politics of Education at the Local, State and Federal Levels.* Berkeley, California: McCutchan, 1970.

Masoti, Louis H. *Education and Politics in Suburbia: The New Trier Experience.* Cleveland, Ohio: Western Reserve University Press, 1967.

Masters, Nicholas A.; Salisbury, Robert H.; and Eliot, Thomas H. *State Politics and the Public Schools.* New York: Alfred A. Knopf, 1964.

Meranto, Philip. *The Politics of Federal Aid to Education in 1965: A Study in Political Innovation.* Syracuse, N.Y.: Syracuse University Press, 1967.

Wiley, Tom. *Politics and Purse Strings in New Mexico's Public Schools.* Albuquerque, N.M.: University of New Mexico Press, 1968.

REFERENCES

Bailey, Stephen K. "Comment." *Leadership for Education.* Washington, D.C.: National Committee for Support of the Public Schools, 1967.

Bailey, Stephen K.; Frost, Richard T.; Wood, Robert C.; and Marsh, Paul E. *Schoolmen and Politics: A Study of State Aid to Education in the Northeast.* Syracuse, N.Y.: Syracuse University Press, 1962.

Browder, Lesley H., Jr. "A Suburban School Superintendent Plays Politics." In *The Politics of Education at the Local, State, and Federal Level,* edited by Michael W. Kirst. Berkeley, Ca.: McCutchan, 1970.

Campbell, Roald F.; Bridges, Edwin M.; Corbally, John E.; Nystrand, Raphael O; and Ramseyer, John. *Introduction to Educational Administration.* 4th ed. Boston: Allyn and Bacon, 1971.

Campbell, Roald F.; Cunningham, Luvern L.; McPhee, Roderick F.; and Nystrand, Raphael O. *The Organization and Control of American Schools.* 2d ed. Columbus, Ohio: Charles E. Merrill, 1970.

Chicago Tribune, 11 January 1973. "Parents Protest Greek Language School Program."

Conant, James B. *The Education of American Teachers.* New York: McGraw-Hill, 1963.

Council for Basic Education. "CBE: What It Is and What It Is Not." *CBE Bulletin* no. 4 (April 1960): 8.

Cunningham, William L. "Some Specific Techniques for Building a Positive Image." Speech made to the National Academy for School Executives, San Francisco, 1 August 1972.

Dickson, George E.; Saxe, Richard W.; et al. *Partners for Educational Reform and Renewal.* Berkeley, Ca.: McCutchan, 1973.

Educational Leadership 31, no. 2 (November 1973). Entire issue: "Women and Education."

Emma Willard Task Force on Education. "Options in Public Education." Minneapolis, Minn., 1973.

Greene, Leroy F. "The Image of Education Today: A Politician's Viewpoint." Speech made to the National Academy for School Executives, San Francisco, 31 July 1972.

Haggart, Robert R. "Survival to Join 3R's, Legislators Seek New School Classes." *Syracuse Herald Journal,* 12 April 1972.

Hawley, Anne. *Contact Washington: An Educator's Directory.* Washington, D.C.: Washington Internships in Education, 1969.

Herndon, Lillie E. "I Strongly Believe in the Power of the Local P.T.A. Unit." *P.T.A. Magazine* 68, no. 2 (October 1973): i.

Hollander, E. P. *Leaders, Groups, and Influence.* New York: Oxford University Press, 1964.

Jamgochian, Richard. "The United States Chamber of Commerce and National Educational Policy." Ph.D. dissertation, University of Chicago, 1964.

Lawrence, Clive. "National P.T.A. Changes Image." *Toledo Blade,* 10 September 1972.

LeBlanc, Jerry. "The Birch Society's Low Profile." *Chicago Tribune,* 1 October 1972.

Lindeman, Tom. "Inspection Chief Planned To Quit, Glad He Didn't." *Toledo Blade,* 20 August 1973.

Marconnit, George D. "A Study of the Current Curriculum Requirements by the Legislature in Each of the Fifty States." *Research Digest Number 21,* pp. 1-32. Iowa City: University of Iowa, 1966.

National Committee for Citizens in Education. *NCCE Report* 1, no. 1 (January 1974).

National Committee for Support of Public Schools. *How To Change the System.* Eighth Annual Conference. Washington, D.C., 1970.

Notre Dame Journal of Education 2, no. 4 (Winter 1972). Entire issue: "Women and Education."

Pharis, William L.; Robison, Lloyd E.; and Walden, John E. *Decision Making and Schools for the 70's.* Washington, D.C.: National Education Association, 1970.

Saxe, Richard W. "The Foundation Fund as Venture Capital." *American Behavioral Scientist* 8, no. 6 (February 1965): 23-29.

———. "Mayors and Schools." *Urban Education* 4, no. 3 (October 1969): 243-251.

———. "Manifest and Latent Functions in Educational Activities." *Bulletin of the National Association of Secondary School Principals* 54 (January 1970): 41-50.

Simon, Paul. "The Eternal Triangle: The Schools, the Legislature, the P.T.A." *P.T.A. Magazine* 67, no. 3 (November 1972): 16-19.

Sitomer, Curtis J. "Mom and Pop Marchers Needle California Schools." *The Christian Science Monitor,* 14 January 1970.

Thimmesch, Nick. "Children's Survival March Scores No Apparent Points." *Toledo Blade,* 2 April 1972.

Toledo Blade, 4 August 1972. "Legal Challenge Brewing Against Schools in Hawaii."

———, 12 September 1972. "School Cancels Jane Fonda Talk."

———, 4 October 1972. "Indian School Protesters."

———, 9 October 1972. "P.T.A. Opposing Ohio Tax Repeal."

———, 1 November 1972. "Abrasive Tactics Notes: Priests, Laymen in 6 Parishes Back Political-Power Drive in Inner City."

———, 3 November 1972. "Membership Breaking Up Brown Berets."

———, 6 March 1973. "Dealing with Disrupters."

———, 20 August 1973. "Diocese Funding To End August 31 for Action Unit."

———, 10 October 1973. "Tar - Feathers Plot Admitted."

———, 27 October 1973. "CTAC Report Cites Progress in Housing Problems Battle."

———, 15 November 1973. "CTAC's Self-Martyrdom."

———, 3 March 1974. "Tea-and-Cookies PTA Starts Twisting Arms."

Walton, Tom. "High School Football Issue Splits Yellow Springs." *Toledo Blade,* 3 October 1971.

Weeres, Joseph B. "School-Community Conflict in a Large Urban School System." *Administrators Notebook* 19, no. 9 (May 1971): 2.

Wolfe, Don. "Young Hunters Aim at Better Grades." *Toledo Blade,* 12 November 1972.

chapter five

Education & Community Power Structures

All animals are equal, but some animals are more equal than others.

George Orwell
Animal Farm

This chapter is the logical successor to the consideration of pressure groups. Pressure groups were seen to be proponents of the particular interests of their members. They were, in general, visible and open advocates of their special interests. Not so the power structure, although the power structure will have its agenda and will favor it above the general interest.

We shall present brief descriptions of the two major approaches to the study of the power structure. We note, in advance, that both are in a primitive stage of development especially in relation to the few studies of the educational structure and educational issues. Implications for educators will be presented. Finally, we shall maintain that the strategies of policy formation of both pressure groups and the power structure are inadequate to represent the majority of citizens and their concerns with the governance of education.

BACKGROUND

Educators, especially superintendents of schools, have long been interested in determining who are influential in decision making about educational issues. It would be strange if they did not have this interest. It stems not merely from idle curiosity or a need for the administrator to retain his employment. Since it is a duty of the administrator to secure and use what resources he can to carry on the educational program of his district, he is almost required to possess some knowledge of the power structure.

It is almost certain that school administrators who have served in a district for more than a few months will have arrived at some conclusions about the influential. They will know "who is in charge," or "who calls the shots." When asked how they know these things about the power structure, administrators will have difficulty in explaining precisely how they arrive at their conclusions. For many, the question appears silly because "everyone around here knows that." Such a reply, far from being seen as avoiding the question, would be seen as highly significant, approximating a proof of the existence and correct identification of the power structure by one school of thought about community power and decision making. It would not at all satisfy another group.

The disagreement touched off by a comment such as that quoted alerts us to a major problem for students of decision making in education—and in other areas as well. There is as yet no generally accepted, all-inclusive way to study the various influences on the control of education. Tyler (1961) acknowledges this condition and notes that each of the social sciences has developed a conceptual scheme and tools to analyze the situation. "Hence, although we cannot obtain a single picture of forces influencing the schools which is comprehensive and accurate we can obtain several pictures, each of which provides a meaningful, accurate, and helpful interpretation of a major aspect of the current situation" (p. 4). This limitation should be kept in mind. It underlies everything discussed in this chapter.

Another caveat is also in order. Much, really most, of what we know about community power structure has been derived from studies of matters other than educational decision making. Cunningham (1971) faced this problem and his conclusion is not reassuring.

> The preparation of this chapter was undertaken on the assumption that the research of an empirical nature on community power, community decision-making, and community change plus certain theoretical models (tested and untested) and the reflections of knowledgeable people in the behavioral sciences would indeed have implications for education. One of the unanticipated outcomes may be the discovery that this assumption is false. [P. 109]

For some there is no need to borrow insights from other disciplines to understand educational decision making. James D. Koerner, of the Council for Basic Education, devotes an entire volume to the question: *Who Controls American Education?* (1968). Koerner's answer is clearly that the professional educators control education. He describes the (deplorable) situation in the final chapter of his book.

> We have seen that the important decisions in education emerge from a labyrinth structure of forces and countervailing forces, but that the interests of professional educators tend to be dominant. We have seen that other interests can have a strong and even controlling influence—as demonstrated, for instance, in the power that public opinion exerted after Sputnik on behalf of educational reform—but only on rare occasions. And we have seen that at least the beginnings of change are now evident in the militancy of teachers, the demands of Negroes in the inner cities, and in the work of the curriculum reform groups. We have, that is, described the complicated political pattern by which American education is presently governed. [P. 155]

Neal Gross, of Harvard University, had previously asked almost exactly the same question, *Who Runs Our Schools?* (1958), ten years before Koerner and received a different answer. Much of the problem, according to Gross, was inadequate financial support for schools. His study showed that the PTA, community officials, businessmen, housewives, and service clubs supported public schools, while community officials, businessmen, taxpayers' groups, older residents of the community, individuals with grudges, religious groups, newspapermen, and the "private school crowd" blocked public schools. The appearance of the same groups on the lists of blockers and supporters is testimony of the way communities vary.

A severe, anticommunist critic of professional educators also finds the answer in an interplay of pressure groups—in this case a collusion of three in a kind of conspiracy

> at the very high levels of learning, tax receipts and tax-deductible donations have combined to establish a three-way line of coded communication between our educational system, the big charitable foundations, and the Federal bureaucracy. For their effective direction of our national policy, it is no longer necessary to let "outsiders" listen in on this esoteric conversation because the audition would serve merely to confuse them. [Manion 1967, p. 2]

Koerner, Gross, and Manion were all dealing with the issue of control of education in terms of the activities of pressure groups as we described them in the previous chapter. They examined the complex, but open rivalries of groups with different objectives in competition to influence the schools to accomplish their set of objectives. The common sense and the folk wisdom of school administrators suggests that the process of decision making is more complex. Those who endeavor to follow the bureaucratic model rigidly soon find ample evidence that outside influences are constantly at work to interfere with the proper functioning of bureaucratic processes. Speculation about which sinister forces are affecting the bureaucracy sometimes leads to the discovery of an informal organization within the school district or school. Often, however, it seems to signal the influence of important persons working unobtrusively.

Many contemporary observers of education assume that there is no longer a need to question the existence of an unofficial community power structure. Consider this comment made in a recent seminar of citizens, businessmen, and educators:

> A public enterprise of such magnitude as the school is bound to be of concern at some time or place to the community power structure. Every community has a power structure which is the relative distribution of decision making among the groups of people in a school district. Decisions which are vital to the school are quite frequently of considerable concern to the power structure. [Darling 1972, p. 9]

Subsequent comments make it clear that the power structure referred to is not that of the regular organizational-governmental structure.

> In the past educators have turned their backs on the power structure in the mistaken belief they were separated from politics by a non-partisan, elected school board and an appointed superintendent. In many instances, they have been brutally manipulated as a result. A major characteristic of the power structure is its lack of social responsibility. Its power is wielded largely in attempts to influence the community to make decisions that coincide with its own ends. [Ibid.]

If the preceding arguments about the probable existence of a power structure are not persuasive, consider the logic of Nunnery and Kimbrough in their book, *Politics, Power, Polls, and School Elections* (1971). They maintain that

> there must be a structure or system for making decisions concerning community living, for executing policies, and for maintaining the system. . . . The power structure of the community is the systematic, relative distribution of social power among the citizens in determining the kind of community they want and the kind of institutional arrangements that will best serve them. The exercise of power by citizens is not equal; there is an unequal distribution of influence in the system. [P. 8]

Early studies by sociologists, although not directed at educational decision making, provided evidence of the existence and the nature of a community power structure. Robert S. and Helen M. Lynd published two important studies of "Middletown" (Muncie, Indiana) in 1929 and 1937. The Lynds investigated community behavior and how the decision makers arrived at decisions. In 1929 they found the Ball family (of the mason jars) ruled Muncie like a "manorial system." In 1937 they found that the business elites were still in power and that there had been little change in power centers. The Lynds did not suggest that Middletown-Muncie was a prototype of all small cities. They did reveal how economic power was used to affect decision making. Now that the Ball brothers have died and only a research division of the glass manufacturing operation remains, it is likely that some new team will replicate the Middletown studies. This will be important to demonstrate that power structure is not a constant; that, with changing conditions, it gives way to new leadership.

Another sociologist, W. Lloyd Warner, and his colleagues studied Yankee City (Newburyport, Massachusetts) (1941) because it seemed to represent a stable, integrated community. Actually, Yankee City was in transition for the local ownership and management of industries (mostly shoemaking) was becoming absentee-ownership and absentee-management. Out of this study came the famous classification system for social class. Despite the interesting effect of this shift, Warner's findings supported the Lynds who had questioned the popular notion that communities were governed by democratic pluralism.

Other early case studies of communities in regions other than the east and midwest are available: see Dollard 1937; Davis, Gardner and Gardner 1941; and West 1945—all of whom also studied the power structures and identified the groups included in and excluded from the elite. The next study that should be reported is Hunter's study of Regional City (Atlanta, Georgia), made in 1953. However, since Hunter precipitated a major controversy between sociologists and political scientists and heightened interest in the study of community power structure, we should take time to define a few of the terms used in the resulting debates.

STUDYING POWER STRUCTURES

Power is variously defined, usually in a manner suitable to the research purposes and orientation of the person using the term. For our purposes—of discussing community power structure—*power* means the ability or authority to cause others to do what we want them to do. *Power* as we use it suggests that one has whatever resources are necessary to get his way.

Influence as we define it is difficult to distinguish from power. *Influence* means the ability to persuade others to act, think, or feel as we want them to. The main difference is that power may be considered coercive and influence persuasive. Many writers, especially political scientists, seem to use influence interchangeably with power. In Banfield's study of *Political Influence* (1961), many of his examples of influence would fall within our definition of power. He offers this example of different kinds of influence: "A mayor for example, is likely to employ in a single act of influence the authority of his office, the respect he commands as a man, rational persuasion, 'selling,' and perhaps both rewards and punishment as well" (p. 5). Clearly, the authority of his office would be a use of power by our definition, as would the application of punishment. Of course, the behavior described would be influence, not power, if the mayor were dealing with persons who were not obliged to respect his authority. For instance, employees in the mayor's office will turn their thermostats down to save fuel because of his power; citizens, because of his influence.

Something like the idea of idiosyncrasy credits is involved in influence. It is also helpful when thinking of a school administrator and a faculty to think of power as "ascribed" status due to any one in the prescribed administrative position and influence as "achieved" status earned by actions perceived as effective and sensible.

Authority is an element of power. It means the rights and privileges that belong to a certain position. It is seen as being the legitimate basis for power, as contrasted to strength, force, and violence, when employed without authority. Authority is usually formal, based on status in an organization. Authority is sanctioned by law, by delegation, or by election.

Community almost defies definition. So many systems interact that it is difficult to construct specific boundaries. To pursue all of the myriad nuances suggested by the term *community* is neither necessary nor feasible in these pages. We will mean by *community* the relatively autonomous political and social systems that together make up a single system. In other chapters we shall need to mean something else by *school community*. Now, *community* is used to refer to the complex of institutions of all kinds that make up a single system. We will need to clarify this usage by modifiers from time to time. Woodlawn can be considered a community within the community of Chicago, which is within the community complex of greater Chicago.

Power structure refers to the relationships among those holding power in a given community. Some students of power structure will be able to show the relationships in a diagram.

Hunter and the Elitists

In 1953 Floyd Hunter, a sociologist, published his discovery that, in effect, a small ruling elite of only a few persons was making the decisions for the entire city of Atlanta. This group, the power elite, was isolated from the mass of people in the community. The leaders were persons of high status and the group of leaders "in specific instances tends to act on policy matters without regard for various community groups" (p. 256). The elite was able to enforce its decisions by persuasion, coercion, intimidation, and even force, if necessary. There was an old guard of elder statesmen whose approval was usually necessary for the projects of a group of younger, new leaders.

The distribution of power suggested by Hunter's findings is illustrated in figure 5-1. At the apex of the pyramid in figure 5-1 would be found the small homogenous group of influentials who direct the affairs of everyone else in the community. Moreover, "there appears to be a tenuous line of communication between the governors of our society and the governed. This situation does not square with the concepts of democracy we have been taught to revere" (ibid., p. 1).

Hunter's data were gathered by a procedure that may be described as the reputational technique. First he identified persons who were at the center of community activities (e.g., members of the Chamber of Commerce, League of Women Voters, community council, and newspaper editors and civic leaders). These persons provided lists of others prominent in economics, government, education, and religion,

FIGURE 5-1 MONOLITHIC POWER STRUCTURE

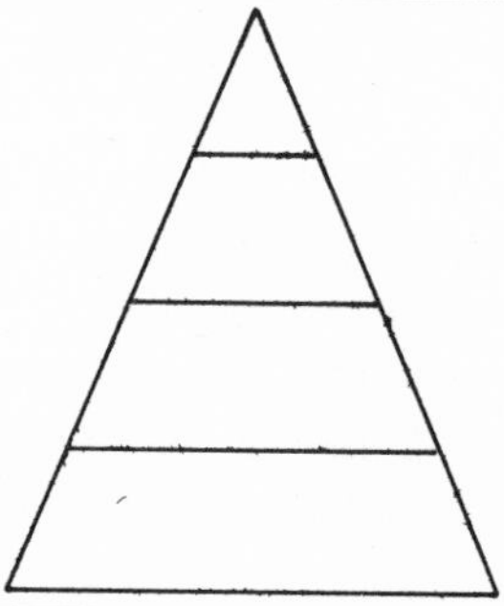

and of citizens of wealth and social prominence. In Atlanta this activity generated a total of 175 names (ibid., p. 61).

The second step was to present the lists to a panel of fourteen judges composed of representatives of three religions, both sexes, various age and racial groupings, business executives, and professionals. The task of the panel was to narrow the list of 175 down to 40—10 each in economics, politics, community affairs, and society.

The third step required interviews of the chosen forty. The interviews took from two to six or more hours. Hunter asked each of the forty to name the five most powerful persons on the list and to add the names of other prominent persons if this seemed appropriate. The forty provided information about issues and decisions in the community, their participation, the participation of other leaders, friendship with other leaders, business ties, estimates of the relative influence of other leaders, kinship patterns, and related information.

Finally, Hunter and his associates organized and interpreted this mass of data to arrive at the findings with which we began the discussion of his work. These are the data that permit the use of the pyramid to describe the distribution of power in Regional City.

Hunter's study was followed by others using his approach. In general, they discovered monolithic power structures, often made of a group of influential businessmen, professionals, and politicians.

Political scientists were quick to respond to the intrusion of Hunter and his fellow sociologists into their territory. They responded with vigorous criticism, some of which provided ideas used later by political scientists in examining power structures. The first of many criticisms was made by Kaufman and Jones (1954) and the first political scientist to complete a study that met the criteria of political scientists was Robert A. Dahl.

Dahl and the Pluralists

Dahl is the person identified with the pluralist-political scientist approach to studies of power structure in the same way that Hunter represents the elitist-sociologist approach. Like Hunter, his study served as a model for subsequent studies by others.

Dahl organized his study (1961) of New Haven, Connecticut to get the answers to questions about urban redevelopment, public education, and political nominations in the major parties. Unlike Hunter, Dahl found that decisions were not made by the same ruling elite. Influence was specialized, few individuals exercised important influence in more than one area, and there were different groups of decision makers for different issues.

Dahl found that the distribution of resources and the ways they are or are not used is a source of both political change and stability in a pluralistic political system. Interestingly, he found that the democratic creed to some extent placed limits on all concerned:

> Citizens are very far indeed from exerting equal influence over the content, application, and development of the political consensus. Yet, widely held beliefs by Americans in a creed of democracy and political equality serve as a critical limit on the ways in which leaders can shape the consensus. [Ibid., p. 325]

Dahl found that the social leaders and the wealthy were only influential in decisions directly concerned with business prosperity. He also found that, despite the many similarities in leadership in public education to leadership in urban redevelopment and political parties, there were significant differences. Most of the associations active in school affairs dealt only with public school concerns and played "a minor part in the political parties and in urban redevelopment" (ibid., p. 84).

Figure 5-2 is a schematic representation of the pluralistic power structure of New Haven. In each of the issue areas a different group is involved. The pyramids are truncated to suggest that the decision makers at the top are not significantly more powerful than those at other levels as they would be in the monolithic mode used to represent Atlanta. Dahl emphasized the importance of the concept of "slack" in the system in that decisions are made by loose

FIGURE 5-2 A PLURALISTIC POWER STRUCTURE

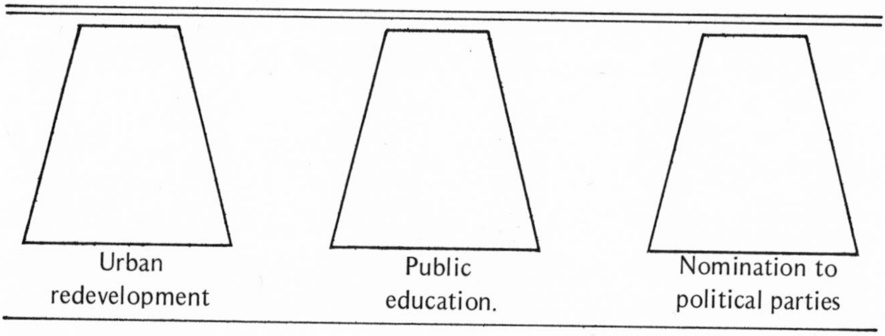

collections of persons, and citizens fail to use their full resources (ibid., p. 141).

Dahl and the pluralists are sometimes referred to as issue analysts or decision analysts, a reference to the method of data collection used in New Haven. The first step in their approach was to select the decision areas—nomination to political office, urban redevelopment, public education—and ask representative persons to identify the most important decisions made in the area during a specified time. The next step was to attempt to reconstruct each decision by documentary analysis, extensive interviews, and direct observation. Lengthy, sometimes multiple, interviews were held with persons who participated in the decisions. Dahl determined who initiated the process of decision making, how people exercised power, who controlled the outcome, how citizens participated, and who carried out the decision. (Dahl's procedure is summarized in appendix B, ibid., pp. 330-334.)

Arguments continue between elitists and pluralists. The literature is too extensive to be reported here, but a colleague, John Spiess, has reviewed this controversy in *Community Power and Influence Studies: Two Positions* (1970). Dahl points out that the elitist position that someone behind the scenes ("they," old families, bankers, city hall, the party boss) runs things is virtually impossible to disprove. He maintains that:

> The ruling elite model can be interpreted in this way. If the overt leaders of a community do not appear to constitute a ruling elite, then the theory can be saved by arguing that behind the overt leaders there is a set

of covert leaders who do. If subsequent evidence shows that this covert group does not make a ruling elite, then the theory can be saved by arguing that behind the first covert group there is another, and so on. [1971, p. 354]

Pluralists have been accused of confusing multiple ruling elites with the pluralistic model out of their dedication to the democratic ideology. The model for the type of power structure that consists of multiple ruling elites is shown in figure 5-3. It would be termed a polylithic power structure (Clark 1968, chapter 2). There are plural

FIGURE 5-3 POLYLITHIC POWER STRUCTURE

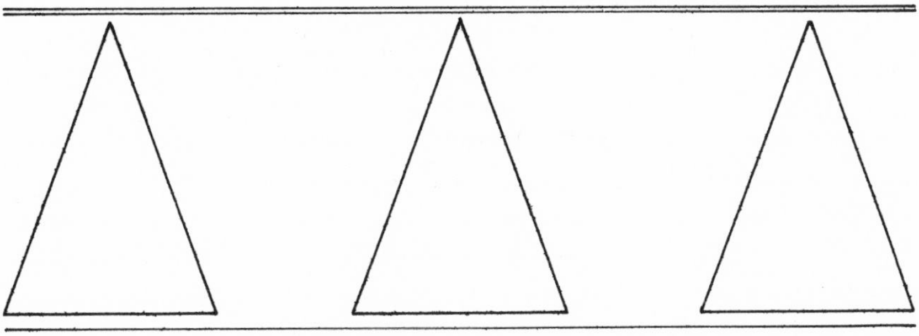

issue areas but within each can be located an elitist monolithic decision-making structure. Even though a given person may be at the top of a pyramid for one issue, he may drop to the bottom for other issues. It is likely that the power structures of several large cities are of this type.

There is one important deficiency of issue analysis as a procedure. The absence of a decision, the refusal to permit an issue to surface may be an important function of power structure. Issue analysis cannot deal with such eventualities.

Combination Studies

As one would expect, there are now studies of community power that use a combination of reputational and issue analysis approaches. From the perspective of a school administrator, it seems most sensible to consider reputational data about the community as well as data about actual participation in important issues. Separately these will not be adequate to analyze the process completely, but taken together the results will be superior to either approach taken alone. Kimbrough (1964, p. 88) and Spiess (1967), among others, support this position.

Apling's study (1970) of the influence of the mayor of a giant midwestern city on educational decision making is an example of the combination approach. It includes the identification and analysis of specific controversial issues as well as the identification of influentials.

A panel of persons knowledgeable about the school system, made up of the superintendent and the past and incumbent presidents of the board of education, nominated the most controversial issues facing the school system during a specified time. Four issues were selected for analysis: the Northwest Project, the Baldwin School, the ten mil levy campaign, and violence at Roosevelt High School.

Data were gathered from personal interviews, mailed questionnaires, news accounts, and minutes of board of education meetings. Each issue was reconstructed and analyzed to determine the relative influence of the mayor over educational decision making. A series of grids was used to represent the mayor's attributed influence for each and all issues. Coalitions of interest and/or action were noted.

The mayor was found to be significantly involved in decisions about the Northwest Project and violence at Roosevelt High School, deliberately less significantly involved in the ten mil levy campaign, and not involved with decisions about Baldwin School. Of the three issues in which the mayor was involved, he was judged to be influential in the two former and lacking in influence in the latter.

Apling concluded that:

1. There is a relationship between politics and education; the relationship between municipal government and the schools is extensive.
2. The relationship of the mayor of this large city to educational decision making is extensive.
3. The mayor is an influential in controversial educational issues.
4. The mayor's involvement in controversial educational issues was largely the result of requests for assistance.
5. There are no coalitions between participants of one sector—municipal government, school government, and community—and participants of another sector.

6. For this particular study, a power elite did not exist to make the decisions about controversial educational issues.

THE STUDY OF COMMUNITY POWER STRUCTURES BY SCHOOL ADMINISTRATORS

The approaches to the study of community power structure discussed above are the best known. There are other approaches and school administrators will find the literature informative, although it should be obvious that schoolmen cannot employ the same methods (see, for example, Bell, Hill, and Wright 1961, pp. 5-23; and Nunnery and Kimbrough 1971, pp. 8-38). Their relationship to boards and to communities would preclude the use of the usual methods of learning about the community power structure by school officials or their representatives. Nevertheless, it is well within the professional role of the school administrator to secure this kind of information. Actually, it is more than proper, it is necessary for administrators to have this kind of knowledge.

Sumption and Engstrom agree that the educator must identify the power structure. They point out that it will be most difficult to discover key figures in the power structure.

> Discreet inquiries, casual conversations, study of past policy decisions, and above all, careful observation are essential. The delineation of a community power structure is somewhat like solving a crossword puzzle; each step toward the solution makes the subsequent step easier. [1966, p. 26]

They then go on to advocate tactics of elitists—asking well-informed persons to identify influentials—and pluralists—list opponents and proponents of defeated and successful issues.

Nunnery and Kimbrough, in *Politics, Power, Polls, and School Elections* (1971), also agree that "studying the power structure is not an avocation of the superintendent of schools and his colleagues, but a serious part of the modern school leader's job" (p. 28). They offer detailed suggestions about how to discover the power structure. The first step is for the school leader to prepare himself by examining the professional literature (such as the works listed at the end of this chapter) and attending conferences, courses, or workshops on the politics of education.

The second step is termed "Learning the problems, issues, and decisions." Educators initiate informal discussions with leaders in areas of importance to the school district. This step is clearly influenced by the reputational approach. The persons to be interviewed will vary according to the characteristics of the district, but might include the executive secretary or president of the chamber of commerce, politicians, bankers, leaders in women's clubs and social activities, union leaders, clergymen, political party chairmen, editors or publishers, farm agents or prominent farmers, and leaders of ethnic and racial groups. The conversations should arise naturally out of the normal activities of the administrator, not by special arrangement. In conversation the educator should encourage discussion about those who are influential in the community and remember the names of persons frequently mentioned in connection with issues and decisions—a pluralist tactic (ibid., p. 28).

The third step is called "Piecing together conversations and documents." The educator records the names of persons identified as prominent and notes the interrelationships among them. Documents of organizations and membership lists also confirm and supplement interview data. Newspapers will help to identify community leaders.

Step four is "Recording and compiling information." Because few can mentally organize and recall all of the information gathered, Nunnery and Kimbrough recommend a clipping and filing system. They also suggest that lists be made of persons interested in working for better schools and of persons "who express predispositions to oppose school proposals" (ibid., p. 29). When they were writing, the famous list of enemies of the Nixon administration had not been revealed (*Toledo Blade* 12/22/73, p. 10). In the light of recent events, it seems most unwise for school administrators to prepare "enemy lists." It needs to be mentioned that the purpose of the list of potential opponents of school issues was to enable the administrator to include such opponents in educational affairs and to provide them with information about educational needs in the hope that opponents will cease opposing once they understand the position advocated by proponents of educational proposals.

The final step is "Direct observation and participation in community activities." As a guide to focus observation, it is suggested that educators formulate ideas (hypotheses?) about the type of power structure they believe exists. Obviously the schoolman-observer must be an active participant in community and civic functions in order to have ample opportunity for observing. Finally the authors recommend "thoughtful engagement in political activities by school leaders [to] provide a 'gut-level' conceptualization of the power structure" (ibid., p. 30).

THE SIGNIFICANCE OF POWER STRUCTURE STUDIES

Although many studies of community power structure were not specifically concerned with educational issues, the conclusions are, nevertheless, of interest to educators. Cunningham wryly notes the "contemporary discovery of local school systems by political and social scientists" (1971, p. 114).

An early study of "Springdale" by Vidich and Bensman (1958) still offers a realistic description of school politics in one type of rural community. Springdale schools enrolled about six hundred students in grades one through twelve from all sections of a township. An informal agreement at the time of consolidation gave four out of five board of education seats to farmer and one to the village. The budget of a quarter of a million dollars made the school the major industry of the village. The school was also the community center for social, cultural, and athletic events.

Decisions of the school board had important consequences for the entire community. The board dealt with such problems as:

1. The budget; specifically [for] school buses, expanded curriculum, and expanded plant facilities, which together determine the school tax rate.
2. The proportioning of the agricultural curriculum as against college preparatory and industrial and business crafts curricula.
3. Appointments and reappointments of teachers and the granting of tenure.
4. The appointment of janitors, bus drivers, and motor repairmen.
5. School food and supply services. [Ibid, p. 172]

Because these are matters of great interest, the Springdale board went to great lengths to make its decisions in secret so as to give the outward appearance of unanimity.

The example of the selection of a new board member by the "invisible government" shows how the prosperous farmers retain their dominance (ibid., pp. 176-180). Village business interests can cooperate with the farm interests because both desire low taxes and a low level of spending. Businessmen speak through the business bureau in favor of law and order (viz., keeping adolescents orderly and off the streets) and local purchasing.

The school principal (in effect, the superintendent, owing to peculiarities of the districting in New York State) attempted to advance his own educational concerns through the PTA. In controversies, the board would often allow the administration "to absorb the resentment and [guarantee] the continuation of rural dominance on the board in exchange for a minor concession to business interests at the costs of the administration's program" (ibid., p. 186).

The principal, always called "The Professor," was perceived as "the personal embodiment of education," a condition that made him a central figure on the political scene. The way in which one school leader responded to his relationship to the particular power structure is shown in the extended quotation from the chapter "School Politics." In order to accomplish his ends "which are necessarily in the selfish interests of education," the principal must:

> recognize differences of power. He must recognize the interests of the farmers, professionals, industrial workers, party politics, the generalized desire for low taxes, and he must give each of these elements their due weight in his educational calculations. To the extent that he makes an accurate assessment of local power relations and acts on this assessment he has a chance, at least in the short run, to succeed with his program.
>
> While giving due weight to these various interests he must at the same time try not to alienate any one of them. As a result he publicly tends to agree with everyone and his public statements are of sufficient generality as to be satisfactory to almost all groups. However, when pressed, he agrees most, in terms of his rhetoric, with the rural interests since this is the dominant group within and through whom he must work.
>
> This he must do even though his underlying educational program is against a lopsided, farm-dominated school system. Vocational training, college preparation, a guidance program and modern methods are central to his educational philosophy. But in order to accomplish his program, he must constantly make concessions to the dominant interests behind school policy and attempt to implement his program through more indirect and subtle means. As a consequence of this, it frequently happens that he is forced to dissociate himself from his own ideas in the PTA and to take public positions which are inconsistent with his long range program. [Ibid., pp. 195-196]

While surely not an admirable stance for the Professor to assume, his strategy seems well suited for survival and long-term change in Springdale schools. Before we condemn the Professor, it would be well to examine the wealth of data presented in *Small Town and Mass Society* and attempt to devise a more ethical strategy that can also be effective.

Alan Campbell would acknowledge the need for the Professor to provide day-to-day leadership in the school district. However, he adds this observation:

> On the other hand, it is probably unrealistic to look to these people (school administrators) to introduce changes on their own initiative. In

> many ways they are captives of the community in which they operate. Further, their day-to-day responsibilities are so great that their primary role is to keep the system operating. They tend to make every effort to avoid controversy and, in general, to keep the boat from rocking. It is ridiculous to be critical of this behavior, for their positions make it inevitable. [1968, p. 50]

We already know, even if some of us will not admit it, that the answer to all our problems is not found in operating a good educational program for the boys and girls in the schools. Make no mistake, a good program is important and it must always be central to the arguments of educators. But, in fairness to the Professor in Springdale and to his counterparts, we must acknowledge that there can be no good program without a successful vote on the next operating levy, no outstanding open school if the bond issue is defeated.

The question of what difference knowing the power structure makes and how to deal with the power structure remains to be answered. The Springdale example showed how one particular school administrator responded to one particular power structure. There are any number of variations of power structures and there is some evidence to suggest that school boards and superintendents are both forced into different types in order to respond appropriately (see McCarty and Ramsey 1967). For what it is worth, we can assume that life would be simpler for a superintendent working with an uncompetitive, monolithic power elite than it would be for his counterpart working with competing elites or competing pluralistic power structures. But, and this is an important, albeit obvious, analysis of the literature on power structures: knowing is not enough! Knowledge of the power structure will not, of itself, result in more effective administration. Teasing out the existing power structure will not yield a panacea. This seemingly gratuitous truism is a response to the positions of many colleagues who conclude their discussions of power structure with the observation that his possessing such helpful knowledge will undoubtedly make the administrator more effective. Maybe it will.

Nunnery and Kimbrough (1971) list seven ways in which educators may act on the basis of knowledge of the power structure. Simple inspection of the list will reveal that if administrators adopted *some* of these ways of acting, they would most probably be less effective! Here is their list of ways in which to approach the power structure:

1. Attempt . . . to organize latent centers of power (e.g., managers of absentee-owned corporations) and the public to defeat the existing power structure.
2. Bring . . . pressure from outside sources to bear to change the opinions of some of the influentials (e.g., the threat of losing the school's accreditation or eventual loss of economic growth, because of poor schools).
3. Organize . . . studies of school needs in which key influentials participate and grow in their understanding of school needs (e.g., cooperative school surveys, citizens committees).
4. Acquiesce . . . in the wishes of the influentials until school conditions get bad enough for public pressure to force a change in their opinions.
5. Forget . . . about the idea of pressing for school improvement.
6. Consider . . . changes in the school proposal that might make it acceptable to the leaders of the community. . . .
7. Attempt . . . to bargain with the influentials for their support by promising advantages to them for supporting the proposal. [P. 35]

The authors point out that these strategies will have different results with different power structures and that all have been used in practice.

Another pair of authors, although surely aware of the infinite variety of power arrangements possible, offer some specific general "guidelines for his personal conduct which will stand the administrator in good stead in meeting this problem." Sumption and Engstrom advise administrators to avoid entangling alliances by observing these rules.

> First, he will maintain a complete independence and freedom of action. This means he will make no deals and accept no favors which are predicated on a return in kind. To do this he need not isolate himself. He can, and should, be active in community affairs . . .
> Second, he will judge each issue on its merits and act accordingly. Insofar as possible, he will avoid personalities and give battle only on the issues.
> Third, he will never align himself with any group which is self-serving at the expense of the people he serves . . .
> Fourth, he will conduct himself in such a manner as to develop a reputation for fairness, consistency, and impartiality in his relations with all groups in the community. Even members of the power group respect a man who will not yield to influence from any quarter and as long as he treats all groups alike, are more or less content to leave him alone most of the time.
> Finally, he will recognize that losing his job is not as bad as losing his integrity. [1966, p. 32]

Sumption and Engstrom take an ethical position based on the assumption that the power structure is hostile to the best interests of school programs. The advice will surely serve the administrator until he has been able to identify the power structure. Then, it would seem that a more pragmatic, less moralistic orientation might enable him to make good use of information about decision makers, hidden and visible. For example, it might be better in the long run for the school administrator to pull out of a hopeless struggle at least until his estimate of the situation gives him some hope of winning. Putting a forty-eight million dollar bond issue before the voters when all the community spokesmen except for a school-supportive PTA oppose it is sometimes a good strategy, if the subsequent defeat will help arrange a compromise that can win. It is perhaps courageous, but probably harmful to education in the long run to stick to one's guns and go back time and again for the same, ideal forty-eight million dollars.

One hears, sometimes from the ubiquitous "reliable sources," of administrators who invariably arrange an informal assessment of major proposals by the power structure before making the project public. In the forty-eight million dollar issue mentioned above, such an administrator would first secure the approval of the identified influentials. This would need to be done covertly lest the schoolman be perceived as a tool of the power structure. There would be a vigorous campaign, supported by the power structure, which could—in the present state of affairs—go down to a crushing defeat because of opposition coming from persons who were not under the influence of the elite. As the losing superintendent goes back to the drawing board to plan his next move, he needs to ask himself whether it makes any difference losing with the support of influentials or without it. The answer to this question will be easier after he has analyzed the sources and strength of opposition to his program.

Dealing with hypothetical issues is frustrating but so, too, is the political world of schoolmen. Of course, there are issues so important that one must not withdraw even in the face of certain defeat. But is every issue such a matter of life or death? Compromise will sometimes result in an important gain but this must be evaluated against the possible long-term loss. Perhaps the voters will approve a two million dollar levy now but this may make the forty-eight million dollar project forever impossible.

Enough has been said, it is hoped, to support the position that school administrators need to be aware of the power structure and to consider the power structure in their planning. There is unlikely to be a handbook of how to deal with the power structure. However, it should be apparent that knowing the basis of possible opposition makes it possible to deal in advance with important obstacles without injuring an over-all design. That is, if an administrator, by knowing his community, can put together a program that will be sure to bring enough support to succeed, he need not suffer remorse for modifying a plan that will engender enough opposition to ensure its failure.

Two important points remain to be made. The first is that neither pressure groups nor power structures however defined provide adequate means for a citizen to participate in education. A structure that would represent an adequate level of participation by citizens is represented by figure 5-4.

FIGURE 5-4 POWER STRUCTURE FOR SIGNIFICANT PARTICIPATION BY CITIZENS IN DECISION MAKING

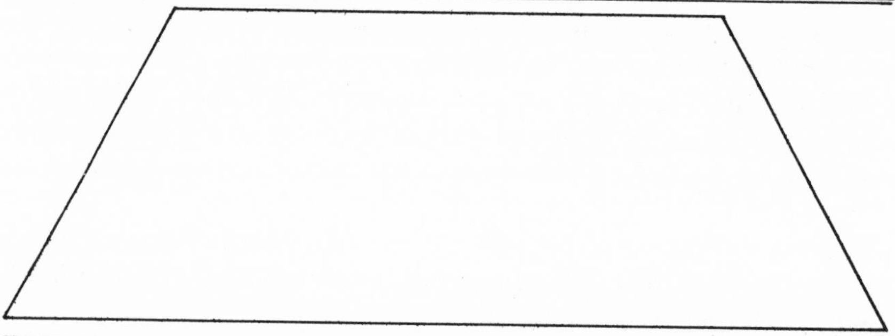

Needless to say, there are few examples of organizations governed in accordance with figure 5-4. The old New England town meetings would be something like this. When one reads A. S. Neill, it seems as though he were trying to make Summerhill become a mass participation model. There are small differences in status and leaders are easily replaced. People participate in any or all issues on an almost equal basis. Clearly, this model can never be achieved in a large, centralized system. We do not yet know if it is even feasible with decentralization to small, local school units.

The second point is a bit more optimistic. Power structures and pressure groups may well have denied certain citizens the chance to participate in decision making about education. New forces, including federal support and attendant controls, are providing a vehicle to involve new groups in decision making. What this new development will mean in the long run remains to be seen.

Finally, in opposition to the mass of data we have collected about pressure, influence, and power, there is always the potentially disproportionate influence of one persistent ordinary citizen. School administrators are always sensitive to the effect of valid, vigorous criticism, no matter what their relationship to pressure groups, or power structures, or ethical codes of conduct. It is still likely that the squeaky wheel will be greased if the squeak is persistent and loud enough.

SUMMARY

In this chapter we discussed the community power structure. Sociologists emphasized a reputational approach and were more likely to discover ruling elites. Political scientists stressed issue analysis and more often found different centers of influence, depending upon the area of the issue. School administrators are well advised to use a discreet approach in discovering the power structure. Knowledge of the power structure is one more source of important information to serve as a guide to planning and action. The power structure does not permit meaningful participation by ordinary citizens in decision making about education. The failure of pressure groups and the power structure to offer appropriate means for citizens to become involved and the barriers of bureaucracy and professional hostility contribute to the demand for alternative structures of educational governance.

SUGGESTED ACTIVITIES

1. Using issue analysis, identify influential decision makers in the area of education for your community. Are these the same persons you would expect to find important in another area, such as housing or medical care?

2. Using the reputational approach, try to find the influentials in your community. Which power structure description is most appropriate to typify the relationships among influentials and others?

3. Make a list of the knowledgeable persons you might interview to discover who is important in educational decision making.

4. Interview some members of a board of education. Try to find out what individuals or groups influence their decision making.

5. Interview a school superintendent. Find out if he can distinguish the degrees of influence he has with different members of his board. What explanation does he give for these differences?

6. Read *Small Town in Mass Society* and try to devise a better approach to the power structure than the one taken by the Professor.

7. Describe and compare the power structures for two public service agencies in your community—make one the education agency.

8. Make a table of words or phrases associated with the two major approaches to studying community power structure. Head one column *Elitists,* the other *Pluralists.* Include names of proponents as well as words describing the approaches. Try to find corresponding but different terms for each side of your table whenever possible.

SUGGESTED READINGS

Campbell, Roald F., et al. *The Organization and Control of American Schools.* 2d ed. Columbus, Ohio: Charles E. Merrill, 1970, chapter 14.

Clark, Terry N. *Community Structure and Decision Making: Comparative Analyses.* San Francisco: Chandler, 1968, chapters 2, 4, and 5.

Dahl, Robert A. *Who Governs?* New Haven, Conn.: Yale University Press, 1961.

Hawley, Willis D., and Svara, James. *The Study of Community Power: A Bibliographic Review.* Santa Barbara, California: American Bibliographic Center-Clio Press, 1972.

Hunter, Floyd. *Community Power Structure.* Chapel Hill, N.C.: University of North Carolina Press, 1953.

Kimbrough, Ralph B. *Political Power and Educational Decision Making.* Chicago: Rand McNally, 1964.

Knezevich, Stephen J. *Administration of Public Education.* 2d ed. New York: Harper & Row, 1969, chapter 24.

Maguire, John W. "School Principals and Community Power Structure." *Intellect* 102, no. 2358 (Summer 1974): 510-511.

Spiess, John A. *Community Power Study: Applications to Educational Administration.* Toledo, Ohio: University of Toledo, 1971.

Wirt, Frederick M., and Kirst, Michael W. *The Political Web of American Schools.* Boston: Little Brown, 1972, pp. 67-77.

REFERENCES

Apling, Daniel L. "An Analysis of a Large City Mayor's Influence with Regard to Educational Decision Making." Ph.D. dissertation, University of Toledo, 1970.

Banfield, Edward C. *Political Influence.* New York: The Free Press, 1961.

Bell, Wendell; Hill, Richard J.; and Wright, Charles R. *Public Leadership.* San Francisco: Chandler, 1961.

Campbell, Alan K. "Who Governs the Schools?" *Saturday Review,* 21 December 1968, p. 50.

Clark, Terry N. *Community Structure and Decision Making: Comparative Analyses.* San Francisco: Chandler, 1968.

Cunningham, Luvern. *Governing Schools: New Approaches to Old Issues.* Columbus, Ohio: Charles E. Merrill, 1971.

Dahl, Robert A. *Who Governs?* New Haven, Conn.: Yale University Press, 1961.

———. "A Critique of the Ruling Elite Model." In *Decisions, Organizations and Society,* edited by F. G. Castles, D. J. Murray, and D. C. Potter, pp. 354-363. Harmondsworth, England: Penguin Books, 1971.

Darling, Arthur (conference reporter). *Better School-Community Relations.* Dayton, Ohio: Institute for Development of Educational Activities, 1972.

Davis, Allison; Gardner, Burleigh; and Gardner, Mary. *Deep South.* Chicago: University of Chicago Press, 1941.

Dollard, John. *Caste and Class in a Southern Town.* Garden City, N.Y.: Doubleday, 1937.

Gross, Neal. *Who Runs Our Schools?* New York: John Wiley, 1958.

Hunter, Floyd. *Community Power Structure.* Chapel Hill, N.C.: University of North Carolina Press, 1953.

Kaufman, Herbert, and Jones, Victor. "The Mystery of Power." *Public Administration Review* 14 (Summer 1954): 205-212.

Kimbrough, Ralph B. *Political Power and Educational Decision Making.* Chicago: Rand McNally, 1964.

Koerner, James D. *Who Controls American Education?* Boston: Beacon Press, 1968.

Lynd, Robert S., and Lynd, Helen M. *Middletown.* New York: Harcourt, Brace and World, 1929.

———. *Middletown in Transition.* New York: Harcourt, Brace and World, 1937.

Manion, Dean Clarence E. "Professional Educators Play 'Musical Chairs.' " *Manion Forum,* 5 February 1967, p. 2.

McCarty, Donald J., and Ramsey, Charles E. *A Study of Community Factors Related to the Turnover of Students—Community Power School Board Structure, and the Role of the Chief School Administrator.* ED 014 130. Ithaca, N.Y.: Cornell University, 1967.

Nunnery, Michael Y., and Kimbrough, Ralph B. *Politics, Power, Polls, and School Elections.* Berkeley, Ca.: McCutchan, 1971.

Spiess, John A. *Community Power and Influence Studies: Two Positions.* Toledo, Ohio: University of Toledo, 1970.

———. "Community Power Structure and Influence: Relationships to Educational Administration." Ph.D. dissertation, University of Iowa, 1967.

Sumption, Merle R., and Engstrom, Yvonne. *School-Community Relations.* New York: McGraw-Hill, 1966.

Toledo Blade, 12/22/73, p. 10. "Committee Discloses 'Enemies List' Given to IRS by Former Nixon Aide."

Tyler, Ralph. "The Purpose and Plan of this Yearbook." In *Social Forces Influencing Education.* The Sixtieth Yearbook of the National Society for the Study of Education, part 2. Chicago: University of Chicago Press, 1961.

Vidich, Arthur J., and Bensman, Joseph. *Small Town in Mass Society.* Princeton, N.J.: Princeton University Press, 1958.

Warner, W. Lloyd, and Lunt, Paul S. *The Social Life of a Modern Community.* Vol. 1, "Yankee City Series." New Haven, Conn.: Yale University Press, 1941.

West, James. *Plainville, U.S.A.* New York: Columbia University Press, 1945.

chapter six

Needs Assessment

> Perfection of means and confusion of goals seem
> —in my opinion—to characterize our age.
>
> Albert Einstein

In this chapter we will consider the problem of determining the educational needs for a given school population. We assume that this is necessary no matter what the pattern of educational control—centralized or decentralized—no matter who is "in charge"—bureaucrats or the citizens. The manner by which educational needs are determined and the use made of this information both fall within the definition of community relations adopted in chapter 1. Experience and a review of the literature suggest that the entire issue of needs assessment has been too long neglected by educators.

BACKGROUND

Readers who wish to review the origins of the public school curriculum in America will find a plethora of comprehensive sources (my own favorite is Edwards and Richey 1963; see also Butts and Cremin 1953). These will reveal that some things were brought to colonial education from the Old World and that this inheritance was augmented and modified through interaction with the needs of the New World. Since then there have been vast changes in society (e.g., industrialization, compulsory education, expansion of knowledge, social awareness) that have had some reflection in the school curriculum. Pressure groups have added studies. The curriculum has grown, but it has been an uneven, unplanned growth. And, except for periodic national studies, there has been little serious attempt to relate the curriculum to the needs of learners and society at a particular time. See, for example, Educational Policies Commission 1938.

In a previous chapter we noted the confusing structure for the governance of education in the United States. This would seem to be the same legal network that would enable us to find out how the needs of the people are translated into goals for educational systems. The Tenth Amendment to the Constitution explains the preeminent position of the states. A tradition of localism contradicts, in practice, the dominant position of the state, in theory. And all of this is in a state of change. Some needs are mandated by the federal government, some by state laws and regulations, and some by local districts.

Educators and citizens alike have inherited this mixed bag of objectives from the Old World and the New. They have also inherited the ungainly mixture of centralized and decentralized—national, state, and local—governing bodies. That is why we must attend to all three areas when we consider the task of assessing educational needs. Our real focus is on the local level but the inherited curriculum and governance structure requires that we be aware of the importance of the national and state levels as well. Before taking up needs assessment, however, we need to recognize other ambiguities, this time semantic.

THE SEMANTIC PROBLEM

There are several thorny issues connected with the determination of the educational needs of a community. Consider first the question of who shall determine the needs. Would there be one set of needs if they were determined by scholars, who are experts in subject matter, another if determined by humanists, another by vocational guidance persons, another by economists, another by theologians, and so on? Could the lists of all these different people be combined in one master list? Who would be empowered to accept or reject the inventory of needs, to add to it, subtract from it?

How should needs be determined? Does the absence of some desirable skill or ability necessarily mark that skill or ability as a need?

Should the educational system be designed to serve the particular needs of a given community or do the needs of a larger community take precedence? Is there some way of determining a priority of needs so that schools can respond selectively to the more essential needs to the limit of their resources? And, most perplexing of all, what of the community that "needs" selfish, mean, or trivial things? Consider, for instance, the community that needs a winning football team or 100 percent admission to renowned colleges for its high school graduates and so omits or short-changes "lesser" needs, e.g., guidance programs, special education, life-long recreation skills, fine arts.

Some communities will "need" pupils to develop attitudes based on the unquestioned assumption that persons with similar social and economic (or ethnic, religious, or racial) characteristics are inherently and everywhere superior to those with different characteristics. It is true that such a "need" would be found in the hidden curriculum of latent purposes of schooling, but it would, nevertheless, be met. Are there good needs and bad needs?

All of the questions raised above, and others not mentioned, are valid issues that educators "need" to face when they assess the educational needs of a community. The process selected to make the assessment will automatically answer some of the questions. For example, if a group of content specialists were given the task of assessing needs, we would not need to be concerned about their having doubts about recreation and vocational skills. Being human, they would tend to see the needs of others, any others, through the selective screen of their own area of expertise. (I once worked with a very able psychologist on general curriculum issues for the public schools. His first recommendation was that the study of psychology should begin in the first grade! This example, of course, proves nothing. The psychologist might even be right. It merely illustrates the problem of objectivity in assessing the needs of others. How many of us would expect the mathematician or the reading expert to recommend that the study of psychology should begin in first grade?)

If the process selected to assess educational needs does not provide for philosophical and psychological legitimation of the needs determined, we may attempt to do the undesirable or the impossible, if not both. That is to say, just because something can be done does not mean that it should be done. Also, unfortunately, just because something should be done does not mean that it can be done. There remain problems of feasibility and order of desirability. And, although overlooked by some and deliberately denied by others, there is the issue of function, of specificity of purpose. In effect, not only can, but *should* schools attempt to meet all types of needs identified?

This, too, is a difficult decision. Traditionally, schools have taken on other tasks by a process best described as accretion, an adding on. The humanitarian argument is simplistic: if something important is not being done for children and children will suffer for the lack of it, the schools should attempt to do whatever needs doing. Politically and pragmatically this strategy has flaws. If schools begin meeting, however poorly and at whatever cost to other functions, the new need, the pressure or bargaining power of those seeking to meet the need in other ways is destroyed. Pragmatically, bypassed institutions, already weak, are further injured if schools assume their functions even if the institutions are defaulting. For example, if a settlement house is not providing a program of evening arts and crafts and a public park that has a field house does not permit evening recreational activities, would it be better to attempt to persuade them or enable them to offer the programs, which are really in their specialty area, or to offer the activities in the school?

This argument should in no way be interpreted as a defense of a three R's, 8:30-3:30 public school. The Mott version of the community school does deliberately seek to provide all of the types of activities mentioned and others within an extended school day (see Campbell 1969; and Gehret 1973). There is evidence of a trend for schools to become the site of more community activities (see, for example, McMurrin 1972). Our point remains that schools cannot do everything. The concept of a consortium of youth-serving or community-serving agencies has much to commend it. A close working relationship among several public and private agencies—including those with broad decision-making powers—could do much toward making *someone, somewhere* more responsive to the needs of the community.

These kinds of important issues should not be overlooked. Their resolution may, however, be postponed until we have obtained some idea of the actual educational needs of a community. So, with all of the several semantic nuances in mind, we shall adopt a temporary, working definition of *community educational need* as: some educational objective identified by members of the community (as narrowly defined) and requested or demanded by them. To put it simply, a *need* will be posited when the community wants the school to do something new, or differently, or to stop doing something.

ASSESSING NATIONAL EDUCATIONAL NEEDS

We know that pressure groups attempt to inform Congress of their perceptions of educational needs and seek the passage of legislation to enable or require educators to help meet the needs concerned. We saw (and some of us enjoyed the benefits of) the response of Congress to needs of veterans of World War II. We saw (and *some* of us put the equipment to good use) the frantic response to our national need for science and mathematics arising from a Russian space satellite. The federal government, like some super school board, continues to respond to perceived educational needs. (Campbell, et al. 1971, chapter 10, provide a helpful conceptualization of the process of policy formation; see also Campbell and Layton 1969.) Policy formation at the national level is now receiving careful attention from educators as well as political scientists (see, for example, Kirst 1970 and 1972).

Commissions, Committees, and Task Forces

The appointment and convening of national blue ribbon committees or task forces to prepare recommendations on education (as well as on other areas) has been a common practice in recent years (see President's Commission on National Goals 1960, chapter 3). Associations, educational and other, often convene their own commissions or panels with a mission similar to that of groups appointed by the government. Depending upon their sponsors, the recommendations of these unofficial commissions have some influence.

The American Association of School Administrators appointed such a commission (1966) and charged it "with responsibility for identifying and stating in clear and concise fashion major educational imperatives that must be at the forefront as curriculums are modified, instructional methods revised, and organizational patterns reshaped to meet the educational needs of this country in one of its most dynamic periods" (p. i). After two years of study, the commission published a report in which it identified and discussed nine "imperatives in education":

> To make urban life rewarding and satisfying.
> To prepare people for the world of work.
> To discover and nurture creative talent.
> To strengthen the moral fabric of society.
> To deal constructively with psychological tensions.
> To keep democracy working.
> To make intelligent use of natural resources.
> To make the best use of leisure time.
> To work with other peoples of the world for human betterment.
> [Ibid.]

Phi Delta Kappa, a fraternity of professional educators, formed its own Commission of Education, Manpower, and Economic Growth. The report, titled *Educational Requirements for the 1970's* (Elam and McLure 1967), consisted of seven position papers by nationally known authorities in different areas. Of special interest is chapter 6, "Educational Policy and National Goals," by Gerhard Colm.

In the approaches mentioned above, official and unofficial groups of experts come together to make their own estimate of the needs of education and then formulate recommendations for the public and educators to consider. Sometimes the government appointed commissions may take on a global type of representative basis (e.g., labor, farm, professional) but the basic approach remains one of assigning to experts or acknowledged leaders the task of making recommendations for education without consulting the citizens or referring to other than the most general statistical data (viz., census reports). The equivalent of this approach can be observed at state and local levels as well.

Nationwide Polling, Testing

In discussing pressure groups, we noted the approach of the newly reconstituted National Committee for the Support of the Public Schools (NCSPS). Although the committee asked members to rank educational needs in order, the list of needs was generated solely by NCSPS and, moreover, the respondents cannot be said to be representative of any population other than members of NCSPS.

The Education Commission of the States sponsors the National Assessment of Educational Progress (NAEP), which reports periodically on its assessments of knowledge of different content areas at various age levels. The NAEP has studied science, writing, citizenship, reading, literature, and music. Almost ninety thousand persons participated in the social studies survey reported recently in the first of a series "that will present survey findings on what Americans—age 9, 13, 17, and 26 to 35—have learned about human relations, geography, history and government and their attitudes about the concepts implicit in these subjects" (National Assessment of Educational Progress 1973, p. 3). Exercises for the testing were based on objectives selected by educators, content specialists, and citizens from all sections of the country and "were administered to small groups of students and to individuals through interviews. Paper-and-pencil questions, discussions and actual tasks were included among the exercises" (ibid.).

The general findings reported in the National Assessment of Educational Progress *Newsletter* were that "Americans Lack Knowledge of Civil Rights." Although the objectives were derived from a three-part sample (of educators, content experts, and citizens), the assessment was based on a subject-matter oriented survey. It is possible to replicate these national surveys on regional, state, or local bases.

Polling has become ubiquitous at the national level. Friends and foes of the Nixon administration waited eagerly or apprehensively for the reflection of the latest Watergate revelations on the president's confidence-popularity rating. For the first time in history the Senate authorized the Harris firm to measure public confidence in key institutions. A cross section of 1,594 adult Americans was asked (between 13 and 22 September 1973): "How much confidence do you feel in the people who are running (a list of categories of public administration departments was read)—a great deal, only some, or hardly any confidence?"

Because educators will be interested in the relative ranking of schools, the findings for a "great deal of confidence" are presented below by the percentage of the total cross section making that response (Harris 1973):

Local trash collection	52%
Local police department	44%
Local public schools	39%
State highway system	34%
Local government	28%
State government	24%

Local tax assessment	19%
White House	18%

It does take a bit of rationalization to make this kind of poll an instance of needs assessment. However, congressmen could conceivably infer a need to do something about institutions rated low or those showing an abrupt decline.

This particular example of polling does help us to recognize an important effect of polls. Polls are not merely assessing knowledge, opinions, attitudes; they are also a potential source of influence. Here we ignore deliberately biased polls (e.g., Should the superintendent be fired? How soon should the superintendent be fired?), which seek to persuade rather than to secure information. Any poll both by its process (the way it is done) and its product (the reported results) can become an influence in and of itself. To stay with the unhappy example of Watergate, it is quite likely that some congressmen and party figures began to add their voices to criticisms of the administration only when they considered that it was the right time, a consideration based on the way their constituents were reacting.

George Gallup, another prominent poll analyst, has surveyed a national sample about educational issues. Interestingly, in terms of our previous discussion of pressure groups, Gallup is assisted by a philanthropic foundation (Charles F. Kettering, CFK Ltd., and the Institute for Development of Educational Activities) and a professional educational fraternity (Phi Delta Kappa). The results of the polls are regularly published in the *Phi Delta Kappan* and the *I/D/E/A Reporter,* which provide a potential audience of over ninety thousand, are circulated in libraries and reported in newspapers and other journals.

> The *raison d'etre* of these annual surveys sponsored by CFK Ltd. is to help guide the decisions of educators. Progress is only possible when the people are properly informed and when they are ready, through their tax dollars, to bear the costs of progress. For these reasons, these surveys are directed chiefly toward appraising the state of public knowledge and ascertaining public attitudes toward present practices, readiness to accept new programs, and ideas for meeting educational costs. In the performance of this work, we, too, sincerely hope that we are making a contribution to the field of education. [Gallup 1973, p. 1]

Gallup points out the apparent inconsistency in the public belief that education is the road to success and its negative view "about meeting the full financial requests of their school boards." He notes that discipline is the chief concern of the public. Militancy in teachers is another area of concern. Gallup also signals a growing insistence on holding teachers and schools accountable (ibid., pp. 3-5).

Gallup has found that the public supports sex education in the schools, performance contracts, management experts to advise on costs and educational goals, year-round schools, ungraded schools, and alternative schools. However, Gallup points out that, because other widely heralded innovations have not lived up to their expectations, objective proof will be necessary to convince a skeptical public in the future (ibid., p. 5).

Gallup concludes that schools have had a "poor press" but believes that with "a properly organized information program [to] overcome the bad publicity which too often colors the public's thinking, there is the very real possibility that this situation can be changed" (ibid., p. 6). Since the Gallup poll is deliberately designed and made available for local community use, we can postpone a consideration of its substance until we take up the assessment of local community needs.

REGIONAL NEEDS ASSESSMENT

Any of the practices mentioned above can be applied at a regional and state level as well. For this reason, we shall discuss only one study each at the regional and state levels. An interesting and informative survey of four geographic regions in the United States and one in Canada was completed by a group at the Midwest Center of the University of Chicago in 1960. They secured a sample from the New England states, the Deep South, the Midwest, the West Coast, and the prairie provinces of Canada. (The way in which the sample was selected is described in Downey 1960, pp. 30-31.) The instrument used to gather data for the study was called The Task of Public Education (TPE) Opinionnaire.

People completing the TPE had to make decisions about the relative importance of sixteen tasks (four each drawn from intellectual, social, personal, and productive dimensions) described on cards:

A fund of information about many things.

Efficient use of the 3 R's—the basic tools for acquiring and communicating knowledge.

A continuing desire for knowledge—an enquiring mind.

A feeling for other people and the ability to live and work in harmony.

An understanding of government and a sense of civic responsibility.

Loyalty to America and the American way of life.

Knowledge of world affairs and the interrelationships among peoples.

A well-cared-for, well developed body.

An emotionally stable person—prepared for life's realities.

A sense of right and wrong—a moral standard of behavior.

Enjoyment of cultural activities—the finer things of life.

Information and guidance for wise occupational choice.

Specialized training for placement in a specific job.

The homemaking and handyman skills related to family life.

Management of personal finances and wise buying habits.

The exact method of ranking is called a *Q* sort. This permits a statistical analysis to take advantage of properties of a normal distribution (ibid., pp. 28-33).

At the bottom of the TPE form were seven slots. The sixteen cards were placed in those slots after being sorted according to directions (only the directions for the final sorting of the cards are quoted).

> Now, sort them further into seven piles—the one most important in the first pile, the *two* next important in the second pile, *three* next important in the third pile, *four* in the fourth, *three* in the fifth, *two* in the sixth, and the *one* least important in the seventh. When you have finished, your sort will look like this:

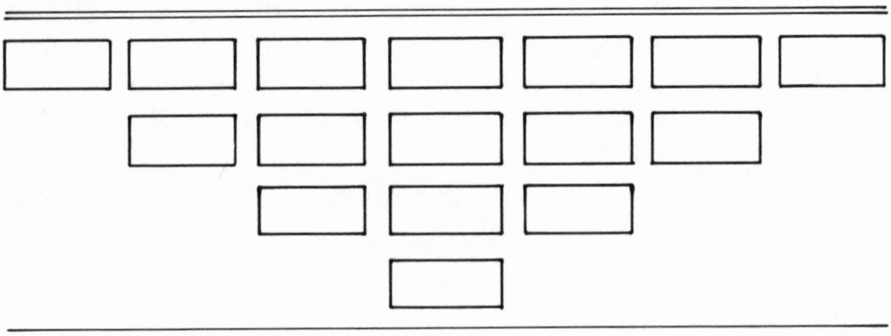

We are not interested in the findings of the task studies so much as in the methods used. However, it may be noted that there was considerable agreement about the task of the public school; geographic region appeared to be a determinant of educational viewpoint; occupation and amount of schooling were the best predictors of educational belief; age, race, and religion were less reliable predictors; community-type, income, sex, and proximity to school were not closely associated with educational viewpoint; and three different educational philosophies and three groups of respondents were discovered. These are responses to a set of needs derived by experts and presented to citizens for ranking. There may well have been important needs not included on any of the sixteen cards for either elementary or secondary schools. This study is of interest because of its scope and because elements have been adopted by subsequent students of educational needs.

A STATE NEEDS ASSESSMENT

The Ohio Department of Education recently completed a four phase, fifteen-month, statewide "Search for Consensus." The result was to be: "Bicentennial goals for elementary and secondary education in Ohio, objectives for meeting those goals, and an accountability model" (Ohio Department of Education 1972*a,* p. 1). The entire process involving "more than 125,000 Ohioans, has included local, county, and regional meetings and a culminating statewide seminar" (Ohio Department of Education 1973, p. 3).

To put the Ohio search for consensus in the over-all perspective of community relations it is important to note that

> the impetus for the April 28 Conference was Amended Substitute House Bill 475, in which the 109th General Assembly enacted a five-point accountability provision. The mandate required the Department to perform five functions and report its progress to the General Assembly by June 30, 1973. The five functions are:
>
> 1. Define the measurable objectives for which schools are to be held accountable.
> 2. Develop a process to determine the extent to which the objectives are met.
> 3. Identify the relevant factors relating to the teaching-learning process.
> 4. Develop uniform accounting methods.
> 5. Report findings to all interested persons.
>
> Following the enactment of House Bill 475, the State Board of Education's Committee on Redesign and Improvement met and concluded that determination of the goals and objectives for which education should be held accountable . . . should come from the citizens of Ohio. Thus, the concept of "Search for Consensus" was initiated. [Ibid., p. 6]

Readers will recall that our consideration of pressure groups in a previous chapter suggested that states would soon be responding in some way to demands that schools become accountable.

Phase 1 of Ohio's search began at the local level where 605 of the 623 school districts in the state held "Local Citizens' Seminars." From these meetings 12,500 written recommendations were received. Two out of the 10 concerns mentioned most often among the recommendations were about school-community relations—numbers 1 and 6:

> Communication between the school and community must be improved.
>
> The public should be kept informed about their schools through additional printed materials such as a school newsletter or the local newspaper. [Ohio Department of Education 1972*b*, p. 1]

Almost 56,000 citizens completed an 88-item questionnaire during phase 1. Results were processed and returned to local school districts for their use.

Phase 2 involved 20,000 persons meeting in 88 County Citizen Assemblies during October 1972. These assemblies reviewed tentative goals that had been drawn from the local meetings in May and analyzed by the Ohio State University Evaluation Center.

During phase 3, 12 regional meetings were held. During February 1973, 4,000 persons met in the different regions of the state to express their opinions about the goals derived earlier and related issues.

Phase 4 was the concluding conference attended by 1,500 persons in the state capital on 28 April 1973. Participants were divided into 44 small seminars directed by a chairman who was assisted by a resource person and a recorder. Twenty-three of the seminars considered accountability models, the other 21 took up the goals derived in earlier phases.

The information of most interest to our present concerns is shown in table 6-1, which is based on data abstracted from the complete report of action taken on fifty different items (based on data in Ohio Department of Education 1973, appendix I, p. 19). The data speak for themselves. In all cases these participants give overwhelming endorsements to practices intended to increase communication and provide more opportunities for citizens to participate in school activities.

These small group seminars offered other recommendations about school-community relations.

TABLE 6-1 VOTE BY PERCENTAGE OF REPRESENTATIVES AT STATE CONFERENCE ON GOALS FOR EDUCATION APRIL 1973

Issue	Percentage Voting	
	Yes	No
Would you favor the inclusion of visitation and study of various community resources as part of the requirement that students be in school six hours per day?	95	5
Would you recommend that local school districts periodically hold citizen assemblies so that the public will have the opportunity to review goals and objectives for their schools?	98	2
Would you favor periodic (at least twice a year) reporting of student profiles to parents?	94	6
Would you favor the expanded use of suitable publications (on a monthly basis) between the school and persons without youngsters in school?	95	5
Would you favor greater cooperation between and among school and community officials over the use of facilities?	99	1
Would you favor the sharing of construction and operation costs for facilities such as libraries, swimming pools, etc.?	96	4
Would you favor use of the community school concept which provides that schools be open during the evening for educational and recreational use by the citizenry even if such services required additional local taxes?	94	6

Local school districts should hold citizen assemblies so that the public will have the opportunity to review and evaluate methods, goals, and objectives for their schools.
Yes: 19; No: 8.

The increased use of school buildings for community use should be at the discretion of the local community.
Yes: 17; No: 0.

School buildings should be used only for approved educational and recreational activities, with sensible rules and regulations developed by the school board.
Yes: 28; No: 0. [Ibid., p. 24]

The problems of a statewide assessment such as this are apparent. The goals attended to are, of necessity, general. One wonders what happened to goals endorsed by a minority of participants during any of the four phases. The very title, "Search for Consensus," makes it clear that objectives put forth by less than 50 percent (in most cases 75 percent) will be eliminated. Consensus, after all, implies not only majority but unanimous approval. Unanimous approval is not easily secured for any but the most general objectives at a statewide level.

The problem of representation needs to be addressed if the search is to signal a significant change in direction. It then becomes necessary to clarify the basis on which persons are empowered to speak for others.

Finally, what authority is vested in the recommendations of the 125,000 Ohioans? Clearly the recommendations are the result of much thought and effort. As such, they will have some influence. But, at what level? This brings us back to the first question raised about statewide needs assessment. If the decisions are being made at a local level, the recommendations of a statewide body are advisory at best. The Ohio effort is a sensible response to conditions of the day. Its significance will be determined by future actions of the Department of Education. For most purposes, the important area for assessing educational needs is the local community or school district.

ASSESSING COMMUNITY EDUCATIONAL NEEDS

Many of the same approaches used at state, regional, or national levels have been applied to the local community level as well. As we noted above, the Gallup poll is designed to permit this and the originators encourage the use of the poll items at any level. They do not permit the names "Gallup" or "CFK Ltd." to be used in reports of the surveys but this is the only restriction placed on the use of the materials. The advantage, aside from work saved in designing materials, of using these materials is that they permit comparisons with the national sample, and specific types of respondents within the sample. The disadvantages are probably that the benefits of the process of involving persons in the design of the survey materials are lost and, of course, the nationwide approach may not be suitable to assess particular local concerns.

Gallup Polls

The national Gallup Poll includes more than 100 questions. Gallup advises those selecting questions for local use to cut the number of questions used to those that can be answered in an interview of thirty minutes or less. They also advise limiting the number of "open" questions–those for which the respondent himself supplies the answer and does not select from among answers prepared in advance by the interviewer. A complete word-for-word script is provided to guide potential users (Elam 1973, pp. 191-193).

Users of the Gallup Poll materials are advised to consult the head of the sociology department or school of education at their nearest college to get help on drawing a sample population for their adaptation of the interview (ibid., p. 193). There is nothing wrong with this advice, but it will be a rare school administrator who does not either have a competent staff member or a continuing relationship with some kind of educational research center for this kind of help. The smallest districts have no sampling problem; they will interview the entire population.

Interviewers must be recruited.

> Parent organizations, A.A.U.W., Jaycees, and other groups of concerned citizens are prime sources of volunteer interviewers. In recruiting try to obtain a large cross-section of citizens; this helps to prevent a bias in influencing responses to questions. Explain that the assignment will take about 10 hours of each person's time, including a training session. [Ibid., p. 194]

One survey handled the problem of bias by selecting two interviewers from each of eight categories: professional, managerial, technical, sales and clerical, unskilled labor, unemployed, retired, and skilled labor (Project Kansas 76, 1972*a*, p. 3). More interviewers than the exact number needed should be recruited to make substitutes available.

Another survey group was able to adapt the poll to a mailed questionnaire response. This was followed up by telephone calls to those who did not respond. They drew their sample by requiring each principal to select a random sample of students and send the names and addresses of their parents to the project staff (30 students from each elementary school, 92 from the junior high, and 98 from the high school). Out of this sample of 430 parents, they received 158 responses (Project Kansas 76 1972*b*, p. 3).

When the interview procedure is used, it will be necessary to furnish baby-sitting service during the training session. The training session is used to explain the importance of the survey and to emphasize the need for interviewers to be completely neutral. They should then be given a few procedural rules before role playing sample interviews—actually interviewing each other in pairs. The volunteers receive their assignments and materials at the close of the training session. The packet of materials for each interviewer using Gallup materials contains: an instruction sheet, identification button or card, questionnaires, hand-out cards, assignment sheets, maps. It is suggested that each volunteer take no more than five or six interviews, preferably on streets where he is not known (Elam 1973, pp. 195-196).

The results of the polis should be processed so that all of the data can be reported in a few pages of tables. Responses to both open and closed questions are coded and punched on cards. The cards are counted and sorted and the report can then be prepared. To suggest the capability of this approach to those not yet familiar with the Gallup reports, we cite summaries of answers to two major open questions from the fifth annual poll. Table 6-2 shows the percentages of the national sample (N.=1,627) who mention each item as a big problem of the public schools. The break down into subgroups shows the variance for each item and permits a more complete analysis of the results. Table 6-3 presents the findings elicited by the question: What's right with the schools?

The data from the national sample speak for themselves. In general, they confirm our impressions of how the different subpublics would respond (e.g., professional educators are most likely to be aware of parents' lack of interest, and private school parents are most likely to perceive that nothing is good about the public schools). Local communities using the same data have some basis for comparison. For example, in Wichita, Kansas, citizens responded similarly when questioned about what was particularly good about their public schools, but 53 percent chose not to answer that question! In regard to the question on problems, again responses were similar but the most frequent response for the Wichita sample was: "Teachers' lack of interest/ability." Elaborations of this response included criticisms of teaching methods, lack of a system to evaluate teachers, use

TABLE 6-2 ANSWERS BY PERCENTAGE OF SAMPLE TO: WHAT DO YOU THINK ARE THE BIGGEST PROBLEMS WITH WHICH THE PUBLIC SCHOOLS IN THIS COMMUNITY MUST DEAL?

Problem	Percentage Reporting				
	National totals	No children in school	Public school parents	Private school parents	Professional educators
	N=1,627	928	620	124	306
Lack of discipline	22	20	24	32	24
Integration/segregation	18	22	14	15	19
Lack of proper financial support	16	14	20	10	35
Difficulty getting good teachers	13	9	16	21	8
Use of drugs	10	11	8	12	4
Size of school/classes	9	7	10	17	13
Poor curriculum	7	7	7	10	16
Lack of proper facilities	4	3	5	4	9
Parents' lack of interest	4	4	5	2	11
School board policies	4	4	5	2	5
Pupils' lack of interest	3	4	2	2	9
Communication problems	1	1	1	1	3
There are no problems	4	3	6	2	2
Miscellaneous	4	3	5	3	7
Don't know	13	16	7	8	1

Source: Stanley Elam (ed.), *The Gallup Polls of Attitudes Toward Education 1969-1973* (Bloomington, Ind.: Phi Delta Kappa, 1973), p. 171. Reprinted with permission.

TABLE 6-3 ANSWERS BY PERCENTAGE OF SAMPLE TO: IN WHAT WAYS ARE YOUR LOCAL PUBLIC SCHOOLS PARTICULARLY GOOD?

Item	Percentage Reporting				
	National totals	No children in school	Public school parents	Private school parents	Professional educators
	N=1,627	928	620	124	306
The curriculum	26	21	34	28	34
The teachers	23	17	32	23	38
School facilities	8	7	9	7	16
Extracurricular activities	7	7	6	5	7
Up-to-date teaching methods	5	5	6	4	14
No racial conflicts	4	4	3	1	5
Good administration	4	3	4	4	8
Small school/classes	3	3	3	2	8
Good student-teacher relationships	3	3	3	3	3
Equal opportunity for all	3	4	1	4	5
Parental interest/participation	2	2	3	2	7
Good discipline	2	2	3	3	3
Close to home	1	1	1	1	—
Good lunch program	1	1	2	2	1
Kids are kept off the street	1	1	1	—	1
Nothing is good	6	5	6	15	4
Miscellaneous	2	1	2	1	2
Don't know	28	37	15	22	4

Source: Elam, ed. 1973, pp. 171-172. Reprinted with permission.

of abusive language by teachers, and student-teacher relations. Obviously, the Wichita survey is adding to the findings of the national sample and revealing more local concerns (Project Kansas 76, 1972*c*, pp. 1-2). Project Kansas 76 used 215 volunteer interviewers for the survey.

Determining Goals

A program, "Educational Goals and Objectives," is sponsored and made available through Phi Delta Kappa. The entire program provides "for the involvement of members of the community, the professional staff and students in ranking educational goals in order of importance; determining how well schools' current programs meet ranked goals; and developing performance objectives to meet ranked goals" (Rose et al. 1971, p. 1).

The basic task to which carefully selected groups attend is to rate and rank order this list of eighteen goal statements:

> To gain a general education.
>
> To develop skills in reading, writing, speaking and listening.
>
> To learn how to examine and use information.
>
> To develop a desire for learning now and in the future.
>
> To learn about and try to understand the changes that take place in the world.
>
> To help students develop pride in their work and a feeling of self-worth.
>
> To develop good character and self-respect.
>
> To help students appreciate culture and beauty in their world.
>
> To learn how to use leisure time.
>
> To develop the ability to make job selections.
>
> To learn to respect and get along with people with whom we work and live.
>
> To learn how to be a good citizen.
>
> To understand and practice democratic ideas and ideals.
>
> To learn how to respect and get along with people who think, act and dress differently.
>
> To practice and understand the ideas of health and safety.
>
> To prepare students to enter the world of work.
>
> To understand and practice the skills of family living.
>
> To learn how to be a good manager of time, money, and property. [Ibid., appendix, p. 12]

Participants get a packet of materials that contains the goal statements on eighteen cards, a display board and forty-five red discs. The cards are placed on the display board in any manner. Discs are placed next to the cards to indicate the importance of the statement on each card, the most important statement getting five discs. Of course, the participant must soon reorder his priorities as he quickly runs out of discs.

After making his decisions, the participant enters the data on a form, leaves his display board in place and joins a small group that attempts to reach consensus on each goal statement. The group leader prepares a summary sheet of the group's ratings of the eighteen goals. These are collected and a master composite display board is made.

The next phase, using the same materials, is to get the perceptions of the community, staff, and students on how well goals are being met. The manner in which goals are being met is marked on a scale from 0 (not at all) to 200 (way too much).

The third phase consists of translating district needs into performance objectives. A district task force selects volunteer teachers to serve as a training cadre and an inservice training program on how to write performance objectives is arranged. The performance level objectives are set by building level or by districtwide program level according to the plan selected.

This is an overview of the plan. There are explicit directions for all aspects of the program in the materials packets and manual. Advantages and disadvantages of five ways of selecting the committee of participants are described and range from arbitrary selection by the superintendent to an unstructured technique of selection by which the superintendent believes "an open invitation should be extended to all citizens residing within the boundaries of the district to participate in the identification and ranking of the district's educational goal" (ibid., p. 7).

The advantages of these materials is, again, that the work of devising the instrument has been done and a careful procedure has been perfected. Moreover, the cost is modest. A major disadvantage is that the focus on eighteen predetermined goals almost insures that only those eighteen will receive careful consideration. The designers attempt to provide for the possible introduction of new goals but it is not reasonable to expect this to happen.* It is something like the

---

* At the bottom of the instruction sheet in a footnote are these directions: "Those Committee members who have developed goals in addition to the original 18 goals, must inform the program moderator at the beginning of the meeting for additional directions."

probability of the write-in candidate winning an election. He starts at a real disadvantage. Then, there is a concern with all of the approaches we have discussed so far. The process of contributing to the creation of goals or the rank-ordering of goals can cause participants to believe that the results of the process *will be implemented.* And, ideally, implementation should follow the process. The constraints of time and resources may slow or block some promised goals. This kind of frustration could rebound and turn a supporter into a skeptic. Hence, care must be taken to point out obstacles and to involve the goal designers in the subsequent search for resources and legitimation by the entire community.

Commercial Materials

Other inexpensive materials are available from several sources. One publisher, Allyn and Bacon, provides alternate modes of data collection. A "School Goals Questionnaire" is designed to be completed at home and mailed to the school. One hundred and six different goals are briefly described. Citizens are asked to rate each from one to five with accompanying verbal designations:

1. Unimportant, Irrelevant.
2. Marginal Importance.
3. Average Importance.
4. Moderate Importance.
5. Most Important.

The first paragraph of directions reads:

> In order to do the good job of teaching you want done, our school has sent you this questionnaire. The questionnaire was developed to enable you to give your opinions on what should be taught in your community's schools. The school wants and needs your opinions. Please take the time to participate in the survey of parents and other members of the community by completing this questionnaire.

Another form, "Rating School Goals," from the same publisher uses a pack of cards with the same 106 goals, one on each card. Five rating mats are provided. The citizen-respondent sorts the cards out on the mats, which are coded from one to five exactly as the response blanks on the "School Goals Questionnaire." The directions require the respondent to put at least five cards in each pile. When the sorting is completed, there is a form, with the same information, which is used to record the rating of each goal. All materials: cards, rating mats, and the form are to be returned to the principal or his representative.

The same comments made about the advantages and disadvantages of commercial materials apply to these as well. One wonders at using both the card sort and the rating in the second example. Perhaps it is to introduce an element of novelty or fun. It does seem to require the user to perform an extra operation.

In Ohio, the Battelle Center for Improved Education "has developed a needs assessment technique that school districts can use to determine their needs in a systematic way . . . the Battelle Needs Assessment Survey" (n.d.). The Battelle materials are similar to the others already described. They feature a "needs profile," which presents a graphic illustration of the discrepancy between the extent to which the stated goal actually exists and the extent to which it should exist. They also compare the perceptions of groups of respondents—students, faculty, parents, community-at-large, administrators, and board members. A representative of the Battelle Center advises the local coordinator about how to administer the survey. The Center codes and analyzes the data and provides copies of the statistical report.

Our next example of professional assistance comes also from Ohio. (Readers are assured that comparable institutions exist everywhere; the Buckeyes have no monopoly.) The Public Opinion Center in Dayton, Ohio, provides survey services in many areas—from water quality to public awareness of national affairs. Recent studies include one on student rights and another on discipline in Dayton's middle schools and high schools. This Center is prepared to take on all phases of the survey. Among the services offered are: research; obtaining feedback from citizens; evaluating current projects; serving as a resource agency for information on polling methods, factual data, and publications; and coordinating institutions, government, and citizens (Public Opinion Center, n.d.).

A Research Approach

Eva Baker of the University of California at Los Angeles designed a study to get parents' responses to more specific goals and to involve students in the survey as well as teachers. For Baker, "needs assessment requires an appraisal of the operation of a system to determine what program goals should be established" (1972, p. 403). The objectives used in the study were drawn from the collection of the

Instructional Objectives Exchange, a nonprofit agency (see, for example, *Measures of Self Concept* n.d.). The study concerned fifteen mathematics objectives, although teachers received and rated forty-three objectives for research reasons. All groups rated the importance of each objective. Teachers estimated the level of performance for their class on each objective. Parents were asked if their child could now master the objective. Students predicted their own performance on the objectives and were subsequently tested to determine their actual performance level (Baker 1972, pp. 410-411).

Baker's substantive findings do not concern us here except to note that seven of the fifteen objectives received high importance ratings and four of these were the lowest in terms of student achievement. What does concern us is the positive reaction from parents—84 percent thought the project was a good idea and 83 percent were willing to do the same kind of thing again.

In this study we can see the relationship of school-community relations to the process of needs assessment. Although this was not a major concern of the study, it seems fair to conclude that school-community relations were improved by the involvement. Such a conclusion could be supported by building a way of pre- and posttesting attitudes about the school into the design. This seems a bit contrived and almost self-fulfilling. In practice it would seem better to look for informal, unobtrusive measures of change in the parents' attitudes rather than to complicate the design of the study by including a formal assessment.

As far as needs assessment goes, this study suffers from the same disadvantage we have noted so often. When a collection of goals is presented to groups, we forgo the consideration of other goals. Certainly this comment is not a criticism of Baker's research. It is a reminder to school administrators not to assume that a valid needs assessment can be obtained by treating in some way (rate, rank order, change) the existing array of objectives. There is a problem for users of the Instructional Objectives Exchange here. They need to ask to what extent objectives set forth by others (no matter what others) can be transported and applied in their localities.

One Local Needs Assessment

A sixth-grade teacher in a Pittsburgh area school designed and supervised a needs assessment survey without using any of the materials described above. John D. Phillips reports that he attended a board of education meeting where "there was general agreement among the board members, administrators and the audience that [policies] should be geared to the expectations of the community. However, no one was able to say what those expectations were" (*Pennsylvania Education* 1972, p. 9). Mr. Phillips then secured unanimous approval from the board to conduct a survey.

"The plan required maximum community involvement beginning in the earliest stages" (ibid.). Cooperation was sought and secured from "key groups in the district," such as business associations, church organizations, PTA, and civic action groups. There was a representative of each group on the survey committee. Mr. Phillips, the only representative of the school system, served as an advisor and provided liaison with the schools.

A series of meetings of the survey committee was held to determine the questions to be asked, methods and timing of the survey. The first draft of the questionnaire was given a pilot administration with a small random sample of residents. The final draft included these sixteen questions:

> What do you think of the educational program in grade schools, junior high and senior high? Would you rate it: excellent, good, satisfactory, poor, very poor, or don't know?
>
> What type of job do you think the administration is doing at the school your child is now attending: excellent, good, satisfactory, poor, very poor, or don't know?
>
> Do you believe the administrative staff to be: understaffed, overstaffed, or about right?
>
> Do you believe that the teachers of the school system, on the whole, are well qualified?
>
> Are fundamentals (reading, writing, spelling, etc.) adequately learned in the elementary schools?
>
> Are fundamentals being learned adequately in the junior high schools?
>
> Are fundamentals being learned adequately in the senior high schools?
>
> Are you satisfied with the school system: very well satisfied, satisfied, dissatisfied, very much dissatisfied, or no opinion?
>
> Do you believe that the school system has a problem with overcrowded school rooms?
>
> Should the school system provide: adult education after regular school hours? Adequate academic program for college preparation? Vocational program for noncollege preparation? Band and chorus? Kindergarten program? Interscholastic sports?

> Do you consider your responsibility to the school system as a continuing one whether or not you have children in school?
>
> If one or the other must be done, should taxes be increased or should school services be cut?
>
> Do you believe teachers should be employed on a nine-month or a twelve-month contract?
>
> How would you rate school-community relations in the school district: excellent, good, satisfactory, poor, very poor, or don't know?
>
> What, if anything, do you think is wrong with the school system?
>
> What are some things or areas you believe commendable about the school system? [Ibid.]

The revised questionnaires were mailed to a random sample of twenty-four hundred of the ten thousand families living in the district. The forms were coded to show which of the nine attendance areas they represented. Slightly more than half (1,275) of the questionnaires were returned. The interview approach was rejected because of the potential expense of hiring poll takers. "The use of the mails kept the cost of the survey at a level low enough to be attractive to all but a most frugal school board" (ibid., p. 10).

One of the findings of this survey was that the community desired to be more actively involved in school affairs. Over 20 percent of the respondents rated school-community relations "poor" or "very poor"; less than 10 percent rated them "excellent." In the open-ended question asking what is wrong with the school system some comments were:

> Parents should have more to say about the curriculum.
>
> You keep information away from the public.
>
> Teachers should be more friendly and cooperative with parents.
>
> Why doesn't the school make use of capable people from the community?
>
> It should be made easier for people to find out what's going on.
>
> It's about time somebody did this.
>
> I appreciate this opportunity to express my views. [Ibid.]

Following the survey, a two-day workshop was held at each school for board members, faculty, and parents. Recommendations and provisions for further study resulted from these meetings. Phillips maintains that this type of survey can be easily replicated elsewhere.

This example of a low budget assessment should be reassuring to those who find even the modest fees of the professional materials and services to be prohibitive. It also has the added virtue of continued involvement at all stages and focus on particular local concerns. It is especially noteworthy that something happened as a result of the survey. We can quarrel with Phillips on minor issues (e.g., the wording of his questions, his decision not to try to recruit volunteers) but the extent of his project with little or no additional resources is impressive.

Charrettes

An approach with the intriguing name, Charrette, has been used to permit wide involvement of citizens in educational planning. One advantage of the approach is that people are brought in to consider a problem that is important to them but that is not in their area of specialization. This is done in the hope that such groups may come up with creative, feasible ideas that the experts, because of their disciplinary focus, would not consider.* The example we have selected, "Charrette 71," was an intensive effort to involve inner-city residents of Des Moines, Iowa, in planning for new schools. In education, the charrette procedure has generally been associated with a facilities planning task.

Before considering the use of the charrette concept, educators are advised to secure affirmative answers to all of the following questions:

> Are educational planners willing to 'share their role' with community residents?
>
> Is the school district interested in cooperating with other local agencies to 'revitalize the community'?
>
> Are funds available to assure community participation in planning activities?
>
> Will the school administration and Board of Education allow residents to 'participate in the decision-making process'?
>
> Is the school system willing to solve problems by 'entering into meaningful dialogue' with representatives of the community? [Educational Facilities Charrette 1971, p. 4]

When these conditions were all met in Des Moines, a director was appointed and a representative steering committee was created. Com-

---

* See Chase 1970 and *Appalachian Advance* 1971. Literally, a charrette is a two-wheeled cart. Charrettes were used by the Paris School of Architecture to collect the students' drawings at the end of the term—hence its usage here emphasizes time constraints, frantic planning, deadlines, and creativity.

munity residents, elected at open meetings, had a voting majority on the steering committee. Eight additional committees, each chaired by a resident, were organized to implement the charrette.

The charrette itself was a ten-day (evenings included) session, with working lunch hours. Residents received twenty-five dollars per day or their regular daily income (whichever was larger). High school students received ten dollars a day. All twenty-seven steering committee members participated as did sixteen representatives from each of four elementary school districts and nine representatives from the community at large. Steering committee members selected the other members from a pool of applicants. Each elementary district sent two students, six adults between nineteen and thirty years of age, five adults between thirty and sixty-five, and two adults over sixty-five. Care was taken to reflect the racial composition of the school and to represent both sexes as well as different viewpoints (ibid., p. 7).

The activities of this particular charrette were organized around four topics. Each topic area had a resource team that stayed in one place as four different community groups were rotated through the stations before selecting one area for special attention. The outcomes of all of this concentrated attention and effort were portions of the program and building specifications; preliminary proposals, which were developed and presented to the community and decision makers during the charrette; and an account of the formation of an interim community advisory committee to carry on the work of the charrette. The sponsors of the project did not expect several finished products. In their estimation "the charrette has produced an assessment of needs, an evaluation of current activities, and a series of value decisions which form the basis and the beginning of activities for improving education and life in these communities" (ibid.).

The charrette example reinforces important aspects of needs assessment surveys. The process of involvement is almost more important than the product—the list of needs. The work and considerable expense of the charrette ($54,700) seems, by implication, to have been justified by the process of creating trust and cooperation. Some of the subjective data cited suggest that this attitude may be right. For example:

> Participants revealed a relatively high degree of suspicion at the beginning of the charrette. However, this distrust diminished toward the end of

> the charrette. Some continued skepticism is shown by 84 percent of the participants who believe that "the community will have to be a watchdog to be sure the charrette work does not go down the drain." [Ibid., p. 22]

Despite the repeated assertions in regard to the charrette and all of the means of needs assessment noted that the widespread benefit of participation is a significant outcome in itself, there are dangers that need to be acknowledged. First, to rouse the public with high expectations may, as we have already warned, turn believers into cynics. Even more disastrous for the unwary, unwise educator, who seeks to manipulate a survey committee by letting it go through the motions of forming policy, is the danger of large-scale alienation, followed by opposition, followed by controversy.

A high-powered citywide committee of citizens was once brought together in the hope that its participation in the study of needs would make it, and its sponsoring organizations, boost a much needed bond issue. Unfortunately, the committee was not empowered to take on any real activity. Because there was, in its perception at least, no real work for it to do, some of the school district's most staunch supporters drifted away over the months. Others talked of being used and of "bad faith." All of this was used by some real opponents of the public school administration who easily formed a coalition to take over the citizens' committee and use it to attack the school superintendent and raise serious questions about proposed projects. The lesson is simply that there must be a bona fide, clearly identified task for the needs assessment committee. The days of token involvement are no longer with us.

This caution in no way releases the school administrator from the obligation to continue to survey the needs and expectations of his community. Not to do so is to endanger the support of the school program. There is really no longer a need to press this point. Accountability is in the wings. Some states are mandating community needs assessment. (The Superintendent of Public Instruction in Illinois proposes "that each school district provide a state with a plan, assessing its own needs and how it proposes to meet them" [*Chicago Tribune* 12/5/72; see also Kearney, Crowson, and Wilbur 1970].) The emphasis on data collection and the advantages of mechanical processing of information will be a boon to overworked school administrators. However, it is suggested that they, the educators, remain "in charge," for it is they who know the citizens and it is they who must do something about the findings, not Gallup, Roper, Phi Delta Kappa, or the educational research center.

SUMMARY

We have argued that the old needs for education, once unquestioned, have changed. Assessment and reassessment of educational needs are happening at national, regional, state, and local levels. It is as though the schools must reestablish their legitimacy. Commercial and locally designed materials and procedures are available. School administrators are advised to involve citizens in needs assessment and to ensure that appropriate response follows the stimulus of needs assessment.

SUGGESTED ACTIVITIES

1. Run a limited poll with a small convenient sample. Use just two open questions: What are the biggest problems and the particularly good aspects of public schools? Compare your findings with the nationwide results shown in tables 6-2 and 6-3.

2. Find out when the last needs assessment was made in a school district. If recently, try to discover what impact it had; what use was made of the results. In your opinion, how might the results of that survey be different today? On what basis are you able to predict differences?

3. Make a small scale needs assessment of your own, using any of the procedures described in the chapter.

4. Ask some teachers how they know what to teach. Continue to probe until you get past the answers of state laws, board rules, administrative directives, etc. Make a list of the ultimate justification for what educators are doing. Is it a formal statement of philosophy, tradition, a teachers manual? How closely are the sources you discover related to some assessment of community needs?

SUGGESTED READINGS

American Association of School Administrators. *Educational Administration in a Changing Community.* Thirty-Seventh Yearbook. Washington, D.C., 1959, chapter 6.

Conway, James A.; Jennings, Robert E.; and Milstein, Mike M. *Understanding Communities.* Englewood Cliffs, N.J.: Prentice-Hall, 1974.

Elam, Stanley (ed.). *The Gallup Polls of Attitudes Toward Education 1969-1973.* Bloomington, Ind.: Phi Delta Kappa, 1973.

Kerlinger, Fred N. *Foundations of Behavioral Research.* New York: Holt, Rinehart and Winston, 1965, chapters 4, 22, and 26; see also chapter 33 for information on *Q* Methodology.

Little, John D. C.; Sheridan, Thomas B.; Stevens, Chandler H.; and Tropp, Peter. *Citizen Feedback Components, Technical Report No. 76.* Cambridge, Mass.: Operations Research Center, Massachusetts Institute of Technology, 1972.

National Commission on the Reform of Secondary Education. *The Reform of Secondary Education.* New York: McGraw-Hill, 1973, especially part II, appendix A, and appendix B.

National School Public Relations Association. *Polling and Survey Research.* Arlington, Va., 1973.

Richardson, Stephen A.; Dohrenwend, Barbara S.; and Klein, David. *Interviewing: Its Forms and Functions.* New York: Basic Books, 1965.

Sumption, Merle R., and Engstrom, Yvonne. *School-Community Relations.* New York: McGraw-Hill, 1966, chapter 10.

REFERENCES

American Association of School Administrators. Commission on Imperatives in Education. *Imperatives in Education.* Washington, D.C., 1966.

Appalachian Advance 5, no. 3 (1971). "Anyone for a Charrette?"

Baker, Eva L. "Parents, Teachers, and Students as Data Sources for the Selection of Instructional Goals." *American Educational Research Journal* 9, no. 3 (Summer 1972): 403.

Battelle Center for Improved Education. "Needs Assessment for Local School Districts." Brochure. Columbus, Ohio, n.d.

Butts, R. Freeman, and Cremin, Lawrence A. *A History of Education in American Culture.* New York: Holt, Rinehart and Winston, 1953.

Campbell, Clyde M. *Toward Perfection in Learning.* Midland, Mich.: Pendell, 1969.

Campbell, Roald F.; Bridges, Edwin M.; Corbally, John E.; Nystrand, Raphael O.; and Ramseyer, John. *Introduction to Educational Administration.* 4th ed. Boston: Allyn and Bacon, 1971.

Campbell, Roald F., and Layton, Donald H. *Policy Making For American Education.* Chicago: Midwest Administration Center, 1969.

Chase, W. W. "The Educational Facilities Charrette." *Educational Technology* 10 (June 1970): 20-21.

Chicago Tribune, 5 December 1972. "Dr. Bakalis and Quality."

Downey, Lawrence Wm. *The Task of Public Education.* Chicago: Midwest Administration Center, 1960.

Educational Facilities Charrette. *Charrette 71: How a Community Planned Two New Inner-City Schools.* Des Moines, Iowa: Des Moines Public School System, 1971.

Educational Policies Commission. *The Purposes of Education in American Democracy.* Washington, D.C.: National Education Association, 1938.

Edwards, Newton, and Richey, Herman. *The School in the American Social Order.* 2d ed. Boston: Houghton Mifflin, 1963.

Elam, Stanley, and McLure, William P., eds. *Educational Requirements for the 1970's.* New York: Praeger, 1967.

Elam, Stanley, ed. *The Gallup Polls of Attitudes Toward Education.* Bloomington, Ind.: Phi Delta Kappa, 1973.

Gallup, George. "The First Five Years: Trends and Observations." In *The Gallup Polls of Attitudes Toward Education,* edited by Stanley Elam. Bloomington, Ind.: Phi Delta Kappa, 1973.

Gehret, Kenneth G. *Getting the Most Out of Our Schools.* Boston: *The Christian Science Monitor,* 1973.

Harris, Louis. "Harris Survey: Who Does the Public Trust Now?" *Chicago Tribune,* 6 December 1973, section 1, p. 20.

Kearney, C. Philip; Crowson, Robert L.; and Wilbur, Thomas P. "Improved Information for Education Decision-Making: The Michigan Assessment Program." *Administrator's Notebook* 18, no. 6 (February 1970).

Kirst, Michael W., ed. *The Politics of Education at the Local, State and Federal Levels.* Berkeley, Ca.: McCutchan, 1970.

______. "Six States and Federal Aid." Paper read at the annual meeting of the American Educational Research Association, Chicago, 5 April 1972.

Measures of Self Concept. Los Angeles: Instructional Objectives Exchange, n.d.

McMurrin, Lee R. "Alternatives for Now and for 2001." In *Opening the Schools,* edited by Richard W. Saxe, pp. 258-281. Berkeley, Ca.: McCutchan, 1972.

National Assessment of Educational Progress. *Newsletter* 6, no. 9 (December 1973): 3.

Ohio Department of Education. *What 125,000 Ohioans Want From Their Schools.* Columbus, Ohio, 1973.

Pennsylvania Education 3, no. 6 (July-August 1972): 9. "A Survey Can Increase School-Community Interaction."

President's Commission on National Goals. *Goals for Americans.* Englewood Cliffs, N.J.: Prentice-Hall, 1960.

Project Kansas 76. *Educational Leadership Planning Survey for the Junction City Public Schools III Community Survey.* Topeka, Kan.: Kansas State Department of Education, 1972*a*.

———. *Educational Leadership Planning Survey for the Manhattan Public Schools III Community Survey.* Topeka, Kan.: Kansas State Department of Education, 1972*b*.

———. *Educational Leadership Planning Survey for the Wichita Public Schools III Community Survey.* Topeka, Kan.: Kansas State Department of Education, 1972*c*.

Public Opinion Center. "How the Public Opinion Center Serves the Community Interests of Dayton." Brochure. Dayton, Ohio, n.d.

Rose, Keith, et al. *Educational Goals and Objectives.* Chico, Ca.: Program Development Center of Northern California, Chico State College, 1971.

chapter seven

Determining Community Resources

Ask, and it shall be given you; seek and ye shall find; knock, and it shall be opened unto you.

Matthew 7:7

In this chapter we shall maintain that local community resources are largely unknown and seldom used to full advantage by educators. Some ways of discovering or creating resources will be presented. Finally, we shall discuss strategies to introduce new and unusual resources into the school and its programs.

WHAT ARE RESOURCES?

This chapter is a logical companion to its predecessor on needs assessment. Ideally, there should be a relationship between needs and resources. It is, also, quite possible to combine the search for needs and resources in the same survey. One reason for doing so has been suggested. The requirement that the same group that inventories needs should also determine resources prevents irresponsible demands for programs so expensive that there is no hope of establishing them with available resources. The flaw in this logic is found in our usage of *resources. Resources* will mean *people or materials situated in the school community that can help the school accomplish its objectives.* When used in this way, there is no implication that resources should be sufficient to meet needs. The only important test is to determine whether the resources are related to the needs identified.

Using *resources* in this restricted way also prevents us from using a systems approach to present data. The systems model would identify all resources (inputs) used by the school and process this information to compare it with the product (output), which would be certain changes in learners. This is an economic approach that is both more inclusive and narrower in scope than our usage of *resources.* It is more inclusive in that it is concerned with federal and state funds (resources) as well as commercial materials and professional personnel not indigenous to the community. It is more restrictive in that it would not make provision for learning places outside the school and for personal services performed by citizens without formal contractual arrangements. Put in simplest terms, *resources* are people, places, and things in the community that can help the school.

Some special schools and special programs within some schools organize their entire instruction programs about resources external to and not controlled by the school. (We discuss this type of arrangement in detail in Saxe 1972 and 1973*a*.) Well known examples of this use of external resources are the Parkway Program in Philadelphia and the Chicago Public High School for Metropolitan Studies: alternative schools within the public system. They are characterized by voluntary enrollment and unusual use of learning places outside schools and classrooms. However, to the extent that (because of their unique mission) they use citywide learning materials, people, and places, they are not examples of community resources according to our meaning. That is to say, the Chicago Public Library, the Art Institute, the Museum of Natural History, the Board of Trade, the Planetarium, the traffic court, and similar institutions used by Metro High in Chicago are only resources in a citywide sense. They certainly cannot be claimed by every one of the more than five hundred schools, even though some of them may be used briefly during the year by some group from every school. (For example, is there any school that does not send some class to the zoo, probably always in the same two months of the year?)

Moreover, such citywide opportunities as concerts, demonstrations, and lectures, are, in a way, too conventional to be considered community resources. They are similar in style to the usual modes and materials of learning in the traditional school program. There is, of course, nothing wrong in using conventional resources to the utmost; one would be foolish not to do so. However, our focus is on community relations and the particular ways of relating the needs of local schools to all kinds of resources in their communities. Hence, the long list of citywide cultural resources prepared and distributed by the central office, although a learning resource, is not for us a community resource.

All citizens who participate in school activities will not be viewed as community resources, although they may be, depending upon whether they are there to control or to participate. Members of a governing body, although certainly of great importance to the success of the program, will not be listed as resources. If, however, their involvement is sometimes primarily service and facilitative, they can become a resource. Perhaps the best way of making this kind of distinction is to emphasize the use of the resource to facilitate learning. The other types of involvement of citizens and parents are better considered in chapters on communication, citizen participation, and community control.

KINDS OF COMMUNITY RESOURCES

The professional literature for years has included articles describing the benefits of inviting community residents in to speak to a class or even to an entire school at an assembly. The foreign visitor or the parent of foreign extraction would be brought in to display artifacts and talk about customs and conditions in another country. Parents would come in and talk about their occupations. Business men would be persuaded to discuss the qualities that lead to success. Local celebrities and illustrious alumni of the school would receive a forum to talk about the influence of their schooling in their careers. This use of human resources is well known to all.

Even such prosaic procedures as those described seem to have an aura of innovation, of creativity, about them. Frequently, student teachers seeking to add motivation and a higher dimension of reality to their unit or module, call on a parent, relative, or friend in an occupation related to the subject to come in and meet the pupils. Such "innovation" is generally received with great enthusiasm by pupils and with benign tolerance by the cooperating teachers (i.e., the regular teachers with whom the student teachers are assigned for their field experience), who expect such enthusiastic overdoing by the neophyte. And, after all, it will impress the college supervisor who is responsible for entering a grade for the student-teaching experience.

A recent, dreadful television program portrayed the loss of self-esteem suffered by a psychologist who competed in a "tell about your career" day with persons with more dramatic (to the fourth-grade pupils) occupations. Hopelessly overshadowed by a fireman complete with axe, the psychologist secured a second chance. This time, for "show and tell," he brought a set of Rorschach plates.

Another series dealt with a middle-aged foreign woman who, because of her constant presence in and around the high school, became a nuisance. The enterprising social studies teacher saved the woman's self-concept by bringing her to speak to his students. Their rapt attention was almost believable.

The point of mentioning these programs is not to analyze the weird concepts of education and educators presented by the entertainment media. That is a problem best addressed elsewhere. It is merely to note that such obvious exploitation of an interesting person or glamorous profession is so well established as to be represented in television situation comedies. And, paradoxically, even these awkward, self-conscious departures from normal practice are viewed as praiseworthy events to be recounted in monthly reports of principals or superintendents.

This type of resource is still available to educators and certainly should be sought wherever appropriate to the curriculum. We turn now to more recent examples of the use of human community resources. To set the tone for the new orientation toward community resources, we begin with a statement by Cunningham.

> Central to the concept of responsible autonomy is the belief that school communities have substantial resources to use in solving their own problems. Problems are there; resources are there. The genius is the ability to release those resources and bring them to bear on the problems that citizens of the school community define as most significant for them. A responsibly autonomous school should develop a posture of reaching out for help and resources. The processes of building community-school strength are not well known. Nor have they been taught to teachers and other professionals. Most buildings will need assistance with these matters—intellectual help as well as fiscal resources will be required—but the basic raw material for improvement is in each neighborhood in the country. [1972, pp. 93-94]

Bringing the Community to the School

Although many community resources are by design two-way between school and community, it will be easier to discuss them if we force them into a dichotomy: either bring the community into the school or take the school out to the community. The first problem met here is the issue of whether it is proper for some teaching to be done by persons other than professionals with certificates. This controversy occurs primarily about the ways in which aides, paid or volunteer, may be used. Up to this time affiliates of both AFT and NEA have been adamant in restricting the use of all such personnel to nonteaching, supportive functions. There has been much progress, however, and schools no longer face the hard line of opposition to even the presence of persons without certificates in the school. Our own bias is that whoever can be most effective at accomplishing a given objective should be encouraged to do so in a program coordinated by the teacher and arranged by the school.

It is not fair to accuse teachers and their organizations of self-serving protectionism when they raise barriers to the expanding role of others in instructional capacities. Their concern about the best interests of their pupils is valid. We have pointed out that they have good reason to be concerned about letting other adults observe their teaching because of the possibility of unfavorable evaluation and loss of prestige resulting from a misunderstanding of what is good teaching. Moreover, and more importantly, teachers feel guilty when they share their instructional role with others. They have long been conditioned to believe that instruction is their responsibility.

We have evidence of the problem that some teachers have in changing their roles from presenters of information to facilitators of learning. The widespread use of self-instructional materials has caused teachers much concern about not teaching as much as they did formerly. We even have some accounts of misguided supervisors criticizing teachers of programs in which self-instructional materials are used for not providing dynamic leadership. Such supervisors too, need to be helped to find a new role for themselves as well as learn how to support teachers in new roles.

If some teachers are to become coordinators of learning resources —both people and things—they will need much support. Something analogous to this quandry has for some time plagued the registered nurse. She, too, feels guilty being a coordinator and manager of people and records instead of the bedside ministering angel. After all, the nurse was motivated to seek that career because of a desire to care—personally—for the sick. Teachers, similarly were motivated (theoretically, at least) to enter their careers because they liked children and wanted—personally—to help them learn. (Although we found many other reasons for preparing to become a teacher, they did not change the fact that personally imparting knowledge to learners was an important expectation for future teachers—see Saxe 1969.)

We need to study the effect of this profound change on the role of teachers. (In a study of Teacher Corps team leaders we found that they were concerned that they were "getting away with something" during the times they were not actively involved in working directly with pupils. See Saxe and Ishler 1971, especially pp. 57-60.) If they are not only to permit but also to welcome the intervention of others in the teacher-pupil relationship, this must be a part of their expectation of the job and of their training programs as well.

Before considering some of the many programs involving the use of volunteers in schools, we need to alert educators to at least two somewhat unexpected sources of opposition. The paramount expected source of opposition is of course, the school staff. (Hubley 1972 deals with the proper orientation of the school staff to the use of volunteers.) The unexpected sources of opposition are community control advocates and women's rights organizations.

Advocates of community control have mixed opinions on volunteer assistance. There are those who think it a good initial tactic to get inside the school on any pretext to gather data detailing educational shortcomings to be used in subsequent open attacks on the board and administration. Others, probably the more confirmed opponents of the existing educational governance, fear that community residents will be in danger of being coopted by the school staff and lose their dedication to the cause of massive, violent reform. The importance of this information is that the administrator should expect some reluctance and skepticism when he begins negotiations to involve citizens in school-supportive services.

The other somewhat unexpected source of opposition, the women's rights organizations, specifically the National Organization for Women (NOW), does approve of volunteers participating in the decision-making processes of schools, but considers volunteer service to schools an exploitation (National Organization for Women n.d.). Since the vast majority of volunteers are women, NOW sees the practice as sexist. It seems unlikely that this position would dissuade parents from seeking to improve the education of their own children. It does suggest, however, that caution be exercised about permitting volunteers to perform tasks usually assigned to paid aides, which could be seen as using the volunteers to deprive others of needed income. Further, the assignment of volunteers to dull routine, away from teachers and pupils, could be perceived as exploitation. Administrators need to ask and have a good answer to the question: "What's in it for the volunteer?"

Volunteers serve in a myriad of ways. There is already a considerable body of literature on the various issues connected with securing, training, and supervising volunteers. At a national level, the ACTION agency in Washington, D.C. has been established to coordinate and service several volunteer programs. Many school districts have directors or coordinators of volunteers.

One use of volunteers is somewhat similar to the old and continuing practice of inviting celebrities or professionals in to talk about their activities. In a more highly organized form, this is found in offerings of special courses or activities. In some innovative schools mini-courses are offered several times throughout the school year, for short periods of time, about an hour a day.

The mini-courses may be taught by a combination of staff and volunteers. For example, if one teacher happened to have certain extracurricular skills and interests, he might offer a course for interested pupils. The same would apply for volunteers. A good way of seeing how this plan works is to look at some of the interest groups available at one elementary school (Motley School, Minneapolis, 2-13 April 1973) during a period of two weeks.

> Music—jazz, melody bells.
> Communications—advanced playmaking, black poems, black images.
> Social Studies—Israel.
> Science—magnetism, insects, plant responses, beginning photography.
> Art—nature drawing, pottery, beginning beadwork, needlepoint.
> Physical Education—soccer, wrestling.

All of these courses were taught on a first come first served basis with students checking seven preferences. The mini-courses offered the next session would be different and not necessarily taught by the same volunteers and staff. Parents had to sign their approval of the choices made by pupils.

Other volunteer service arrangements to use the special talents of community residents for one time or a short term are easily arranged. Former nurses and librarians have needed skills. Some primary level teachers have capitalized on volunteers' abilities to cook, do handicrafts, or carpentry. A volunteer working on this basis had some advice for educators.

> Make sure the volunteer will come on the day planned and be prepared with all equipment and materials. Keep the projects simple enough so that children can complete them successfully. Make sure safety precautions have been made. Plan this type of activity no oftener than once a week to keep interest high. [Fireside 1972, p. 57]

We have a wealth of information on this way of enriching the curriculum. For years now teacher education institutions have been advising students to make a file of such resource persons (see, for example, Sommers 1972, p. 62). In some areas a list of volunteer talent and resources available is compiled and coordinated by a professional, full time director (Weinstein 1971, p. 14). However, such services, though helpful, do not discover the rich source of support among persons in the local school community who cannot or will not claim to be expert at anything.

The use of volunteers as tutors is now commonplace. There is a National School Volunteer Program, which claims that 2,031,000 volunteers are working with 5,000,000 children in 3,000 programs.* They have state groups, some of which provide six training sessions to volunteers. Housewives, retired professionals, and young people are the most common sources for volunteers in this program.

Residents in retirement homes and senior citizens anywhere have become a good source of volunteer help. There is reason to believe that the involvement of elderly volunteers is a mutual benefit. This was the subject of a doctoral dissertation by Eileen Bayer at Hofstra University—"The Effect of Male Senior Citizen Intervention upon the Readiness of Kindergarten Children." Bayer tested three prem-

---

* National School Volunteer Program, Inc., 16 Arlington Street, Boston, Massachusetts 02116.

ises: that preschool children, especially boys, would benefit from more regular contact with older male models at the primary school level; that retired men would be a good source of enrichment and excitement; and that contact between very old persons and very young children would be an important experience for both. The study was arranged so that three kindergarten classes in a school were taught with the help of retired men and three other classes in the same school were taught in the usual manner. "Generally speaking parents and teachers—as well as the children—were delighted with the results. Evaluation shows that the experiment has had a positive effect on the children's interest in and readiness for reading" (Hechinger 1972). The principal of the school reported that he was confident that the men had helped the pupils respect the role of older people. The men were enthusiastic about the experience.

Educators adopting this approach to using volunteers are advised to provide training and support for the volunteers selected. If they are not helped by the regular staff, it is not reasonable to expect them to succeed merely because they want to help. Although the research procedure will not be necessary in most cases, the idea of having some kind of an evaluation of the volunteer experience is good.

Parents are often willing to perform school services on a definite schedule. They can staff libraries or media centers (Brady, Donovan, and Buntin 1973-74, p. 33). Years ago they took care of kindergarten registration and lunchroom supervision. In Toledo they help prevent disturbances at athletic events (*Toledo Blade* 12/18/73). Erma Bombeck devotes another of her delightful columns to her experiences as a volunteer on a field trip in "School Trip Rivals Normandy Invasion" (1973). The National Education Association has put together a multimedia kit to help train volunteers.* One of the booklets in this kit has a list of organizations that will be helpful to those establishing regular programs for volunteers (National Education Association 1972, pp. 54-64).

Students are reliable and enthusiastic volunteers. There is a trend toward permitting high school students to help in the elementary

---

* *Parents and Teachers Together (For the Benefit of Children),* N.E.A. Publications Section 26, 1201 Sixteenth Street, N.W., Washington, D.C. 20036. The entire kit costs about seventy-five dollars, but the individual information booklets may be obtained separately for modest amounts.

schools. Sometimes the service is performed for high school credit (Thomasy 1973). Sometimes high school students are brought in through Future Teacher Clubs, sometimes through classes called community service, field work, or volunteer service. Some specially funded projects train the high school students and provide instructional materials for them to use with the elementary school pupils (*New York Times* 1/13/74, p. 74).

There is no shortage of information on ways of using volunteers. As one source puts it: "The range of possibilities extends as far as the imagination is able, and regular staff willing to go" (Mott Institute for Community Development 1973, p. 6).

Another important community resource is the paid aide. Volumes have been written about working with aides. (See, for example, Brotherson and Johnson 1971; Ferver and Cook 1968; and the entire issue of *National Elementary Principal* 46, May 1967.) Aides and paraprofessionals are new types of personnel found increasingly in urban schools. However, since they may be classified as part of the regular school staff, they will not be discussed here as community resources. Administrators will wish to become thoroughly familiar with the many studies of aides and paraprofessionals. They should be aware that, for some communities, people may suffer a loss of status when we call them paraprofessionals, although they are usually people who have occupied leadership roles and are admired in the community (Bowman, et al. 1972, p. 167). Our own survey of aides found many of them concerned about the low salary paid for what they believed to be important service to schools. Most of them reported that they had no preservice training but learned on the job (Saxe 1973*b*).

Finally, to close this section on bringing resources into the school, we turn to an anecdote from our British counterparts. As we frequently confess, such isolated instances cannot be submitted as proof of anything. The one selected is a nice example of the mutual benefit concept of working with volunteers. Moreover, it anticipates an important argument about communicating with people in ways that preserve the dignity of the other person and avoid condescension.

> There was one mother, very slatternly, always dirty, whose child didn't turn up for school very often. The head was acutely aware that this mother was always being given advice, always at the receiving end, getting clothes from people, help from social workers, help from national systems. It appeared that she could contribute nothing to the school; even so, the

> head invited the mother to supervise a lunch period and join the children at lunch. After extending the invitation, she waited with some trepidation to see what would happen. The mother turned up, dead on time, in all her tidy clothes. She was treated as an equal by the teacher. After that, the child never missed school. One morning when the child was ten minutes late, the mother sent a note saying she was very sorry but the alarm clock hadn't gone off. [I/D/E/A 1969]

Such happy endings are, we hope, not uncommon in American schools.

Taking the School Into the Community

An interesting and important change occurs when we reorient our search for resources to the use of such resources outside the school rather than their introduction into the building. There is, first of all, the psychological shift from host to guest. There is also, and this is the antithesis of bureaucracy, a loss of control, of predictability. The concept of territory seems to be helpful in understanding the reluctance of schools to venture into "their" communities. (Frederick M. Thrasher discusses the importance of territory to youth gangs in *The Gang,* a sociological classic first published in 1927; see especially chapter 9. For a scholarly analysis of territory for all species, see Ardrey 1966. For a brilliant application of the concept to education, see Sarason 1971, chapter 2 and page 30.) In one's own territory there are many advantages, not the least of which is security. Roles and relationships are better understood on home ground. Children must develop a kind of schizophrenia in fortress schools—discussed by Wayson (1972)—to accommodate the different forms of behavior expected by the school and by the community. If the school and community are separated by a moat and drawbridge, real or figurative, educators need to be aware of the rules of the game being played in the other arena—the community game.

The concept of territory also helps one to understand the prevalence of the folk wisdom dictum that teachers should reside in their school districts. If teachers are members of the community, it can be reasoned, they will be more disposed to meeting the real needs of the community when such needs differ from the purposes of the school as an institution. Of course, there is an economic basis for the folk wisdom as well, as we learned from the study, *Small Town in Mass Society* (Vidich and Bensman 1968).

The importance of understanding different territories is well represented by clichés in American speech. "Like a fish out of water," captures an important element of the concept. The refrain of the salesman in *Music Man,* "But he doesn't know the territory," includes another nuance of the meaning of territory. These brief comments on territory are not intended to discourage educators from leaving their castles and journeying out into the community. They are intended to emphasize the need for orientation and support for the fish who are out of water and salesmen who don't know the territory and apply to traffic flowing both ways through the boundary (visible or invisible) of the school's territory.

The discussion has prepared us to appreciate the position of many educators that the school must find ways to cooperate with all elements of the community. This perspective is represented by Barry and Tye in their treatment of "External Relations" in *Running a School* (1973).

> Research has clearly demonstrated that . . . the influences of home and environment play a crucial and often a predominant part in a child's education, and that the impact of the school will be effective only to the extent that the child is seen by the school, not only as a pupil, but as a member of a family, of a peer group, and of a community, including the community of the school. It follows that no single factor in this process of interaction can make its full contribution in isolation; all must be aware of and responsive to what the others are doing and are planning to achieve. For the threads which make up the fabric of a child's experience of learning and growing are very closely interlinked, and cannot easily be disentangled. So it is important that, for the sake of its children (and for many other cogent reasons) a school should be sensitively aware of, and involved with, the world outside its walls. [Pp. 209-210]

A more radical approach to the use of community resources is taken by Colin and Mog Ball (1973), a pair of countrymen of Barry and Tye, who cite beautiful examples of school children performing essential and humane services for and with the community. For the Balls, there should be no boundary between school and community and we can all profit from the examples of creative service they describe. But, to some extent it seems as though the radical ideology detracts from the usefulness of their message. They violate one of their own precepts by taking a position that implies that educators are rock-headed conservatives and that virtue is all on the side of the young. They should know that this is not the way to secure the cooperation of the group attacked. Moreover, it seems as though, in their desire for freedom—for doing one's own thing—they place a most difficult burden on children and adolescents. "Young people must serve the community on their own terms. Then they are not 'serving the community' but doing what they can do or enjoy doing, in ways and places which makes them a service for others" (p. 101). It is perhaps because of the Balls' unhappy assessment of educators in Britain that they see no leadership role for school people.

In this country, there is a kind of ideological, missionary force at work that can inspire the revolutionary zeal suggested by the Balls. The concern for the environment and ecology has much to offer science educators and history, government, and civics teachers. This concern and others are apparent in the account of learning activities in a Missouri junior high school:

> Teams of ninth-graders have collected water samples from a stream polluted by a paint manufacturing plant. They took the samples for analysis to the labs of the Metropolitan Sewer District, which found the water polluted. Charges were brought against the company. Several classmates wrote a brochure cautioning teens against shoplifting; the local crime prevention agency circulated the brochure throughout the community. Other students design surveys, prepare data sheets, staff polling booths in elections, attend community meetings in ecology, education, politics, government. Some work as teacher aides in Head Start and Day Care Centers, or assist in devising activities for the elderly. [National Commission on Resources for Youth 1973, p. 1]

Such action projects and internships of varying lengths of time are becoming more frequent for high school students. This is one approach to taking full advantage of community resources and an important one. Irving Rosenstein, a professor of urban education, believes that "only when teachers and administrators begin to perceive the community as a learning resource for individuals rather than entire classes will they really be able to exploit the local community for meaningful educational experience" (1972, p. 129). We can agree with Rosenstein about the merits of learning from the community, not about it, by activities that involve students. We must disagree with the implication of his statement that students individually, rather than entire classes, must learn in this way. Doubtless both approaches–individual and group learning–as well as others have merit. In anticipation of a consideration of public relations in another chapter, we must also question the use of "exploit" in regard to community resources.

Janowitz supports the use of the community as a learning laboratory by means of community service or work:

> For the bulk of youngsters in the slum school, the formal academic and vocational programs alone are not able to afford sufficient gratification to be an adequate basis for self-esteem and a moral order. If students have to remain under educational supervision until sixteen, school experiences must be fused with community and work experiences. [1969, p. 106]

Janowitz notes further that:

> again and again, for reasons that are only dimly perceived, youngsters will find in an outside educational program involvement and satisfaction that they cannot develop in a school setting. Success in an outside academic program can, over time, dampen negative attitudes toward the school. The existence of educational field stations in the community [is as] indispensable as second-chance agencies . . . thus the school system must take the initiative to insure that a variety of facilities are available in the community for the slum students to do their homework, pursue musical and cultural activities, and form associations based on these interests. [Ibid., p. 107]

There seems to be widespread support in the literature for arranging for students to go back and forth from school to community to serve, to learn, and, sometimes, to earn. Teachers and new types of educational personnel also work "both sides of the street"—school and community. Teacher Corps has the distinction of being the first program of teacher education that mandated continuing involvement in poverty-level communities throughout the entire duration of the program. In our own research, we found that Teacher Corps team leaders reported that they were not effective in the community component of the program although they did rank it as being important (Saxe and Ishler 1971, p. 2). Only 5 percent of the total group of team leaders responding to our query reported that they most enjoyed community work compared with 54 percent who reported that they most enjoyed supervision (ibid., p. 3).

As a result of our survey we suggested these objectives for training programs for team leaders:

1. Team leaders will prepare a comprehensive list of community agencies and write a brief description of the goals and functions of each.
2. Team leaders will select five agencies (from above list) and describe ten important activities in which the interns might participate.
3. Team leaders will personally visit five agencies in their respective communities and hold exploratory conferences with agency personnel regarding the objectives of the Teacher Corps program.
4. Team leaders will visit the homes of ten pupils and discuss how Teacher Corps is changing what the pupils do in school. [Ibid., p. 41]

Corwin's extensive study of the Teacher Corps program supports our findings about the role conflict and other difficulties arising when teachers go into the community (1973, p. 147). Despite the difficulties encountered, Teacher Corps accomplished much in articulating school and community efforts. They must surely be a rich resource of suggestions, tactics, and knowledge about sensitive problems of school-community cooperation.

There are several new classifications of paid personnel who devote a major portion of their time to working in and with the local school community. Those who serve several schools or an entire district will be discussed elsewhere.

Parent Partners are a group of community residents, usually mothers of pupils, funded by Title I of the Elementary and Secondary Education Act. They work with a group of parents to enable the parents to help their children with learning problems. They establish a parent advisory committee for their programs and have an extensive inservice program coordinated by a full-time director. They are a resource to the school, of course, in facilitating learning, but especially as a means of communication between school and community. See *Operation Success: Parent Partners* (n.d.); *The Right To Know* (n.d.); or *Toledo ESA Title I Newsletter* (n.d.). (A similar program in Omaha, Nebraska, is described in *Education Summary* 1974, p. 8.)

Other services to help parents help their children are available, especially in large cities. One such is PAR, Parents as Resource,* which provides workshops and materials for parents (Cushman 1973). Although educators will wish to know about such organizations, they are not community resources in the restricted meaning we are using in this chapter.

Members of organizations such as Parent Partners are intended to give their primary attention to problems of learning. Other types of personnel have a more broad service mandate. One such, a home-school counselor for a school in the Flint, Michigan, Community School Program, believes that "anything that's going to help the child is our job." The counselor not only interprets the school to the community, but also serves as an advocate and promoter of needed community services. A description of her activities includes examples of finding resources in the community and making them available for school use (Gehret 1973, p. B3).

A similar orientation toward helping students in any way possible appears to influence a federally funded home-school coordinator in a

---

* PAR Project, 464 Central Avenue, Northfield, Illinois 60093.

small city in Ohio. The story of this man's activities includes incidents of securing needed community resources for school use. Again we note the additional potential for better communication between school and home made possible by the work of new types of personnel such as home-school coordinators. According to a newspaper report, the coordinator was asked to take a new kindergarten pupil home because of the lack of a required birth certificate.

> He was all dolled up. This was the proudest day in his life, because he was going to school. You can imagine what attitude might have been produced by being escorted home that first day. So (the home-school coordinator) left the boy in school, discovered that the boy's parents both were working, and finally ran down a copy of the birth certificate at a doctor's office. [*Toledo Blade* 1/7/74]

There is a need for administrators to insure that new types of school-community personnel have a clear and thorough orientation to the scope of their duties. It occasionally happens that a coordinator becomes so involved in meeting various needs of residents that he fails to perform his role as a resource to the school. One coordinator known to us was acting in much the same style as a precinct captain in a large city. Whatever citizens needed, he helped them get it. He reported that he was working night and day for the school, always doing something for someone in the community. The principal and teachers did not question his dedication to the community, but had to counsel the coordinator to devote more of his on-duty hours to school-related concerns.

We cannot inventory ways of using business and industry facilities in the community. There is a tradition for this sort of cooperation that is well reported elsewhere (see, for example, Buffer 1972). The tactics of "scrounging" and making instructional aids out of locally available materials we must leave for another time or for colleagues in media or curriculum materials centers to explain. (But, for a good introduction to this task, see *Changes* no. 22—from *Changes* Magazine, 2314 Elliott Avenue, South, Minneapolis, Minnesota 55404—and any issue of *The Whole Earth Catalog, The New Earth Catalog,* of *The Mother Earth News.*) We turn now to some ways of finding what resources exist in a school community.

FINDING COMMUNITY RESOURCES

A routine survey of a school community is helpful to persons new to a community. At the risk of boring veteran teachers, it is probably worthwhile to review basic data about the community from time to time. Occasionally one meets teachers and sometimes even administrators who are not aware of other agencies that serve youth in the community. Moreover, there are times when it matters for a teacher to know whether a given address is in the Robert Taylor housing project or the Thomas Jefferson group. But that is another issue, not related to finding community resources.

To locate volunteer speakers, an Ohio school district placed a coupon in the monthly district newsletter. The coupon provided space for identifying information, profession or hobby, topics, and employer. Accompanying the coupon was an explanation:

> The Washington Local Schools are attempting to enlist the help of talented parents and other persons willing to talk to school children on unique hobbies or professions. Topics may include special interests, handicrafts, travel experiences or subjects dealing with any profession such as dentistry, carpentry, auto mechanics, printing, etc.
> Requests for speaking engagements will be made by the individual teacher. A list is being compiled through the Information Services Department. . . . [*School Life* 1974, p. 3]

Another district offered several daytime "Renewal Classes for Adults." They, too, provided a coupon for several types of school involvement. The information was secured by the form reproduced below.

HOME-SCHOOL PARTNERSHIP PROGRAMS

I wish to become involved in the Newark Schools. Please send me information about:

. . . . The school district resource and talent bank.

. . . . The Community Advisory Program.

. . . . The Golden Pass Program for Senior Citizens.

. . . . The Tutorial Program.

. . . . Daytime Renewal Classes.

. . . . The Volunteer School Aide Programs.

. . . . The Music-Action Committees.

. . . . The Booster Clubs.

. . . . The Parent Surveillance Programs. [*Superintendent's Newsletter* 1972, p. 3]

The Huntington (Pennsylvania) schools had no extra funds, yet they needed materials for a new elementary curriculum that included comparative culture studies in every grade.

> So the district ran an ad in the local paper asking people in the community to give or lend articles from foreign countries they had at home. Many worthwhile items came in, often on a gift or long-term loan basis. To

get more objects, school officials contacted local people who were planning trips abroad, gave them $25.00 each, and asked them to purchase authentic and educational items for the schools.

Results? Huntington's students now have access to genuine articles from foreign countries: A Mexican sombrero, a handmade Japanese walking stick that converts to a cue stick, wooden shoes from Holland, dolls from India, an entire clothing ensemble from Japan, Eskimo dolls from Iceland and many others.

The artifacts supplement instructional kits stocked with pictures, tapes, transparencies, films and filmstrips. [*Pennsylvania Education* 1972, p. 23]

It is more than likely that some readers are not impressed by the items resulting from the ad. Apparently, however, they were helpful to the school concerned. We mention the incident as an example of what one school found effective. It is possible that educators who hesitate to follow such a procedure out of consideration for the lack of resources possessed by their communities could be surprised. True, they would probably not come up with walking sticks that convert to cue sticks but then, how many times does one need something like that? It is more than likely that the school-community relationship will benefit by the school's appreciatively borrowing a family possession.

Before beginning the search for community learning resources, educators would do well to begin by reading the *Yellow Pages of Learning Resources.** Some of the learning resources identified in this publication will be present in any city. On people as resources, the *Yellow Pages* has this comment: "Everybody can be a teacher" (ibid., p. 2). On places as learning resources, the *Yellow Pages* offers this advice: "As well as being spaces for meeting and learning in, many places are themselves learning resources. Very often things can best be learned by experiencing them first hand. . . . Any place where special things happen or that possesses unique characteristics . . . can be a rich learning resource."

There are other systematic ways of unearthing community resources. Quite often, however, their location and utilization depends upon the ingenuity of the educator in the situation. Despite the psychological benefits derived from using community resources, educators need to keep their basic purpose in mind. The enhancement of

---

* Group for Environmental Education, Inc., 1214 Arch Street, Philadelphia, Pennsylvania 19107. The book is also available from the National Association of Elementary School Principals, MIT Press, and Educational Facilities Laboratories.

learning opportunities for children is the primary goal. Hence, if the educator has good reason to believe that a given objective can be more effectively accomplished outside the school (and the costs are comparable), that is what should be arranged. Conversely, if the classroom, or the library, or the science laboratory are better learning places, that is where learning should be arranged. As for resources and talent, they may turn up in the most expected places as well as in the most unexpected places.

SUMMARY

We accepted a broad definition of resources to mean people or materials in the school community that can help the school accomplish its objectives. Some resources can be brought from the community into the school. There are predictable, but not insurmountable, obstacles to having other persons in the school, especially if they serve in an instructional role of any kind. Sometimes learners must go out into the community. Leaving the school territory has problems, but the benefits are worth it. Using community resources builds community support at the same time as it helps accomplish other learning or service objectives. There are many ways of locating community resources. They should be used whenever they are the most effective (and feasible) way of meeting objectives of the school.

SUGGESTED ACTIVITIES

1. Make a list of all community resources—people and things—brought into a school during a given time. Put the items in categories that describe their contribution.

2. List all the incidents of individual students going out of the school into the community to take advantage of community resources. Classify the items in any way that seems appropriate to you.

3. Find out if a list of external resources is available for a school. How recent is it? What kinds of resources does it include and exclude? On what basis is the list distributed (who has copies)?

4. Make your own list of community resources along the same lines as the *Yellow Pages for Learning* or the *Whole Earth Catalog.*

5. Find out what school or district policy applies to:
   a) bringing resources into the school, and
   b) taking or sending students out into community learning places.

6. Make a survey of parents of one school class similar to the one taken by the Washington Township Schools. Analyze your results. If you are the teacher, include an item asking whether respondents would be willing to share their resource with other classes as well as your own.

SUGGESTED READINGS

Ball, Colin and Mog. *Education for a Change.* Baltimore, Maryland: Penguin Books, 1973.

Cronin, Joseph, and Hailer, Richard M. *Organizing an Urban School for Diversity.* Lexington, Mass.: Lexington Books, 1973, chapter 13.

Educational Leadership 30, no. 2 (November 1972): editorial and eight theme articles.

Levine, Daniel U., and Havighurst, Robert J., eds. *Farewell to Schools???* Worthington, Ohio: Charles A. Jones, 1971.

National Education Association. *Parent Involvement: A Key to Better Schools.* Washington, D.C., 1972.

National Elementary Principal 52, no. 6 (April 1973): entire issue.

Saxe, Richard W., ed. *Opening the Schools.* Berkeley, Ca.: McCutchan, 1972.

REFERENCES

Ardrey, Robert. *The Territorial Imperative.* New York: Atheneum, 1966.

Barry, C. H., and Tye, F. *Running a School.* New York: Schoken Books, 1973.

Ball, Colin and Mog. *Education for a Change: Community Action and the School.* Baltimore, Md.: Penguin Books, 1973.

Bombeck, Erma. "School Trip Rivals Normandy Invasion." *Toledo Blade,* 2 December 1973.

Bowman, James; Freeman, Larry; Olson, Paul A.; and Pieper, Jan. *Of Education and Human Community.* Lincoln, Neb.: University of Nebraska, 1972.

Brady, Charlotte; Donovan, Myrtle; and Buntin, Joseph. "Parents Staff Center." *Ohio Elementary School Principal* (Winter 1973-74): 33.

Brotherson, Mary Lou, and Johnson, Mary Ann. *Teacher Aide Handbook.* Danville, Ill.: Interstate, 1971.

Buffer, James. "Tested Alternatives: Industry and Education." In *Opening the Schools,* edited by Richard W. Saxe, pp. 179-212. Berkeley, Ca.: McCutchan, 1972.

Corwin, Ronald G. *Reform and Organizational Survival: The Teacher Corps as an Instrument of Educational Change.* New York: John Wiley, 1973.

Cunningham, Luvern L. "The Reform and Renewal of American Education." In *Futures Conference: New Directions in American Education,* edited by Carroll F. Johnson and Joan Booth. Washington, D.C.: Proceedings of the Conference, 1972.

Educational Leadership 30, no. 2 (November 1972): 128-130. "Using Community Resources."

Education Summary 26, no. 14 (15 January 1974): 8. "Community and Society."

Ferver, Jack, and Cook, Doris. *Teacher Aides.* Madison, Wisc.: University Extension, University of Wisconsin, 1968.

Fireside, Byrna J. "Use a Parent's Special Talent." *Instructor* 82, no. 1 (August/September 1972): 57.

Gehret, Kenneth G. "Woman with a Cause." *Christian Science Monitor,* 4 August 1973, p. B3.

Group for Environmental Education, Inc. *Yellow Pages of Learning Resources.* Philadelphia, 1972.

Hechinger, Fred M. "Grandpa Goes to Kindergarten." *New York Times,* 29 October 1972.

Hubley, John. *School Volunteer Programs How They Are Organized and Managed.* Worthington, Ohio: School Management Institute, 1972.

I/D/E/A. *British Infant School.* Dayton, Ohio: Institute for Development of Educational Activities, 1969.

Janowitz, Morris. *Institution Building in Urban Education.* Chicago: University of Chicago Press, 1969.

Mott Institute for Community Development. *The Use of School Volunteers.* East Lansing, Mich.: Michigan State University, 1973.

National Education Association. *Parent Involvement: A Key to Better Schools.* Washington, D.C., 1972.

National Organization for Women. *Volunteerism: What It's All About.* Berkeley, Ca., n.d.

New York Times, 13 January 1974, p. 47. "Teen-Age Tutors Go Back to Schools."

Operation Success: Parent Partners. Pamphlet. Toledo, Ohio: Toledo Public Schools, n.d.

Pennsylvania Education 3, no. 6 (July/August 1972): 23. "Huntington Finds Local Materials."

Resources for Youth Newsletter 3, no. 1 (October 1973): 1. "Community Participation Class."

Sarason, Seymour B. *The Culture of the School and the Problem of Change.* Boston: Allyn and Bacon, 1971.

Saxe, Richard W. "Motivation for Teaching." *Teachers College Record* 70, no. 4 (January 1969): 313-320.

———. *Opening the Schools.* Berkeley, Ca.: McCutchan, 1972.

———. "Can We Have Alternatives and Schools Too?" *The National Elementary Principal* 52, no. 6 (April 1973): 102-104.

Saxe, Richard W., and Ishler, Richard E. *Final Report: Team Leadership Development Project.* U.S.O.E. Project No. 452272. Toledo, Ohio: University of Toledo, 1971.

Sommers, Kathryn. "Make a Resource Person File." *Instructor* 82, no. 1 (August/September 1972): 62.

School Life 4, no. 3 (January 1974): 3. "Community Support Asked for School Speakers' Program." (Washington Local Schools, Toledo, Ohio.)

Superintendent's Newsletter, Newark (California) Unified School District 2, no. 1 (August 1972): 3.

The Right To Know. Pamphlet. Toledo, Ohio: Toledo Public Schools, n.d.

Thomasey, Bernadette. "Volunteer Work Is Education in itself for High School Students." *Toledo Blade,* 30 September 1973.

Thrasher, Frederick M. *The Gang.* Chicago: University of Chicago Press, 1927.

Toledo Blade, 18 December 1973. "Parent Groups Praised for Athletic-Event Aid."

———, 7 January 1974. "Home-School Coordinator Also Pal."

Toledo ESA Title I Newsletter. Toledo, Ohio: Toledo Public Schools, n.d.

Vidich, Arthur J., and Bensman, Joseph. *Small Town in Mass Society.* Princeton, N.J.: Princeton University Press, 1968.

Wayson, William. "Educating for Renewal in Urban Communities." *The National Elementary Principal* 51, no. 6 (April 1972): 5-19.

Weinstein, Grace. "Tapping Community Talent." *Scholastic Teacher* (November 1972): 62.

chapter eight

Two-Way Communication

Except ye utter by the tongue words easy to be understood, How shall it be known what is spoken? for ye shall speak into the air.

I Corinthians 14:9

In this chapter we shall maintain that communication is of major importance to school-community relations. We believe that there is not sufficient communication, that it flows almost exclusively one way, from school to home, and that much of the communication is poorly designed. In short, what we have here, is a failure in communication.

Some of the problems of communication will be analyzed and promising practices presented. Although the chapter is all about communication, it is most certainly not about all communication. Our focus will be on communication between schools and communities. The vast literature on communications as art and science cannot be reviewed here. There are departments and even entire colleges given over completely to the study of communication. Unfortunately, we cannot simply refer educators to these resources—the colleges and departments of communication—and move on to other concerns. Because of the particular interpretation of community relations adopted in chapter 1, communications is the fundamental issue underlying the entire concept of community relations. We have been discussing communications indirectly in the chapters on needs assessment (chapter 6) and community resources (chapter 7). In these pages we specifically and directly consider issues in school-community communication.

It is especially difficult to distinguish between communications that are primarily community relations and those that are primarily public relations. Just as *public relations* can be considered a category of the more inclusive term *community relations,* its procedures can also be considered a subdivision of communication. Thus, communication is the main element in the process of school-community relations and the particular procedures of public relations are one aspect of this communication. The distinction is arbitrary to a large extent, but it does help to arrange the mass of data for study and discussion.

The purposes of school-community communications are many. Sumption and Engstrom (1966) list ten objectives, four of which are better considered under public relations. Those that deal with community relations are:

> To provide the people with information about their schools.
>
> To provide the school with information about the community.
>
> To develop a commonality of purpose, effort, and achievement.
>
> [To] keep . . . the people informed of new developments and trends in education.
>
> To develop, through a continuous exchange of information, an atmosphere of cooperation between the school and the other social institutions of the community.
>
> To secure an unofficial but frank evaluation of the program of the school in terms of educational needs as the community sees them. [Pp. 105-107]

A more general statement, which emphasizes the importance of two-way communication, is provided by Marx and Milstead. They maintain that there are two broad goals for school-community communications: "(1) to make the community aware of the policies and practices of its schools and the reasons behind them, and (2) to determine the opinions and expectations of the community relative to education" (1970, p. 27).

In discussing communication, we continue to opt for a broad inclusive meaning that permits us to include almost everything that happens in the school and a great deal of what happens in the school community. Thus, we view all behavior as communication. Recognizing that this position, although indicative of the inclusive meaning of the term, "communicates" little of specific use to readers, we need to attempt some refinement. *Communication* will refer to transmitting and receiving information, attitudes, ideas. It matters greatly whether the message intended by the sender was the same one perceived by the receiver, but even if this is not the case, we shall maintain that something has been communicated. We shall even insist that buildings, physical arrangements, and things communicate something, even though there has been no deliberate attempt to formulate a message to be sent by these means. (A locked gate at the school playground on weekends communicates something to persons seeking to use that facility. A schoolhouse with the lights on at night communicates something else.)

There are many ways of discussing school-community communication. A common approach is to deal with person-to-person communication separately from mass media communication. Because of our assumption that two-way communication—originated by either school or home—is essential, we find it more reasonable to organize the information under the general headings of "school initiated" and "community initiated" communication. Communication of the public relations type will be discussed in the next chapter.

SCHOOL-INITIATED COMMUNICATION

According to Cronin and Hailer: "Community relations cannot be improved without frank recognition that the problems of the past few years are based partly on the failure of school people and parents to listen to each other. This failure is a reflection of communication problems within the system itself" (1973, p. 43). The same emphasis on communication appears in a report of an extensive survey of the Cincinnati public schools. The survey, arranged by the Midwest Administration Center of the University of Chicago, began the discussion of "School-Community Relationships" with this statement:

> Effective communication is essential to a school system—particularly a relatively large one which is located in an urban area, like Cincinnati. The successful functioning of such a school system—even its mere operation—is dependent to a great extent upon the degree to which the myriad units involved in public education achieve understanding of one another. Communication is the primary means through which such understanding is sought. It is a process characterized by complexity and variability in terms of the persons and groups involved and particularly with reference to their respective values and understandings, the nature of the messages transmitted, and the means of conveyance utilized. The units involved may be institutions or individuals, directly or indirectly concerned with education,

and internal or external to the formal structure: the messages transmitted may vary all the way from a student's response on a test to the public's refusal of a requested operating levy; the means of conveyance can include everything from walkouts to report cards, from television to apples for the teacher. [1968, p. 9-1]

Statements such as those quoted above are found throughout the professional literature. Indeed, it seems as though the argument for improved school-community communication has been accepted. If this is the case, as it seems to be, it will be revealing to consider some of the more common communications practices used by schools.

In a study of communication between her school and its parent community, Sloan (1973) examined communication between school and home and vice versa. Table 8-1 summarizes the findings for the survey of communication between school and home. There were 286 forms returned out of a total of approximately 350 families with children attending the Edgewater Elementary School in Toledo—a response of over 80 percent. Parents were invited to check all the ways in which they learned about the school. The school newspaper and being told by one's own child were almost invariably checked, followed by parent-teacher conferences in third place.

TABLE 8-1 WAYS PARENTS LEARN ABOUT SCHOOL (N = 286)

Communication Channel	Number of Responses	Percent
My child tells me	272	95
Neighbor children tell me	57	20
Conversations with adult friends and neighbors	160	56
School newspaper	280	98
Classroom newsletters	104	36
Teacher notes or phone calls	129	45
Parent-teacher conferences	237	82
Report cards	196	68
Notes or calls to school	101	35
Personal visits to school	128	45
Classroom visits or observations	111	39
PTA meetings	151	53
Other	7	2

Source: Bonnie Sloan, "School-Home Communications" (Educational Specialist's thesis, University of Toledo, 1973), p. 39.

Sloan also asked parents to indicate ways in which they *preferred* to learn about the school. Table 8-2 shows the difference, in rank order, of ways in which parents *are* informed about schools and the ways in which they *prefer* to be informed. Only the five most frequently checked preferred ways of learning are reported. Table 8-2 reveals general agreement between the preferred and actual ways of learning about schools. However, Sloan notes that the absence of items in the preferred list may be because these ways of communicating are not used at Edgewater and hence unknown to these parents. Items dropped out of the preferred list were report cards (fourth in actual rank) and conversations with friends and neighbors (fifth in actual rank).

TABLE 8-2 RANK ORDER OF ACTUAL AND PREFERRED WAYS OF LEARNING ABOUT SCHOOL

Channel	Actual Rank	Preferred Rank	Difference
School newspaper	1	1	0
Parent-teacher conference	3	2	1
PTA	6	3	3
My child tells me	2	4	2
Teacher note or phone call	7	5	2

Source: Sloan 1973, p. 40.

In our survey of multiunit school principals in Wisconsin, we asked principals to report how the school communicated to parents. The replies are shown in table 8-3. Except for items in table 8-1 not under the control of school (e.g., my child tells me), the ways of communicating illustrated in tables 8-3 and 8-1 are similar. The common media for communication between school and home seem to be newspapers or newsletters, conferences, notes, and phone calls. The Cincinnati survey mentioned above identified six major ways through which the public learns about schools: informal conversation, community meetings, personal communications from teachers and administrators, visits to schools, school publications, and the mass media (Midwest Administration Center 1968, p. 9-13).

Although informal conversation with children, friends, and

TABLE 8-3 WAYS PARENTS ARE INFORMED BY MULTIUNIT SCHOOLS (N = 121)

Media	Number of Principals Reporting
Newsletters and bulletins	97
Teacher-parent conferences	28
PTO/PTA meetings	20
Newspaper	20
Group parent meetings	19
Radio	13
Special letter	12
Open house	11
Telephone	7
School visits/tours	6
Unit-parent sessions	6
Television	5
Community clubs	4
Room meetings	4
Quarterly reports	3
Parent handbook	2
Pot-luck supper/coffee groups	2
Inservice education for parents	2
Parent Advisory Committee	2
Audiovisual presentations	1
No entry	4

Source: Richard W. Saxe, "Multiunit Schools and Their Communities," *Elementary School Journal* 74, no. 2 (November 1974): 103-111.

neighbors is the most readily available source of information about schools, it is not noted for its accuracy. Some schools attempt to supplement and correct information conveyed by conversation. They may employ parent aides or orient school volunteers about school activities. School employees who live in the district often help supply needed information and stop the spread of misinformation. This explains, in part, the once widespread practice of requiring teachers and other school employees to make their homes in the school district.

The Parent Partner program mentioned in the chapter on community resources is an example of a program that helps improve the informal school-community communication. There are many such programs. Unfortunately, the continued existence of too many of them seems to depend upon additional federal or state funds. Educators are ignoring an important means of communication if they do not make every attempt to keep all categories of employees—paid or volunteer—aware of school activities.

Citizens learn some things about schools from the regular progress reports. These, once called report cards, are prepared in as many different ways as there are school districts. We need not take up the psychological and philosophical questions of whether it is effective and proper to assess and report students' progress in one form or another. We should be concerned about whether grade progress reports communicate clearly whatever it is they are supposed to communicate. All of us who have survived even one change in reporting practices know that this—unambiguous communication—is not easily, never universally, achieved.

The problems that can accompany a change in reporting systems are well represented by the experience of the Dallas Independent School District. As reported in *Time* (18 February 1974), the new report cards "may well have completely eliminated any communication between home and school." An 8½- by 14-inch sheet was used for kindergarten through third grade reporting. A 32-page manual was supplied to help parents interpret the numbers entered on the sheet by teachers. The manual was titled: *Terminal Behavioral Objectives for Continuous Progression Modules in Early Childhood Education.* A board member termed the procedure "a monster" and stated that "70 percent of the parents will never raise the lid on a cover with a title like that."

Inside, the explanatory manual were terms familiar to most, but not all, educators: "seven to 23 specific skills in 39 'modules' under seven basic curriculum areas." To explain the technical language, examples were offered: "Skill number 5 in the basic concepts module in the communications curricular area, for example, is 'oral response on a concrete level using objects.' " That means, the manual explains helpfully, that a child can "identify a toy car by saying a word, phrase or sentence about it." Another writer is now hard at work writing a pamphlet to explain the manual that explains the report form. (For another treatment of this same issue, see Hechinger and Hechinger 1974.)

We can sympathize with the educators in Texas as well as with the bewildered recipients of the new report forms. The school was, in this case, striving for a new level of clarity, of specificity. It proposed to replace an *A, B, C, D,* or *F* in four or five subjects with new lists of exact behavioral competence. This is a commendable effort. However, if the report of the school's efforts is accurate, it has seriously underestimated the problems of communicating information coded in technical terms to persons not familiar with the new code and the developments that lead up to it. This is easy to do for those of us who live daily with the terms and observe the introduction of variations and new meanings.

At a recent school meeting there was a long discussion of the advantages of career education. The first question from the audience was, "What is distributive education?" This is a fair question but should have caused the educator-speakers some concern because they had been using the term throughout their entire presentation. We are always willing to define terms for persons who raise questions but there are many who will not raise a question. They would rather remain uninformed than go to the trouble of finding out what educators mean by words such as *multiunit, behavioral objective, SMSG, NDEA, Title I,* and the like. Moreover, for those who do ask for clarification, there is a psychological cost involved. They must interrupt the flow of discussion as well as signal their own lack of knowledge. (Neil Postman and Charles Weingartner have prepared a book for amateurs "who want to know what all the hollering is about": *The School Book* 1973.) It would be best to save technical terms for the technical audience. When they must be used for others, such terms should be explained when they are first introduced.

Educators have long believed that report cards, even sophisticated "monsters" like the Dallas innovation, are inadequate. One way of supplementing objective information was to write brief, pithy comments descriptive of some attribute of the learner that the teacher thought to share with the parent. Sometimes these unsolicited comments were complimentary, sometimes severely critical of the child described. We extracted a list of such comments from the margins of one set of report cards from one second grade class in a predominantly middle-class town in Indiana. The comments are verbatim; pupils' names are changed.

TABLE 8-4 REPORT CARD NOTES

Robert Brown. Robert should practice reading at home. He needs to pay attention and leave others alone.

Bonnie Butler. A delightful child—high ability—a good student.

Marie Casebeer. Marie is moving at an average pace.

Sarah Carson. Encourage to do extra reading at home for practice. Also work on number combinations with her so she can gain speed in her answer.

Gregg Collet. Gregg still needs to pay attention and to get busy with his work. He is reminded about that each day. Encourage reading at home for extra practice.

David DeLong. David has shown improvement, but he needs a lot of extra help.

Sue DeReamer. Sue has improved. She must learn to concentrate. She needs a lot of opportunity to read in her spare time.

Gene Fontana. Gene is a capable child. His work has improved.

Beth Fulka. A very pleasant young lady to have in the room.

Jeffrey Glass. A good, cheerful student. He follows directions well.

Julie Godlewski. Julie is a very fine young lady and a delight to work with. She'll make a fine third grader.

Jon Hendricks. Jon should strive to become a more attentive listener.

Stephen Huber. If Stevie would improve his work habits, his school work would be much better. He has days when he concentrates on what he is doing and his work is much better.

Patricia Jarrat. Pat has improved some about her attitude towards doing arithmetic and other work. She had to be reminded for a while to turn in her arithmetic which was hardly started even.

Jack Johnsen. Jack is an underachiever. Has a greater potential than his daily work indicates.

Donald Jones. Don's independent work in reading has been very poor since our conference. If he does not show some improvement within the next few weeks, he will not be able to remain with his present reading group.

Cathy Kay. Cathy is doing satisfactory reading with her reading group, but the group is reading below the level at which they should be at the present time.

Janet Kussmaul. Janet has a good quiet manner. Her fluency in reading is improving.

Jeffrey Lange. Jeffrey could do better work if he would pay attention and leave others alone.

Lori Lorcas. Lori is doing poor work—doesn't complete assignments—talks and plays most of the day and is very inattentive. We need a conference.

Deborah Matheny. Debbie talks and wastes time. Could do better in independent work.

Chris Patterson. Chris is a very good worker and helper.

Jimmy Savia. Jimmy is extremely weak in all areas.

Michael Schroeder. An excellent, cooperative worker.

Bill Shucker. No data.

Richard Springer. Will not take things seriously—laughs at everything! Below average.

Pamela Tappen. Encourage Pam to do extra work, extra reading on her own for practice.

Brian Ulich. Brian's attitude seems to have improved just during the past few weeks. He is still very careless about his work. I think he is capable of doing good work when encouraged. I hope this improvement will continue next year.

Bonnie Varga. A delightful child. She enjoys everything.

Dale Van Alt. Encourage Dale to do extra reading for practice. Also help him with his numbers so that he can gain speed.

Nita Sue Warner. Nita Sue does very careless sloppy work which is seldom completed. Orally she does a very nice job which indicates her written work should be better. I think she is capable of doing good work.

Robin Williams. She is doing satisfactory work. She can do better, but needs time to gain self confidence. Lately she has seemed very nervous in class.

The statements in table 8-4 have been used in several classes of teachers preparing to become school administrators. Rarely do teachers find anything objectionable in the content, or the tone of the marginal comments. Most seem to feel that it is the work of a conscientious teacher who deserves credit for going beyond the bare minimum of information required on the grade report forms.

There is no doubt about the motivation of the teacher concerned. She was popular and considered a good teacher who maintained a pleasant, although firm, classroom environment. What educators should consider is the propriety of passing judgment on the overall worthiness of children (e.g., "a delightful child"), of directing of parents to engage in specific instructional tasks at home, and the kindness and compassion of "publishing" harsh judgments for the families and friends of pupils to read. I am told that there are still homes in which the child's report cards are placed in the family Bible for posterity. Siblings and cousins, if no one else, may pick up comments such as garrulous Debbie Matheny's or giddy Dickie Springer's. There is also a classic example of pedaguese that rivals the best of the Dallas confusions: "Cathy is doing satisfactory reading with her reading group, but the group is reading below the level at which they should be at the present time." One might hope that there are better ways of communicating such information if, indeed, it should be communicated at all.

Individual notes and calls from educators to parents are common ways for parents to learn about schools. Sometimes the most carefully worded notes are misinterpreted by parents. The notes can themselves become a source of resentment either because of a real or imagined insult to the parent. The notes may be mailed or sent home with children. Some of them will arrive promptly, some will not. In some schools there have been so many unfortunate incidents connected with notes from teachers to parents that none is permitted to be sent until the principal reads and initials the note. This system has obvious disadvantages, but it does suggest the need for some assistance from time to time.

Nearly all educators send notes or letters to parents. The great majority of these are about problems. They signal something amiss to the recipients. The practice of calling or writing parents to compliment them or their child is still rare enough to be reported as a kind of creative innovation in educational periodicals. A letter from the school is still only slightly more welcome than one from the Bureau of Internal Revenue. This can be easily changed if some in-service time can be set aside to help teachers with the substance and the form of friendly letters. A collection of "over 170 model letters that school administrators, teachers, counselors, and central office personnel can use," has been published. The authors claim that it contains "every kind of letter you will ever need, already written for you" (Larson and McGoldrick 1970). We seriously doubt the latter claim but such a collection (whether the published collection or one plucked from files and borrowed from colleagues) may be useful to beginning educators. In many situations, we believe, there can be no substitute for an individualized communication prepared for the particular occasion.

Bulletins, announcements, reports, newsletters, and newspapers all tell citizens something about their schools. Sometimes the quality of the reproduction is marginal. Sometimes they communicate clearly. Just as with letters, there are collections of bulletins available for beginning educators (see, for example, Keith, Infelise, and Perazzo 1965). There are also excellent sources on the technical aspects of printed bulletins, newspapers, newsletters (for example, Kindred 1960). We shall consider these media in more detail when we examine public relations oriented communication in chapter 9.

The mass media (newspapers, radio, TV) serve as both community relations and public relations communicators. For years, schools resisted releasing comparative data that might present the schools in an unfavorable light. Finally, after much pressure, nearly all records and reports (excepting personal data about students and staff) are available. When requested data are not forthcoming or are provided in only the most general manner, citizens or pressure groups are likely to seek assistance from the courts.

When the Business and Professional People for the Public Interest and the Lakeview Citizens Council asked the Chicago Board of Education and the city treasurer for detailed information on school spending, they received only the board of education's annual financial report. They termed this incomprehensible and complained that:

> For example, there is no way to determine how much money the board actually spent on any individual school for teachers' salaries, textbooks, lunchrooms, maintenance, or anything else. We also found items such as $10 million for professional and special services and $21 million for administration, with absolutely no breakdown or explanation of what these items are. [Lauerman 1974]

The citizens' groups went to the Circuit Court, charging the board of education with failure to comply with the Illinois School Code. The requested data are now being assembled.

The reluctance of educators to release some kinds of data is understandable. Readers of local papers can now contemplate discouraging headlines, such as: "S. Arlington Pupils Scores Are Lower" (Shaffer 1973) and "Lag in Reading Scores Blamed on Teachers and Establishment" (Peterson 1972). However, there is editorial approval and possibly increased effort by citizens as suggested by a *Chicago Tribune* editorial:

> It is good—and not to be taken for granted—that the reading scores were made public. Supt. James F. Redmond has taken few if any braver or better decisions than when several years ago he decided to make an annual public report on test scores in reading and arithmetic. Not all school systems release such figures. Chicago Public Schools did not do so until recent years.
>
> Public knowledge of the low achievement of Chicago pupils has contributed to the decision by the Board of Education to put $3 million of its own money into an intensive reading program. . . . If test scores had remained top secret, locked up at headquarters, despairing board members and teachers might still be hoping to get by with shrugs and resigned remarks about "what can you expect?" But that will not suffice when the public has factual information, school by school and grade by grade, showing that our expensive schools are not achieving the literacy upon which future learning and earning depend. [9/23/73]

The argument against releasing test data was reported by Kenneth Gehret, education editor of the *Christian Science Monitor.* He quoted educators' concerns that comparisons can be misleading and could lead to a national (totalitarian) curriculum. All schools, regardless of their local purposes, could be forced to conform to the curriculum measured by the tests. A more temperate educator commented that assessments (testing) "have the propensity to be very good, very bad, or mediocre, depending on how they are handled" (*Chicago Tribune* 8/14/73). (See also Connie Lauerman, "8th-Grade Readers 14 Months Behind" [*Chicago Tribune* 3/3/74]. This headline appeared on the front page of the newspaper. It is doubtful that most readers will take the time to read and understand the discussion and interpretation of the tests results. Most are more likely to take literally the message that all eighth-grade students are severely retarded in reading ability.) It is well to note the problems that can accompany full disclosure of information about schools. The data will not speak for themselves, so there will be a need for educators to interpret the reports. There is, however, no point to debating the issue of whether information should be released or not. That issue has been resolved for the general public in the affirmative. The situation is analogous to the right of the individual parent to examine all school records pertaining to his child. This decision was reached by the State Education Commissioner of New York, despite the New York City Board's argument that "some unofficial or informal file data, such as teachers' personal comments about children, should not be available to parents in the best interest of their children" (*Scholastic Teacher* 1972; see also National Committee for Citizens in Education 1974*a* and 1974*b*; Divoky 1974; and Mouat 1974). The effect of these two positions—open general information to groups and the press and open particular information to parents—is to require educators to be like Caesar's wife, to be carefully objective in their reporting.

As we mentioned previously, the physical environment of the school communicates something to the community. The several locked doors may be an unhappy, but, we hope, temporary, symptom of social disorganization, but the absence of a clear designation of how one is able to secure entrance is an unnecessary irritant to the visitor who must sometimes walk entirely around a building before discovering the open door. The manner by which one is greeted by the teacher, security guard, or student at the open entrance is also a kind of communication.

When the visitor is required to register in the school office and secure a pass to his destination, more communication occurs. The appearance of the office itself and the demeanor of the school secretary can be either hostile or friendly. Some administrators take advantage of the opportunity to meet the visitor and perhaps escort him to his destination. Others have prepared materials discussing school activities. Some administrators seem not to notice the curt, sometimes rude, reception given to visitors by the secretary. This encounter is rich in its potential for communicating attitudes and ideas about the relationship of the school to the community.*

Before taking up the processes of incoming communication—from the community to the school—we consider one additional concern of educator-communicators. This can be best discussed under the head-

---

* An extreme example of the prompt creation of a hostile attitude is the way in which a receptionist answered the telephone at one institution. Her usual answer was "Yeah, whadaya want?" Surprisingly, fearsome dragons such as this are often associated with friendly, kindly administrators. There is a possibility that they—the administrators—are unaware of the behavior of the receptionists. This in no way absolves them of responsibility for discourteous behavior. In effect, an administrator has no right to be uninformed of such practices performed under his authority.

ing of: What does the community want to know about schools? The answer to this question is not as we might predict, everything. Parents and others desire only partial information about the schools. One of the problems for educators, therefore, is the necessity to prepare different messages for different groups of receivers. (Parents differ from business men or retired persons in the information they need about bond issues. Some writers use the terms *publics* or *subpublics*.) Another problem is that of determining the more important communication concerns of citizens.

Before considering the desirability of concentrating on specific communication needs, it is important to note that the frequent complaint of most groups about schools is the lack of sufficient accurate, understandable information. The need to concentrate on the most important information—as perceived by the group with which the educator seeks to communicate—in no way relieves the educator from the responsibility of providing free and open communication about all educational matters. (We always assume that information about individuals is privileged and provided only to those with a valid claim, such as parents and counselors.) If one must err in communicating, he would be better to err in over-communicating rather than in under-communicating. Much information that is meant to be disseminated to entire faculties stops at the principal's desk. Much information meant to be disseminated to parents stops at the teacher's desk. This kind of block to communication is a problem of any organization with a hierarchical structure.

The reasons for this block vary. Often, administrators see information as power and seek to retain power by retaining information. Other administrators may act out of more benevolent motives, seeking not to bother teachers with information that they do not need. This denies teachers the opportunity to decide for themselves whether they need information or not. A common example of this error is the official report of the board of education. Many administrators never make these reports available for the faculty to read. The caveat to be rigorously observed in this regard is that information directed to an administrator as the designated head of a school or district must not be considered personal communication. Many communications of vital interest to teachers are lost because of the failure of the administrator to move them off his desk. Sometimes secretaries route communications addressed to principals or superintendents to the persons actually interested in the content. In this case, care must be taken not to deny the administrator access to the same information.

Teachers might fail to share information with parents for the same reasons of misguided benevolence (thinking they will not bother parents with superfluous information). It is also possible that teachers may be less than enthusiastic about disseminating information with which they are not in sympathy. This is a serious concern for communicators in hierarchically structured organizations. The policy board at the top may officially take a position that can, in effect, be negated by failure to communicate at lower levels. (For example, some parents may never receive the pro forma invitation to visit schools; others may not be requested to contribute to the community fund.)

It is good practice for educators to be certain that citizens receive information about issues that are of great importance to them. Failure to do this will seriously endanger school-community relations. The other extreme—saturating citizens with information about which they care little—although not as harmful, should also be avoided. For these reasons, educators will need to be aware of the concerns of the community.

Sloan investigated this question in her study. The results are shown in table 8-5. Parents were asked to check the extent to which they wished to be involved in thirteen selected school activities. They were also encouraged to enter other activities in which they wished to participate.

Inspection of table 8-5 supports the concept of complete and open communication. Most of the parents want to be informed about all of the activities listed. The more important conclusion is found in the center column on participation. Here the faculty at this one school could quickly get a good idea of the activities that require particular attention and more complete communication: "learning problems of my child," "dress code," and "discipline."

Interestingly, an activity that would seem to be especially newsworthy—"purchase of major school items"—was the one in which the largest percentage of parents requested no involvement of any kind. That parents (in this study) were willing to trust educators with the technical aspects of education but showed concern about activities relating to their own child, is a hopeful sign that someday we will find a resolution to problems of the relationship between school and community.

TABLE 8-5 TYPE OF INVOLVEMENT DESIRED BY PARENTS IN SELECTED SCHOOL ACTIVITIES (N = 286)

Activity	Type of Involvement by Percentage		
	To be informed	To participate in making decisions	No involvement of any kind
Purchase of major school items	64	8	20
Hours of the school day	67	14	6
Safety concerns	77	16	4
Field trips	83	11	4
What subjects are taught	73	14	7
Size of classes	62	15	8
Clothing children wear to school (dress code)	60	31	4
Homework	79	12	5
Pupil evaluation (report card)	80	11	3
New programs/changes	72	16	1
Discipline, policy, and procedures	69	27	3
Lunch program	62	16	11
Learning problems of my child	62	36	.9
Other (only 14 replies)	4	.3	.3

Source: Sloan 1973, p. 48.

The contrasting attitudes can best be conveyed by citing the comments of two parents. One wrote: "I always wanted to know about anything concerning my children" (Sloan 1973, p. 49). Another wrote: "I am not a teacher. Therefore I believe that I should leave teaching to those who are qualified. The size of classes and subjects taught should be left to educators. But, discipline problems and learning problems are business of both teachers and parents" (ibid.).

The data in table 8-5 do not show the extent of parents' interest in a particular activity. Some may be intensely interested; others only moderately so. Moreover, even the percentage reporting that they wish no involvement at all in some activities can be deceptive. For example, the 11 percent reporting that they wished no involvement in the lunch program could reverse their position if the activity changed significantly. They may merely be satisfied with the way things are at the moment. All of these limitations aside, this survey did provide the faculty with information needed to plan a more effective program of school-home communication.

COMMUNITY-INITIATED COMMUNICATION

In previous chapters we examined the ways pressure groups and power structures communicate with the schools. In the chapter on bureaucracy and school organization, we noted some communication problems associated with large, bureaucratically structured institutions. In these pages we consider the typical communication channels available for messages between the community and the school.

The most visible of these channels—the PTA—has been discussed as an interest group. Nevertheless, it bears repeating that the PTA is commonly considered the most generally accessible channel to provide a dialogue between community and school. The discussion of the image of the PTA and its changing role need not be repeated here, but educators are advised to reexamine their relationships with the PTA. In most situations there is much room for improvement. The PTA may be unable to function in some situations. In others, it may be a communication medium to be developed and improved. Readers will recall that the legacy of the PTA of middle-class morality (Harper Valley PTA*) and puppet spokesman for the schools must be rejected before the organization can become effective in most urban areas.

Sloan asked the parents of one school to check the most effective way and the least effective way of communicating with the school. The results are shown in tables 8-6 and 8-7. Since parent councils and open forums are unknown to the parents completing the survey, the results for these two channels are meaningless. The two tables do show a correlation between the effectiveness of the channel and the personalization of the communication. That is, one-to-one communication is better than one-to-group communication and oral communication in person is better than printed forms or surveys. Although

* When Jeannie C. Riley sings: "The day my momma socked it to the Harper Valley PTA," she is conveying a long-standing resentment felt by those who have been intimidated or alienated by the image of the PTA as a sanctimonious repository of middle-class Puritan values.

TABLE 8-6 HOME-SCHOOL COMMUNICATION CHANNELS CONSIDERED VERY EFFECTIVE BY PARENTS

Communication Channel	Number Rating Very Effective	Rank Order
Direct approach by phone or in person	227	2
Parent-teacher conferences	261	1
Periodically scheduled open forum	70	5
PTA	167	3
Representative parent council	35	6
Surveys done by the school	92	4
Other	5	

Source: Sloan 1973, p. 43.

it does not show in the tables, Sloan found that parents differentiated between channels used for general information about the school (indirect is acceptable) and specific information about their child (direct is desired).

In our study of multiunit schools in Wisconsin, we asked principals to list the ways in which parents communicated with the school.

TABLE 8-7 HOME-SCHOOL COMMUNICATION CHANNELS CONSIDERED LEAST EFFECTIVE BY PARENTS

Communication Channel	Number Rating Least Effective	Rank Order
Direct approach by phone or in person	26	5
Parent-teacher conferences	11	6
Periodically scheduled open forum	128	2
PTA	64	4
Representative parent council	142	1
Surveys done by the school	112	3
Other	9	

Source: Sloan 1973, p. 45.

These data are reported in table 8-8. The procedures listed are generally well known to educators. However, some of the items reported by only a few principals suggest that administrators may be willing to receive communication from parents at all sorts of functions perhaps because (although this is only conjecture) of the lack of easily available regular communication channels for some parents.

TABLE 8-8 PROCEDURES FOR PARENT-INITIATED COMMUNICATION
(N = 121)

Procedure	Number of Principals Reporting
Phone calls	51
Individual conferences	26
Parent visits	26
Note/Letter	25
PTA/PTO	24
Group decision meetings	21
Parent-teacher conferences and report card conferences	20
Questionnaires/Surveys	14
Curriculum Advisory Councils and Policy Committees	6
Teacher-parent coffees and luncheons	6
Unit discussion sessions	5
Small group meetings	4
Parent volunteers	4
Gossip grapevine	3
Local bars and social functions	1
Old fashioned school picnic	1
Inservice seminars (includes parents)	1
No entry	23

Source: Saxe 1974.

It may seem as though this chapter is unbalanced, with a long treatment of school-initiated communication and a rather perfunctory consideration of community-initiated communication. This impression reflects the reality in most situations. There is much more evidence of outgoing—from the school—communication than there is of incoming communication. The Midwest Administration Center's survey on Cincinnati supports this position:

> Another generalization which needs emphasizing is that the school-community communication program in Cincinnati appears to be largely a one-way effort, in that the Division of School-Community Relations is devoting most of its resources to the dissemination of information, to the relative neglect of improved 'feedback' techniques. While the Board has recently employed a consultant to reflect feelings of the Negro community to the school system, it is questionable whether such a part-time effort is a real solution to the need for more effective opinion analysis and 'feed-back.' [1968, p. 9-53]

The use of school employees, paraprofessionals, and volunteers as well as teachers, as communication agents has been noted. In this case communication flows both ways. Additional ways by which the community initiates communication will be noted when we take up the topic of public relations. Because the predominant emphasis of such procedures (e.g., open house, budget hearings, science fairs) is public relations, they will be considered under that heading.

SUMMARY

In this chapter we adopted a broad definition of communication to include the transmission and reception of information, attitudes, and ideas. Public relations is one type of communication. School-initiated communication was discussed in the light of the findings of three studies. One of the problems observed was the need to translate the technical terminology of education into something intelligible to citizens. Community-initiated communication was seen to be relatively neglected and new channels will need to be devised.

SUGGESTED ACTIVITIES

1. Collect all the routine forms currently in use at a school. Assess their legibility, clarity, and tone. Select the least effective of your collection and try to improve it as much as you can.

2. Go through all of the incoming communications from parents to the teacher for one class for one month. Put them in appropriate categories (e.g.: excuses for absences, permission notes, requests for information). What can you say based on your examination of this correspondence?

3. Prepare a one-page letter to parents of your class telling them what you expect to accomplish in the next month (term, year,

whatever). Try it out on your colleagues and revise it until you are confident that it is clear. Then try it on some friends who are not educators and get their impressions of the meaning of your letter.

4. Make a survey of citizens on one city block. Find out what concerns they have about the schools. Try to find the appropriate communication channel to supply the information needed. If one doesn't exist, invent it.

5. Attend meetings of the PTA, Mothers' Club, or equivalent organization. Compare actual attendance with potential attendance. Interview some parents to find out why they do not attend. Suggest procedures that could remove obstacles to attendance.

6. Go over the report card form in use in your school with a pupil and his parent. Compare their perceptions of what the entries mean with your own. Do the same with another teacher, an administrator.

SUGGESTED READINGS

Abbey, Davis S. *Now See Hear!* Toronto, Ontario: Ontario Institute for Studies in Education, 1973.

Culbertson, Jack; Jacobsen, Paul; and Reller, Theodore. *Administrative Relationships, A Casebook.* Englewood Cliffs, N.J.: Prentice-Hall, 1960, pp. 380-411.

Erickson, Donald. "Major Communication Problems in the Schools," *Administrator's Notebook* 14, no. 7 (March 1969).

Kindred, Leslie W. *School Public Relations.* Englewood Cliffs, N.J.: Prentice-Hall, 1957, chapters 8 and 9.

McCloskey, Gordon. *Education and Public Understanding.* 2d ed. New York: Harper and Row, 1967, chapters 3, 4, 5, 12, and 14.

McLuhan, Marshall. *Understanding Media: The Extensions of Man.* New York: McGraw-Hill, 1964.

National Elementary Principal 45, no. 6 (May 1966): "Reporting to Parents." Entire issue.

Olson, David R., ed. *Media and Symbols: The Forms of Expression, Communication, and Education.* Seventy-Third Yearbook of the National Society for the Study of Education. Chicago: University of Chicago Press, 1974.

REFERENCES

Chicago Tribune, 14 August 1973. "Hidden Dangers in Standardized Tests."

______, 23 September 1973. "The Bright Side of Reading Scores."

Cronin, Joseph M., and Hailer, Richard M. *Organizing an Urban School System for Diversity.* Lexington, Mass.: Lexington Books, 1973.

Divoky, Diane. "How Secret School Records Can Hurt Your Child." *Parade,* 31 March 1974.

Hechinger, Grace and Fred M. "Remember When They Gave A's and D's?" *New York Times Magazine,* 5 May 1974, pp. 84-92.

Keith, Lowell; Infelise, Robert S.; and Perazzo, George J. *Guide for Elementary School Administration.* Belmont, Ca.: Wadsworth, 1965.

Kindred, Leslie W. *How to Tell the School Story.* Englewood Cliffs, N.J.: Prentice-Hall, 1960.

Larson, Knute, and McGoldrick, James H. *Handbook of School Letters.* West Nyack, N.Y.: Parker, 1970.

Lauerman, Connie. "Schools Sued; Asked Cost Data." *Chicago Tribune,* 12 January 1974.

Marx, Dionne J., and Milstead, Robin J. "A Better School/Community Dialogue." *Batelle Research Outlook* 2, no. 2 (1970): 27.

Midwest Administration Center. *Supplementary Papers Cincinnati School Survey.* Cincinnati, Ohio: Cincinnatians United for Good Schools, 1968.

Mouat, Lucia. "Can You Find Out Your Child's Record In School?" *Christian Science Monitor,* 22 March 1974.

National Committee for Citizens in Education. "Children, Parents and School Records." *NCCE* (April 1974*a*): 1.

______. *The Privacy Report.* Washington, D.C., 1974*b*.

Peterson, Iver. "Lag in Reading Scores Blamed on Teachers and Establishment." *New York Times,* 3 December 1972.

Postman, Neil, and Weingartner, Charles. *The School Book.* New York: Delacorte Press, 1973.

Saxe, Richard W. "Multiunit Schools and Their Communities." *Elementary School Journal* 75, no. 2 (November 1974): 103-111.

Scholastic Teacher, May 1972. "Parents May See Children's Full School Records."

Shaffer, Ron. "S. Arlington Pupils Scores Are Lower." *Washington Post,* 7 December 1973, section C, p. 7.

Sloan, Bonnie. "School-Home Communications." Educational Specialist Degree Thesis. University of Toledo, 1973.

Time, 18 February 1974, p. 59. "The Dallas Monster."

Sumption, Merle R., and Engstrom, Yvonne. *School-Community Relations.* New York: McGraw-Hill, 1966.

chapter nine

Public Relations

> Neither do men light a candle, and put it under a bushel, but on a candlestick; and it giveth light unto all that are in the house. Let your light so shine before men, that they may see your good works.
>
> *Matthew* 4: 14

In this chapter we consider some public relations activities of schools. Our focus is on the local school and typical educators rather than on specialists in public relations. We shall advocate both an increase in the number and an improvement in the quality of public relations activities.

Another compelling reason for attention to public relations at this time is the widespread evidence of a weakening in the public's trust in the schools. We need not report the evidence of this educational malaise here. The critics are so prolific and creative that their indictments of education monopolize the space available for educational literature in bookshelves and on coffee tables.* The situation is not as one sided in the daily press and in periodicals but even there there is heavy emphasis on free schools and remedies imported from Great Britain, such as open classrooms.

---

* In a survey of ten bookstores in the Toledo area, we found little space given to education. Except for study guides and reference works, almost all the books displayed were those of critics (for example, Holt, Kohl, Kozol, Herndon). The remaining 10 percent were, in effect, descriptions of alternatives to public schools, such as Summerhill and Montessori.

In the first chapter we adopted a meaning for public relations that restricted it to efforts by the schools to inform and influence the community and bring about cooperation and support. There is no impropriety associated with public relations. On the contrary, public relations practices are necessary to respond to the public's right to complete information about its schools.

Professional public relations personnel are commonly assigned to the school district central office. They prepare publications and press releases. They maintain liaison with representatives of all communication media. They can compose, edit, crop pictures, arrange multimedia presentations. They are able to advise and assist school administrators and should be consulted early and often. There is a wealth of information on the techniques of public relations for professional public relations personnel. (See, for example, *ERS Circular* no. 3 1971, and National School Public Relations Association's "Educational Public Relations Standards for Programs for Professionals.")

Having taken note of the availability of expert help, we turn our attention to the amateurs. When it comes to public relations, all educators serve as more or less talented amateurs. Hence, most public relations practices in education are conducted by amateurs.

THE PRESS

The educator who is also the amateur public relations officer must deal with the professional press. This will continue to be necessary no matter what governance bodies are operative or what organizational patterns are adopted. Perhaps another personal recollection may be allowed to emphasize an important point in this relationship between the amateur (the educator) and the professional (the reporter or photographer).

In my early years as a teacher one of my additional duties was serving as sponsor of the school safety patrol. Early in the year one of my patrol boys, Eddie Morlan, was credited with saving the life of a kindergarten pupil by snatching her from in front of an approaching car at some risk to himself. A school assembly was arranged to honor Eddie and present him with an award from the Motor Club, which then served as a patron to all safety patrols.

The newspapers covered this event. They took several pictures. At the end of the program, one photographer asked Eddie to pose standing on a table with his award with all of the other pupils crowded around pointing at him with fully extended arms. This seemed absurd to me at that time (it does even now) and I told the photographer what I thought of his idea. He looked at me a moment and then remarked, in a pained manner, "Do I tell you how to teach school?"

The absurd picture was the one that appeared on the back page of the paper. The photographer knew his business, or at least he knew what his editor wanted and that may amount to the same thing. As a slow learning amateur (I especially disliked the predictable shot of the children bursting out of the doors on the last day of school), I have questioned other media professionals over the years with predictable results. They know their craft.

Another lesson neophyte administrators should try to learn vicariously is that reporters are always on duty. Casual remarks made en route to a scheduled event may turn out to be more prominent in the report than the formal event. The simple lesson for educators who are relating to the press is this: if you do not want to see something in print, do not tell the reporter about it.

Some advice often given by veteran administrators to beginners is likely to lead to embarrassment for the educator and to a strained relationship with the third estate. I was often advised to insist on seeing all news reports in print before permitting them to be published. I can assure readers that this is a futile request. The press does not and will not operate in this way. Not only that, they will probably be offended by the request. Presumably such advice is offered by persons who feel that they have been misquoted, but have not attempted to apply the remedy they suggest to prevent this in the future.

Problems of press relations can be kept to a minimum if educators can acknowledge the freedom of the press. It is not that educators seek to censor news or even to deny access to the news. The trouble is that some of us do not admit that the press has the status of a basic institution in American democracy. When educators internalize the attitude that the press is present as a basic right and not on sufferance or with the permission of educators, the relationship should improve. When approached from this perspective, few reporters will not give careful attention to the suggestions of the amateur PR-educator.

If the press does not choose to use school press releases, it is the concern of the professional PR person. It is not grounds to favor friendly papers and ignore others. Finally, the press is entitled to all the news, good and bad and entitled to receive it promptly. Important events (sometimes called hot news) cannot wait for a carefully composed press release. It is good practice to let the school PR person know when you have been interviewed by a reporter.

ROUTINE PUBLIC RELATIONS EVENTS

We turn from the press—where educators are the amateurs dealing with a professional press—to other public relations activities where educators are the experts. Some of the examples will ostensibly exist for purposes other than public relations. We maintain, however, that their public relations impact is as great or greater than the impact of the officially acknowledged purpose. If readers cannot recall this argument from previous chapters, it may be suggested by one example—sports. The ostensible purposes are physical education and the inculcation of attitudes of sportsmanship and fair play. The PR function is to win support for the school, preferably by fielding a team that wins more games than it loses. A related PR function is entertainment. There are more Machiavellian purposes to be served in some cases (for example, diversion of attention or prevention of boredom and vandalism) but we need not be concerned with them.

Parent-Teacher Conferences

A routine practice with great potential for enhancing or diminishing public relations is the regular parent-teacher conference. The time at which these conferences are scheduled can convey consideration or disdain for parents, especially working parents. The physical setting is important. Teachers everywhere now know better than to expect parents to occupy pupils' desks, but they do not all know that the content of a parent-teacher conference is confidential. One can still see lines of parents waiting their turn for a conference within hearing distance of the conference in progress.

There are many opportunities to convey supportive or hostile attitudes throughout the conference. We can assume that teachers do not wish to convey a negative attitude. We also assume that parents wish to appear at their very best. Yet, so often these conferences, instead of improving communication, create new obstacles. The reasons for this lack of complete satisfaction with the conference are not mysterious. The situation is threatening to both parties. Parents are summoned to hear someone else evaluate their children. Of course, they need an objective appraisal, but it is folly to expect normal parents to be able to be really objective about their own children. This is a most sensitive task. We have already alluded to the reasons that teachers are apprehensive about the contact. Their tenuous role as expert is in jeopardy before a partial judge.

We cannot deal with the expected defensiveness and anxiety of parents except through the actions of the teacher. Unfortunately, this extremely difficult and demanding task is virtually ignored in most teacher preparation programs. All administrators would be well advised to examine the assistance they offer teachers in preparing for conferences. Possibly inservice education will be in order. Role-playing and videotaping will reveal problems. Human relations and communications training may be indicated. Administrators and teachers' bargaining agents will need to acknowledge the wisdom of arranging some conferences before or after the usual school hours.

Bulletins and Newsletters

Most elementary schools and many high schools produce regular information bulletins for parents. Typically these announce the dates of meetings and holidays for special events, charity collections, and the like. Now that there has been a technological breakthrough from the hand-cranked duplicator machines, quality has improved greatly. Nevertheless, illegibility is still a frequent PR error associated with publications produced by schools. The more difficult problem is the distribution system. Small children may lose the bulletins or forget about them for days or weeks. Ask any bus driver to tell you what high school students are likely to do with bulletins.

Despite the problems associated with bulletins for parents or newsletters as communication media, they are likely to continue to be among the most frequently employed by local schools. Educators preparing newsletters or similar publications may wish to begin by consulting their district PR specialist, who can prevent common errors and give sound technical assistance.

One of the common errors is omitting the name of the school or other information that would identify the source of the information.

This is easy to understand since most often the newsletter is carried home by the student. The person preparing the newsletter could easily assume that anyone receiving the publication from a student would know that it originated at the school.

Another common mistake in distributing bulletins and newsletters is to overlook some members of the faculty and staff when the publication is sent out. This is more likely to happen when only part of the school is directly concerned with the information. A moment's thought can provide any number of reasons why everyone should receive the information. For example, a primary grade teacher needs to know if the older student who usually picks up one of her pupils is going to be busy elsewhere—on a field trip or at a special program.

Administrators in other offices and other schools should be on the distribution list for all bulletins and newsletters. This permits them to make appropriate adjustments. For example, in my first principalship, our elementary school was only a few blocks from the high school. Occasionally this high school would have early dismissal for parent interview day or some special event. The first time that this occurred high school students on their way home came through our elementary school playground like a herd of wild horses knocking the smaller children down in the sheer exuberance of unexpected freedom. After attending to an alarming number of bruises and contusions, I persuaded a friend at the high school to inform me of future early dismissals. It is much less time consuming (and in this case less painful) to have advance knowledge and time to make necessary adjustments.

Many of us in education do not believe that proofreading is necessary. It is easy to make a collection of funny and not-so-funny typographical errors to establish the need for careful proofing of bulletins and newsletters. With all the care in the world, some mistakes will end up in print. Without care, the result may well prove embarrassing and cause additional work for those who must clarify misunderstandings.

The tone of the newsletter or bulletin is crucial. I have some in my collection that seem to have been prepared by retired servicemen—To, From, Re. Others seem to be friendly and informative. Even the salutation requires careful consideration. Many are addressed to "Dear Parents" and this is probably as good as any for most purposes. A perfectionist might well raise a question, "whose parents?"

but it is reasonable to use the term when the bulletin is meant specifically for parents and guardians of students and no one else. When a bulletin is intended for the entire community, another salutation seems in order. One school district uses "Friends of the Schools."

It should not be necessary to issue prohibitions or make criticisms in mass distributions such as newsletters or bulletins. Unfortunately some administrators believe it is necessary to include warnings needed only by a few in the broadside announcement. "It is expected that all attending the dance will conduct themselves like ladies and gentlemen." "Failure to comply with standards of conduct in the lunchroom will result in loss of the privilege of eating lunch at school." Such information is quite appropriate and parents and students alike have every right to be forewarned of the consequences of violations of the rules. The objection we raise here is only to the inclusion of such reservations in PR communications. It is as though an acquaintance added a P.S. to an invitation to a party: "Please note that I reserve the right to throw you out if you act improperly."

Bulletin Boards

The bulletin board should be kept current whether its purpose is primarily public relations, administrative, or instructional. The display of students' work, if properly acknowledged, can be a source of appreciation and support. Many schools are favored by a plethora of bulletin boards. These can and should be used and changed frequently. The administrator may have to exert personal leadership in orienting teachers to the use of such display areas. Many teachers mistakenly believe that bulletin boards are only showcases for superior products. Consequently, they devote undue time and effort to putting up the display when it is their turn, and look on the boards as more curse than blessing. The point that I think many administrators miss is that teachers will create their own overload of anxiety about the bulletin boards. Unless the administrator eventually counteracts the impression, they will perceive both the administrator and their colleagues as holding exalted expectations for the bulletin boards.

Everything we have said about bulletin boards can be applied to exhibits at the central office. If the duty is rotated among art teachers on a monthly basis, the excitement and diversion of energy can be as great as putting on a public exhibition. The purposes of the displays must be clearly identified and teachers must be kept from overextending themselves because they misunderstand what is expected of them.

Telephones

For years the telephones of Chicago schools were unlisted. It was frequently stated that at least one more secretary would be needed in each school merely to attend to incoming calls. Now the telephones are listed and the dire predictions failed to materialize. This incident is typical of a continuing problem in public relations. Whenever a request for more data or improved service is made, the protective instincts of administrators seem to take over. The request is too often met with untested reasons why it cannot be honored. For improved public relations, however, it would be better to respond with data rather than opinions. The listing of telephones could have been tested on a small scale forty years before social pressure forced the listing from a reluctant bureaucracy.

The telephone, now listed, needs to be answered and personnel need to be taught the procedures to be followed. The busy-executive-one-upmanship ploy of not getting on the telephone until the designated person is on the line seems presumptuous for public employees. It seems pompous for anyone and should be avoided if at all possible.

If a caller leaves a message, his call should be returned the same day. This is essential if the caller is not to receive the impression that he is being avoided or ignored.

Special Events

The PR purposes of sports and some other activities are fairly evident. Commencement and graduation ceremonies give the schools an opportunity to win friends. Music performances entertain and persuade. Assemblies and programs have long been a part of the educational scene, a way of placing some small part of the school life on display. That the elements seen as appropriate for display are somewhat atypical and represent special areas of the curriculum is traditional. Forensics are the least popular of these programs and even these are designed to be more exciting and competitive than regular school lessons. That hardy perennial, the spelling bee, never was really a teaching device, but even it was too dull to survive as a PR display.*

---

* In Chicago there was a citywide competition until the 1960s. The city champion went to Washington, D.C. for a national competition. All of this was well publicized by the sponsoring *Daily News*.

Some really silly practices have been associated with school PR attempts—even sillier than the bad old spelling bee. Consider the kindergarten graduation complete with cap and gown and Bachelor of Rhymes degree.

Science Fairs

Science fairs are still with us. It is to be hoped that they may some day join the spelling bee as quaint relics of a misguided past. Only the most naive educator believes that a project made by students has a chance of winning—if winning matters and, if one goes to competitive exhibits, it matters. Coaching by parents and teachers is endemic and projects constructed by parents are often poorly explained by their student demonstrators. Private resources, of material or advice, beyond those of the school are usually associated with winning exhibits. It is not fashionable to complain, as yet, about science fairs but, when the dam breaks, we can expect to hear cries of resentment from teachers assigned to sit with students and exhibits during the contest while other unhappy teachers covered their classes—somehow. Surely, if an administrator with any professional autonomy wished to increase public understanding and support for science education, he could think of a better way. It is hard to think of a worse way.

Open Forums, Budget Hearings, and so on

It has become common to schedule occasional open meetings to permit citizens to express their opinions on educational issues and finances. To the extent that this is valid (that what the citizens have to say can make a difference), these meetings will be considered under the heading of citizen participation. Unfortunately many meetings are merely for public relations purposes, so that the board or superintendent can attest to widespread community input and even participatory democracy.

There is nothing objectionable in a PR function designed to persuade the public that the professionals have done their jobs well. However, to pretend that such meetings are more than they are borders on deceit. It is easy to expose the ersatz community-participation meeting. Educators are not urged to give up the meetings, which can serve a useful purpose. They are asked to describe them honestly and not to pretend that they provide opportunities for decision making when they are merely giving information. There is a place for both kinds of meetings, but there is a real difference between the two that is often blurred by dishonest rhetoric. (It would be cruel to single out one example of this practice. It is ubiquitous. Visit one of the participation meetings and compare the actual event with the description provided beforehand.)

Open House

The periodic open house is the most readily accessible, legitimate means of building a good public relations image. The first task in planning this kind of special event is to make an explicit list of the objectives to be achieved. These should be placed in an order of importance, lest the accomplishment of a minor objective lessens the attainment of other more important objectives. For example, the objective of securing maximum adult participation could be ensured by bringing in a celebrity who has no connection with education. This could hurt the accomplishment of other objectives such as: informing parents of an educational innovation, or enabling parents to meet and interact with all teachers who work with their children.

Despite the concern about letting other issues detract from educational objectives, a wide spectrum of interests must be considered in planning the open house. It is good practice to schedule the time so that it does not compete with other events important to many members of the groups you hope to involve.

It is deflating to the egos of educators, but realistic to avoid, if possible, competition with favorite TV programs. In the early days of television, principals knew better than to schedule their open houses on Wednesday evening opposite the Wednesday night fights if they wished to have maximum representation of male participants. Avoiding this conflict is a reasonable precaution. Going to the other extreme of inviting fighters or ball players (or whatever the current object of interest may be) to be featured speakers is shortsighted in view of the hierarchy of objectives to be accomplished by the event.

The actual program of the open house will vary according to the objectives set down. It is common to have parents exposed to the entire staff and curriculum by arranging for them to walk through an abbreviated version of the actual schedule followed by their children. Another common format is the large general meeting with a speaker or a panel of speakers either preceded or followed by visits to individual classrooms, ending with "coffee and" in the cafeteria or gymnasium.

One of the most difficult aspects of combining a large group meeting, and classroom tour is the accessibility of teachers. All parents need to be recognized for at least a few minutes by the teacher and there just is not enough time for this. To complicate matters, some of the more outgoing parents may monopolize large segments of the time available at the expense of less aggressive persons who will be hurt and offended if the final bell rings before they have had their opportunity to chat with the teacher.

As if this were not enough of a problem for teachers, there is the matter of what is discussed. As we pointed out previously, information about the conduct and achievement of students is confidential. To reveal such information to others waiting impatiently for their turn with the teacher is unethical and may well meet the legal conditions of slander. If the physical setting is such that confidentiality is impossible how, then, is the teacher to meet parents' expectations for the answers to the usual queries: "How is Mary doing?" or "Is Johnny behaving himself?" Obviously, the objective of providing an assessment of the student's progress cannot be met in this type of event. Nevertheless, many educators continue attempting the impossible.

One tactic intended to encourage more adults to participate is to provide some kind of attendance register. There may be a guest book in each room or one master register at the main entrance where parents "sign up" for all the rooms that are entitled to credit for their presence. Perhaps parents will be asked to write their names on the chalk board so that students can see the list the next morning. Some teachers place packets of papers at each student's desk to be taken home or initialed by the parent. The variety of practices is unlimited.

Administrators and teachers too will want some kind of record of attendance at the open house. The practice of a symbolic or real reward to the winning class requires careful consideration. Clearly the inducement of a reward is extrinsic to most purposes of attending the open house. It is unfair to make any assumptions about those who do not or cannot attend. In some cases the rewarding of some can result in the unintentional punishing of others. Consider the competition for an ice-cream treat for all students in the room with the most parents represented at open house. Recently, when this happened in a middle-class suburb, the turn-out of parents (admittedly unrelated to the ice-cream prize) was outstanding. Of two fifth-grade rooms, one was represented 100 percent by parents, the other was lacking only one parent. The guilt of being recognized as the student who had personally (by his unfortunate choice of parents) cost his entire class a treat was not easily borne by the one boy. We need to collect our attendance data in less competitive ways.

DISCUSSION

Both routine and special events should be designed with a view to providing public information in a manner most likely to justify public approval and support. This recommendation is so obvious that it seems trite even to state it. Perhaps that has something to do with the perplexing realities of school-community relations, which often seem to ignore this principle. Educators may neglect the observance of the principle because it is taken for granted. That is, schools often provide information in ways that can confuse and alienate the public. This is one violation of good practice that is associated with an overly rigid bureaucratic orientation to the community. This type of error conveys the implication that "lay people" should refrain from meddling in professional business and do only what they are directed to do. The consequences of this syndrome were delineated in chapter 2 on bureaucracy and school organization.

There is another class of error which is at the opposite pole of the bureaucratic-hostility syndrome. This is the hard sell, manipulative approach that places emphasis on impressing the public by any means that work without undue reliance on the facts. The assumption seems to be that if our PR tactics are clever, the public will believe in us, and it is essential that they believe in us for their own good. This huckster approach to PR can be associated with good sound educational programs as well as with chaotic, ill-conceived disasters.

Perhaps a discussion of some PR practices may clarify errors of the second type. An article in the *Toledo Blade* (10/30/73) was headed: "Sultry, Sexy Voice Coos Facts of School Construction Plans." School officials were seeking support of a six million dollar bond issue needed to start a vocational education program, build a middle school, and construct additions to the high school. The article began as follows:

> "Come a little closer while I tell you about some v-e-r-y appealing figures," a sultry sexy voice coos, accompanied by the figure of a seductive, scantily

clad woman. "Sorry, no skinny dipping," Cleopatra says about a proposed swimming pool for ______ High School.
In ______ school district, Cleopatra is everywhere—in slide shows, posters, signs—extolling the virtues of the district's proposed expansions.

Aside from the possible reactions from women's liberation groups (the teacher who prepared the materials thinks that, "it's a compliment to use her [Cleopatra] to tell the story as opposed to Mark Antony"), the campaign seems inappropriate in many ways to represent a school building project. For one thing, the seductive approach of Cleopatra is irrelevant and dishonest in that the Empress of the Nile has nothing whatever to do with the project. As far as an educational project goes, there are certainly more appealing and honest approaches inherent in vocational education and the new school. The adjective "appealing" above may be a poor choice, but for educational purposes it can be maintained that enabling a potential dropout to gain self-respect and an occupation is, in its way, more "appealing" than the cute sex symbol. It is at least honest and related to the project.

Moreover, the campaign suffers from an excess of cuteness—"no skinny dipping!" Here the use of PR tactics has come into what may be a confusion of means and ends. If my analysis is correct, the means are tasteless and dishonest. The fact that a noble end is at stake does not justify deceptive means. We shall never know the effect of this particular campaign. The issue may pass in spite of the approach rather than because of it. If it passes because of the slick campaign, the district may have sold the public something it does not want and will not support.

Other tried and true PR practices are so patently absurd that one can only conclude that their continued existence is a tribute to tradition and a rejection of creative thinking. Consider the fund raising gimmick of "Duck the Principal" or teacher or superintendent. In this carnival event, students buy baseballs to throw at a target that dumps the celebrity into a tank of water. Buying turns at throwing pies is a variation on this theme. The reasoning is that the event shows that the authority figure is a good sport at the same time as it provides an opportunity to raise funds by capitalizing on the student's hostility toward the good sport. This type of event seems ill-conceived and more likely to perpetuate disdain rather than increase respect for authority. Doubtless, it would have vanished long ago if it were not for the implication that one is not a good sport if he does not accept the challenge. There are thousands of ways to use the talents of leaders. This type of activity is one of the least effective imaginable.

Making authority figures appear in the role of victim is related to another common tradition of casting them in the role of clowns for public relations or fund-raising purposes. The athletic contest between student and faculty (volleyball, basketball, baseball) is, if free from pressure to participate, a more harmless version of this. Typically the faculty presents itself in outlandish costume and may or may not participate seriously. The need for promoters of these comic events is to respect the human dignity of the participants, students as well as adults. Failure to do so is to use bad means to accomplish a good end. This will not be effective public relations in the long run.

The specific examples used above may seem extreme. I hope they do. Their use is intended to demonstrate excesses of the improper application of public relations practices that are not appropriate to the purposes to be served. Disdaining all efforts to court public favor is an extreme error of one type. Making the cultivation of public support an end in itself is another kind of error.

CONCLUSION

It must be noted that this has not been a well balanced discussion of the topic. It conveys a lack of enthusiasm for typical public relations efforts by schools in general that accurately represents our own bias. To put things in better balance, readers may wish to familiarize themselves with literature that describes PR practices in more favorable terms.*

This impression—of our lack of enthusiasm for educational PR in general—although accurate is unfortunate. Despite the real or imagined shortcomings of public relations efforts, we maintain that they are now needed more than ever before. Because of the apparent lack of confidence in institutions everywhere, it is necessary that educa-

---

* The National Public Relations Association has an extensive collection of books dealing with public relations. Ask for the list of books in the Edward L. Bernays Foundation Public Relations Library. See also "References on Public Relations for Classroom Teachers and School Administrators," NEA Research Division, 1201 Sixteenth Street, N.W., Washington, D.C. 20036. Copy free on request.

tion, as well as the other institutions, find ways to inform the public. The identification and reaffirmation of purpose jointly by the educator and the citizen, the school and the community, can best be achieved at local levels. Whatever we call this—and it is certainly more than accountability—it will require increased public relations activities. It is important that the PR activities be honest and continuous. Information programs cannot be put forth sporadically at decision-making times (elections) or transformed by glamorizing the spokesman and the message. Full and honest public relations in more and different ways will be required.

In summary, we noted the public relations significance of routine educational activities as well as special events. It is assumed that large school systems will make professional PR help available for consultation and specialized PR activities. Most of the PR work will be done by educators serving as amateur PR persons. The press, like education, is one of the basic institutions of a democracy and educators need to approach press relations in this context. We noted errors in PR ranging from an apparent rejection of PR as a legitimate concern to the embracing of PR as an end in itself. Neither of these extremes is suitable to the present needs of schools and their communities. Because our focus is on the more general issue of community relations, we have not provided a review of the extensive literature on public relations practices.

SUGGESTED ACTIVITIES

1. Collect a number of letters to the editor that deal with education. Classify them by issue and by attitude, approving or disapproving, toward the schools. Try to find out how an editor decides which letters to print. Find out if a school administrator takes any action in response to criticism or suggestions offered in this manner.

2. Make a scrapbook of all school news published during a year. Classify articles in whatever way seems appropriate (for example, sports, innovations, personalities, controversy, finance). Rank order the subjects according to number of articles in each.

3. Prepare a press release about a forthcoming educational event. Ask a PR professional or a reporter to criticize your press

release. Revise the release according to the suggestions offered, secure the necessary approval, and try to get your release published.

4. Attend an open house. Estimate the attendance of men, women, and children. Try to find out what aspect of the event has been most interesting to those present. If some children are involved in the program, find out how many visitors are related to the participating children. If no children are present, find out exactly how they were excluded. Note what the competition on television is for the time involved.

SUGGESTED READING

Fessler, Ralph. "Support and Opposition in School-Community Relations." *Planning and Changing* 4, no. 1 (Spring 1973): 29-34.

Maeroff, Gene I.; Bottomly, Forbes; and Woodring, Paul. "The Schools and the Press." Occasional paper no. 21. Washington, D.C.: Council for Basic Education, 1974.

Mullins, Carolyn. "How to Get Along With Your Local Newspaper." *American School Board Journal* 109 (October 1973): 31-34.

National Association of Elementary School Principals. *Elementary School PR Tool Kit.*
[This is a multimedia package of how-to-do-it resources "that can help principals, teachers, aides, and other school personnel become enthusiastic public relations agents." It was produced in 1974. Available from NAESP or NSPRA.]

National School Public Relations Association. *Ideas for Improving Public Confidence in Public Education.* Washington, D.C., 1972.

Stough, Charles. "When PTA Meetings Are Held in Clancy's Bar." *The North Central Association Quarterly* 48, no. 1 (Fall 1973): 255-261; and *The Education Digest* 39, no. 7 (March 1974): 36-37.

Toledo Public Schools. *The School Administrator and Public Relations.*
[This is a fifteen-page pamphlet dealing with important issues in public relations. To request a copy write: Kay Quealy, Director, Office of Information Services, Toledo Public Schools, Toledo, Ohio 43606.]

Unruh, Adolph, and Willier, Robert A. *Public Relations for Schools.* Belmont, Ca.: Fearon Publishers, 1974.

REFERENCES

ERS Circular 3 (1971). "The School Public Relations Administrator."

National School Public Relations Association. "Educational Public Relations Standards for Programs for Professionals." Brochure, n.d.

chapter ten

Decentralization & Community Control

> Centralized administration . . . may insure a victory in the hour of strife, but it gradually relaxes the sinews of strength.
>
> Alexis de Tocqueville

The several issues considered in the preceding chapters are of importance to educators regardless of the particular arrangements for governance and organization. In this chapter we consider the beginnings of alternatives to the traditional bureaucratic school system: decentralization and community control.

DECENTRALIZATION

The centralization of decision making accompanied the growth of large school districts. For years there has been a constant pressure to consolidate small districts in order to secure the blessings of centralization—increased special services, economies in purchase and use of materials and facilities, flexibility, a broad base of support. There is still evidence of this press toward centralization in plans to create metropolitan districts composed of central cities and the surrounding suburbs. Area service units and educational parks are based on combinations of increased numbers of districts for some purposes. Teacher Centers or Teaching Centers, when they come to fruition, seem to expect centralized resources. For these reasons, it is important that the increasing decentralization of some functions of education should not be interpreted as an all-encompassing trend. The confusing reality is that there are concurrent pressures to decentralize some aspects of education and to centralize others.

Pressure to decentralize decision making in education preceded the racial and ideological concerns of recent years. Our discussion of the typical bureaucratic school organization revealed that it failed to offer sufficient opportunities for citizens to participate. One observer described the problem more dramatically. "We've allowed our public schools to be effectively isolated from the people" (Askew 1973). Another observer of public participation reinforces this comment and discusses its consequences.

> The remote and dilute nature of electoral opportunities and the inauthentic nature of local opportunities have probably contributed to the drive in many places for community control, or at least for decentralization combined with more adequate vehicles for representation. That drive is often referred to as "community involvement" and the phrase has passed into the professional litany without much analysis. It is neither fashionable nor feasible to be against increasing community involvement. [Mann 1974, p. 279]

In response to the concerns of educators as well as the public that parents should participate in educational planning and that the centralized, bureaucratic model prevented this, boards of education and superintendents have considered appropriate remedies. The best known, first attempted response has been termed *decentralization*. The notion is that some elements of administrative authority are given to the local districts or schools. The decentralization may be to areas or districts or to individual schools. It is seldom released to the classroom level. If the necessary authority for decision making has been delegated down the organization, the flow of communication up and down can be significantly short circuited.

The failure of the simplistic response of decentralization is so well established in urban areas as to require no documentation. Often the decentralization was merely a semantic arrangement that sent another copy of each piece of correspondence to the newly designated site of authority. Even done in good faith, it was seldom accompanied by a freeing of resources and sufficient controls to the lower levels. Administrators were still tied to the same line allocations on budgets. The districtwide adoptions of textbooks were still observed. Personnel were assigned and reassigned by the central office. Conditions such as these made it impossible for lower level administrators really to accept and exercise the new autonomous leadership that was supposed to accompany decentralization.

The decentralization model just discussed really makes no provision for a change in the role of the citizen. He still participates in policy formation at the board level and still approaches the professional at the building level as a lay client of the professional educator. True, many decentralization plans provided for community advisory boards at district or even building level. But these boards were not to be involved in policy formation. They were to be antennae of the schools or sounding boards.

The presence of the schism between citizen and educator was shown in the constitution and functioning of many community boards. These were often chaired by the district superintendent or principal concerned. In one city district of Chicago, large numbers of these advisory boards had never been convened by their principal-chairmen, despite a directive from the board of education that established such boards as part of a citywide school-community study of education. This could be interpreted as arrogance. I see it rather as defensiveness based on fear.

After three years of experience with such community boards, the Chicago schools were forced to admit that they were failures (*Chicago Tribune* 3/27/69). The boards were then functioning in only six of the city's twenty-seven districts. One board member complained that "part of the failure may stem from the fact that some school officials lack respect for parents and others who are highly educated." Another board member deplored "the limited interpretation the administration seems to have put on the councils, leaving most of the power in the hands of the district superintendents." Other board members agreed that the plan had failed in its purpose of giving the board some way of hearing from the "grass roots."

The district superintendents predictably were concerned that councils wanted to "play an increasing policy making or executive function" and refused to follow the guidelines established by the board. The superintendents balked at forming councils because "the prospective members run the gamut of polarized opinion from extreme liberalism to extreme conservatism." The superintendents reasoned in advance that councils formed of persons holding such conflicting views about schools would be unproductive battlegrounds. At early stages in the effort to establish community councils, many of the potential members found that they were able to have more of a voice and gain their objectives more effectively through pressure groups that dealt directly with board members.

It seems that the remarks about the councils to accompany decentralization programs represent well the limitations of this attempt to modify the typical model. In retrospect, what happened might easily have been predicted. That is, schoolmen would resist even the limited influence intended to be allowed to the councils. Unless the board mandated in the most forceful terms that councils be formed, they were not formed. If forced to form councils, schoolmen would make them as "friendly" as possible. Citizens would accurately perceive the limitations of councils and would rapidly abandon them and redirect their efforts where there seemed at least a chance of influencing a decision maker rather than going through motions with a middle management administrator. That is what we could have predicted and that is, in essence, what happened with administrative decentralization accompanied by advisory councils.

The administrative decentralization discussed above is only one type of decentralization wherein decision making for some issues and a few resources were transferred from a central office to several regional offices. Of concern to most communities are matters of personnel, budget, and curriculum. If decision making in these areas is retained in the central office, the power of the decentralization plan is negligible.

Other types of decentralization are identified in an appendix to *Decentralization: Achieving Reform* by Fantini and Gittell (1973), the most prolific writers on this topic. They credit Edward N. Costikyan with developing a typology of decentralization which includes: administrative, coordinative, and functional decentralization, and participative-program implementation and creation (ibid., p. 129). The administrative decentralization we have noted is representative of the first category.

Coordinative decentralization would bring together the efforts of various municipal employees within an area to solve common problems. That is, clinics, schools, welfare agencies, and others might cooperate on a health problem. This type of decentralization is not responsive to pressure for more participation by citizens.

Functional decentralization would be represented by a system that transferred the control of services and the necessary funds to local areas but retained ultimate control. That is, goal setting would occur at the central level but implementation of functions would be decentralized.

Participative-program implementation involves the local councils in supervision of some services. One version of this would be represented by allowing local boards to appoint personnel but retaining over-all budget control at the central level.

In the participative-program creation type of decentralization, the community would be involved in policy formation for some programs.

These types of decentralization were designed for municipal services in general. In applications to education, the first type is the simplistic shifting of bureaucratic procedures from one location to several. The other stages represent more complete decentralization on a continuum that would end in a version of the participative-program implementation. This would most closely approximate the "community control" arrangement in education.

A more familiar way of conceptualizing gradations of citizen participation is shown in figure 10-1, which represents types of citizen participation along a continuum ranging from very little (a central board dominated by the superintendent) to almost autonomous local arrangements. The Costikyan typology found in Fantini and Gittell could be superimposed on the left side of figure 10-1.

Obviously figure 10-1 shows only a few of the several possible arrangements that might be made in school districts as we know them. I am not certain that the different arrangements are properly situated. It is simply a rough way of representing variations in school governance. It may be interpreted as an increase in centralization, bureaucratic control, and lack of citizen participation as we move to the right of the center and the opposite to the left. I originally placed *responsiveness* to the left, but reluctantly took it off the diagram, because it is quite possible for a highly centralized bureaucratic system to be very responsive to community needs if those at the top of the hierarchy are so inclined. The terms *open* and *closed* refer to the ease of citizen participation. As we move to the left, the organizational arrangements shown become progressively more open to participation than those to the right.

There is no compelling evidence to demonstrate the superiority of either centralized or decentralized school systems when the criterion

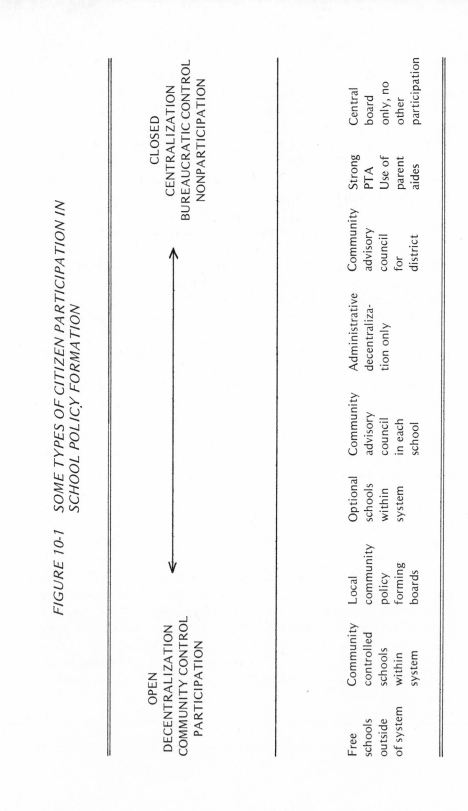

FIGURE 10-1 SOME TYPES OF CITIZEN PARTICIPATION IN SCHOOL POLICY FORMATION

OPEN DECENTRALIZATION COMMUNITY CONTROL PARTICIPATION	←					→		CLOSED CENTRALIZATION BUREAUCRATIC CONTROL NONPARTICIPATION
Free schools outside of system	Community controlled schools within system	Local community policy forming boards	Optional schools within system	Community advisory council in each school	Administrative decentralization only	Community advisory council for district	Strong PTA Use of parent aides	Central board only, no other participation

is student achievement (Greer 1970, ch. 2). Nevertheless, the demand for decentralization persists. It is motivated chiefly by political objectives, by the concerns of ethnic and racial populations that see themselves without power to influence education.

The same forces that we identified as opposing increased citizen participation also serve as obstacles to decentralization. The school bureaucracy is reluctant to release its monopoly on decision making. The teachers organization (whether union or NEA) is obligated to give rhetorical support to decentralization, but the vested interests of members require them to oppose vigorously anything that permits more citizen participation. Another potent obstacle "to the development of an effective program of decentralization [in New York City] is the use of decentralization for political ends" (Brown 1973). This had led to controversy and conflict without improving schools.

Although these obstacles seem formidable indeed, the trend toward decentralization prevails. Advocates stress responsiveness, simplification of the process of changing schools, increased flexibility, and *accountability*. These benefits may or may not accompany decentralization. We lack sufficient data to determine the effects of decentralization. The important concern for educators is that, in many instances, the school communities will perceive some form of decentralization as essential to improved schools. Given this condition, decentralization becomes necessary (although far from sufficient) before improvement can be obtained and perceived. In many cities, educators cannot wait for data to support or refute the arguments about decentralization before initiating plans and at least pilot studies. When data become available it is not likely that decisions can be supported solely by student achievement gains or losses. There is really no guarantee that the actual processes of teaching and learning will change in response to a major reorganization of a school district.

Although data on all aspects of decentralization are essential, they will not be easily interpreted. Ornstein advocated caution because "decentralization, community control, even community participation—are mainly slogans rather than closely worked out concepts with consequences understood and accounted for" (1973, p. 613). Bernard Watson quickly took issue with Ornstein's position, noting that

> the very real and important question from which Ornstein attempts to distract us is whose value system will prevail in educational decision making,

> and not whether we can substitute "objectivity" for ideology. Power may be a nasty word as Mary Parker Follett once remarked, but it is the name of the game, in education as in most other human endeavors. [1973, p. 199]

Ornstein's reply to Watson's rejoinder contained this paragraph:

> Watson rejects professional insight on the ground of "massive school failure." Interestingly, he does not mention student input, although the research repeatedly informs us that this is the most important variable associated with school learning. He does exactly what many community control advocates do: He rejects the research when it suits his purpose, then attacks school people and urges conflict tactics. [1973, p. 200]

The exchange between Ornstein and Watson should signal to educators that decentralization can engender vigorous contention. This is to be expected when the issue is value-laden and not readily available for objective, factual analysis.

Even the same program of decentralization can be perceived completely differently by observers from different philosophical or political positions. Consider this excerpt from an article by an associate superintendent of the Los Angeles Unified School District.

> In only three years, the second largest school system in the nation has been reorganized, has significantly shifted its principal responsibilities to a local level and has opened its structure to greater participation by the public. Change has occurred with serious and often heated debate, but without a harmful division of the community or political structure and without negative effect on the school population. [Halverson 1973, p. 42]

Now, consider this conclusion by two participants in the same decentralization project, one of whom was Commissioner on the Mexican-American Education Commission and the other an attorney for Los Angeles Neighborhood Legal Services.

> The major criticism (and the ironic flaw) of the plan is that, in effect, it adds an additional layer to the bureaucracy through which citizens must wade to get to the Board of Education. Decentralization as it functions in Los Angeles is a creation of the Board of Education and the Board claims that it cannot legally delegate its authority to others. Consequently all important decisions still have to be made "downtown." [Gurule and Ortega 1973, p. 43]

It is difficult to understand how the two opinions can be drawn from the same reality. Obviously, then, reasonable men may differ on the success of decentralization. This juxtaposition of two contrasting conclusions reinforces our concern about the need to secure objective data.

One final example of the ambiguity about decentralization reveals another concern. Today's proponents can become tomorrow's opponents. The pre-eminent example of this disaffection is Dr. Kenneth B. Clark, an early, influential, much quoted advocate of decentralization. Clark has now reported that school decentralization has been a disastrous experience. His concern was that "selfish forces," including the "racial politics" of local groups, and a United Federation of Teachers that protects teachers regardless of quality, had submerged the basic issue of teaching children (Buder 1972).

Clark's point about the diversion of the goal of decentralization is well taken. Not all advocates pursue decentralization for educational purposes. Some purposes are compatible; some are mutually exclusive. The removal of many incompetent administrators has no doubt been overdue. Others, however, have been summarily pushed out to make room for leadership of the dominant ethnic group in the community.

Both cross purposes noted—visible ethnic leadership and the protection of competent professionals—are defensible. But at any given time the advocates of one purpose could find themselves in direct confrontation with advocates of the other. The dilemma is further complicated by the occasional presence of an administrator who really is incompetent as the object of the dispute.

This problem and others that accompany decentralization can possibly be avoided by advance planning. Too often decentralization happens almost overnight.

COMMUNITY CONTROL

In our discussion of decentralization, we have often dealt with issues involving community control. This confusion is found throughout the literature. The two phenomena are responses to the same stimuli. They differ in their specifics, in particular with regard to the role of citizens. We now focus on community control.

As district and local advisory boards refused to function as so-called rubber stamps or impotent advisors to an absentee landlord central board and its resident administrator, decentralization moved into the community control phase. Initially the semantic preference was for community *involvement* but the issue was quickly identified as community *control.*

In viewing administrative decentralization, we discussed the functions that were released from the central office level to other levels and to what extent they were released. In decentralization, the role of the citizen need not have been altered by one iota even though his local school could have become somewhat more responsive to his needs.

In discussing community control, we confront the much more threatening (to the professional educator) question of how much decision-making power has been awarded to what segments of the community. Just how sharply this controversy could be drawn was quickly demonstrated by the most notorious conflict in community involvement to this date: Ocean Hill-Brownsville.

Controversy

Fred Hechinger of the *New York Times* devoted many articles to Ocean Hill-Brownsville. In one of these (9/22/68) he set the general theme: "Demands by masses of people to run institutions that hitherto have been run for them by a central establishment are rising everywhere." Another item in the same issue introduced a frightening variation on the general theme: "Race: The Third Party in the School Crisis" (Roberts 1968). The teachers' strike and the community's efforts to keep schools open had pitted members of the white teacher's union against black parents. Teachers quite obviously feared that a black community board would deal unfairly with white personnel. The black community, as analyzed by Roberts in the *Times,* did not trust whites and felt that "white people really don't care about us."

Albert Shanker, president of the United Federation of Teachers in New York City, also wrote many columns about the decentralization experiments. Mr. Shanker and occasional guest columnists presented a weekly column in advertising space in the *Times* immediately adjacent to the space usually filled by Mr. Hechinger's column. Shanker was doing on a larger scale what many creative school superintendents have been doing as public relations for years. The difference is that space was usually provided for the superintendent's weekly column whereas the Union purchased its space. The Union's columns presented cogent explications of the inconsistencies and flaws in decentralization plans. The headings of some of Shanker's columns suggest the Union's orientation: "Decentralization: Closer Look at a Sacred Cow," "School Decentralization: Have its Claims Proved Valid?" "Ocean Hill-Brownsville: Why the Experiment Failed," "Decentralization II: The New York Experience," and (by Bayard Rustin) "Community Control: Separatism Repackaged."

Ocean Hill-Brownsville survived somehow and is almost certainly the most thoroughly documented case study of the problems of moving toward community control. (See, for example, Carter 1971, especially "Chronology"; Wasserman 1970; and Levin 1970.) Others learned from the trials of New York and avoided some of the conflict. Meanwhile, the pressure for community control seemed to grow ever stronger as a result of far reaching social forces augmented by well placed foundation funds (Ford Foundation grants assisted early efforts at community control in Ocean Hill-Brownsville) and mandated by the now ubiquitous federal guidelines.

In a debate on what was initially intended to be *decentralization* but became *community control,* Walter Degnan, President of the Council of Supervisors Association of New York City Schools, opposed Mario Fantini, then Program Officer with the Ford Foundation. Mr. Degnan maintained that community control is a false premise because city people do not know one another, there is too much mobility of population, and there is a lack of fiscal control. He went on to cite ten specific weaknesses of community control:

1. Education gets poorer in poor districts because teachers and principals have no control.
2. It is more expensive.
3. Militant activists take over—not parents.
4. Chaos develops from confrontation of local and central school board.
5. An exodus from the city of middle-class families results.
6. Principals are unable to exercise educational leadership and lose the professional attitude toward their jobs.
7. It destroys democratic foundations to suit purely local desires.
8. It sacrifices the education of children to social theories.
9. It ignores due process of law.
10. It does not strengthen the educational process. [1969]

Nevertheless, Mr. Degnan made it clear that he favored community involvement and participation. He emphasized efforts to find the best education for poor children and the need of finding superior teachers.

His opponent, Dr. Mario Fantini of the Ford Foundation, believed that the educational system needs reform at the expense of upheaval if need be. He stressed that:

1. The educational institution is obsolete and needs reform rather than improvement.
2. The present relationships between the school, pupil, and parent are dysfunctional and we are now experiencing a period of realignment.
3. The public must decide what kind of school it wants.
4. Educators become too defensive when challenged.
5. The new option to try to improve education by participation should not be denied.
6. New plans cannot be superimposed on the existing system.

There are many nuances in this controversy about community control. It *is* a vital issue but as it usually develops has not made all that much impact on the learning of school children. Sometimes that—the learning—almost seems to be irrelevant to the arguments put forth by all parties in the debate. And, of course, aspects of this issue are symptomatic of a political and ideological battle that is no less real for being unknown to the majority of participants in the school controversy. This would-be social revolution is a most difficult element. It adds geometrically to the problems of school reform. Thanks to the visibility of Ivan Illich and others, it is now quite clear that there actually are those—invariably among the proponents of community control—who unashamedly seek to destroy the public schools. Hence, a schoolman who suspects a conspiracy need not be paranoid, although it is rarely an element in the usual pressures for more citizen involvement and control.

The undeniable fact that the educational institution is sometimes in some places under attack makes it difficult for school administrators to avoid showing the defensiveness deplored by those who have followed the process of decentralization and community control. It also makes it awkward for reformers who see themselves as friends of the schools.*

---

* One of the more legible journals featuring articles of the type that assumes that schools must go is *This Magazine is About Schools.* Many articles appear in the underground press in publications that are easily accessible but not readable. For a good list of twenty of these counterculture sources, see "Underground Periodicals for Educators," *Newsletter American Educational Studies Association* 3 (April 1972). For a more comprehensive listing, see *Alternative Press Index* (Radical Research Center, Carleton College, Northfield, Minnesota 55057).

Administrators as Targets

If the events reported in the press of any large city are in any way representative of the problems associated with community control, administrators have good reason to fear it. The vulnerability of administrators was noted above under decentralization. It seems that, when even the implementation of full or partial community control fails to remedy the educational problems of a community, the frustration is vented on the school administrator. That community control by itself is not going to make everything right seems patently obvious. Nevertheless, many persons pursue it as if it were an end in itself rather than merely a kind of reorganization as a means toward other actions that can in time improve education.

When improvement is too slow in coming, it seems as though someone must be at fault. In many cases that someone is perceived to be the administrator. That is why decentralization in New York City was accompanied by unprecedented early retirements of administrators and even resignations. (For example, it was reported in the *New York Times* on 6 February 1972 that a district superintendent resigned on the day of a "brawl between Puerto Ricans and members of the Jewish Defense League at a district board session. . . .") It is certain that some of these departing administrators deserved their hard lots. It is equally certain that others were sincere, hard-working persons who were sacrified because they were symbols of authority or, as mentioned before, they were not members of the dominant ethnic or racial group.

A brief review of a few of the cases of attacks on school administrators in Chicago will establish the pattern. In February 1971, all but 265 of 1,529 pupils at Horace Mann School participated in a boycott arranged by parents seeking a new principal (*Chicago Tribune* 2/9/71). On March 18 parents and some teachers argued for the removal of the principal (ibid.). On 8 February 1972, a boycott sponsored by parents was part of a movement to oust the principal of the Whistler School who, they charged, was "an incompetent administrator who refuses to take advantage of federally funded programs to improve [the] school" (ibid.). One interesting situation involved the tripartite (community, school, university) Woodlawn Experimental Schools Project. Across something like a generation gap the students and some younger teachers were aligned with the project director in opposition to a school principal and some parents (*Chicago Tribune* 4/19/71). (Of course, this situation is more involved than my simplistic generalization. The role of a faculty senate and the relationship between the teachers and the principal were important factors.) The director is now superintendent of schools in Washington, D.C., where her aim is to "raise the community's level of anxiety" in order to rid it of apathy (see "The Boat Rocker," *Time* 3/9/73, p. 70).

Later a Mexican-American community secured the removal of a principal at the Jirka School because, they charged, "she is prejudiced against the Mexican-American students . . . and is not responsive to the needs of Latin children" (*Chicago Tribune* 7/22/72; see also 7/21, 7/26, 7/28, and 8/13/73). In this case some believed "that a Jesuit priest and three young seminarians had been instrumental in actions against the principal (ibid. 8/6/72). The priest was trained in Saul Alinsky's methods of organizing communities. (For a discussion of Mr. Alinsky's tactics, see Alinsky 1969, pp. 27-49.)

The Chicago Principals Association reacted vigorously to the ouster of principals. They held a special meeting of the Board of Directors of the Principals Association to express "a vote of 'no confidence' in the Chicago Board of Education for its irresponsibility in capitulating to mob action in the Jirka School situation" (*Chicago Principals Association News Bulletin* 1/8/72). This was accompanied by telegrams and press releases (*Chicago Tribune* 8/3/72). An interesting complication of this controversy is the demand for a new, Mexican-American principal. In retrospect, one could wish that boards would make ethnic matches of administrators and communities during this period of special awareness of ethnic ties. But the use of this concept as a defensible official policy guide to placement quickly breaks down. Clearly, if the Jirka community board were selecting a principal today that would seem to be a starting point.

The several principals under attack in Chicago represent just one of the many possible types of conflict (and, of course, of cooperation) that can occur in the community control or decentralization models. At one time so many principals were ousted by their communities that their presence on one or another special assignment in the central or district offices became an embarrassment to the central board and administration.

An entirely different type of conflict concerned a community that rose to the support of a principal disciplined for ignoring a federal program requirement. In one way this is the reverse of the situation mentioned at the Whistler School where a principal was rebuked for not pursuing federal grants with sufficient vigor. However it does seem as though in this instance the community would have received no direct benefit from the federal monies that occasioned the controversy.

In this case, mentioned briefly in another context as an example of the principal as the man in the middle, the principal of the Murphy School in Chicago was suspended by the board because of insubordination (*Chicago Tribune* 12/3/71). The principal had refused to turn over to the central office a Department of Health, Education, and Welfare survey to determine the amount of federal aid the Chicago schools were eligible to receive. The principal reasoned that since his community did not qualify for aid, supplying the information was a needless invasion of privacy.

The fact that the community in this case supported a local administrator against his central board suggests a new dimension of the administrator's role that may accompany community control. That is, should the principal become an advocate, a participant, a gadfly on behalf of his constituency? This interpretation of his role is almost diametrically opposite that of the typical model in which local administrators were expected not to permit the top of the organization to be disturbed and certainly not to seek to disturb the top by their own actions. This new possibility inherent in decentralization and community control plans merits careful study.

The concept of community control introduces a whole range of new possibilities for cooperation and, of course, for conflict. I have just noted, in the Murphy School case, a conflict of community and central office. More frequently one would find a dispute between a community board, *as a board,* and the central board (see, for example, *New York Times* 3/7/71 "Defiance Vowed by Local Boards"). An incumbent community board opposing a rival, defunct, or disenfranchised board has also been observed (see Buder 1970). And, of course, conflict between community board member and community board member is quite likely to occur (Farber 1971). It would be an interesting exercise to list all the possible pairings or consortia of arrangements for controversy in the new relationships. Quite likely there would be instances of controversy involving each possible arrangement.

Endorsements of Community Control

The controversial aspects of community control are well known. The many successes are not as well known. Since quiet, gradual progress will never become good material for newspapers or television, it is not reasonable to expect the same type of coverage for quiet discussions as we can secure for violent confrontations. Despite this fact of journalistic life, we do have accounts of some positive responses to community control.

It is not surprising that controversy has been associated with a shift in the location of some decision making. The controversy was there. Some of the same forces causing the controversy may also have helped bring about decentralization. Shifting the point of application of pressure is in no way a sufficient solution to educational problems, although it may seem to bring a temporary respite to the hard pressed central administration and board. The pressures are still there and, if those responsible are not willing and able to deal with them appropriately, they will grow stronger and seek other points of entry.

A reorganization of any kind is just that—a reorganization. Things have been shifted around but nothing needs to be any different. Unless some things are done differently, the reorganization will have been futile. And that—what to do now that we are reorganized—is the point at which most plans stop.

Some administrators seem to have possessed or found the skills needed to implement decentralization effectively. One who met early success as a principal and later on as a superintendent commented that

> the new local councils can be an enormous gain for the schools. They will be a test of the principal's ability to live with lay participation, and each council itself will undergo the test of whether it is able to survive. If it only talks, if no beneficial change takes place, it will disappear. If there is apathy in the community about what happens in school, that apathy spreads to the kid. It's critical that neighborhood people be in the inner-city school, showing concern the way middle-class parents do. Seeing parents in the building tells kids a lot. [Joseph Rosen, quoted in the *Chicago Tribune* 4/18/71]

A draft of a proposed "Illinois Program for Evaluation, Supervision, and Recognition of Schools" mandates widespread community involvement and participation. Local goals would have to be consistent with state goals. The state goals "encompass involving the local community in all phases of a school's operations, including but not limited to policy decisions, administration and discipline, curriculum and extracurricular activities" (Justus 1972). We have previously noted the federal insistence on community involvement. The sad fact that we do not have a working model for this involvement means that the mandated involvement can run the gamut from tokenism to destructive power plays. School administrators must quickly accept their new roles as actors in community relations or become targets for others who will act.

Signs of Institutionalization of New Community Roles

There is little doubt that the role of citizens in decision making for schools is in a state of change. It is fair to describe the change as a trend away from political representation on a citywide board toward some more direct involvement at local levels. The new role has not yet achieved either sufficient clarity or stability to be defined.

Evidence of the trend is found in newly created positions designed to expedite community involvement. At one time it was an innovation to add to the central staff someone termed a "Director of School-Community Relations" or something similar. Usually this person prepared press releases and planned special events. With increasing integration, another position was created, usually called a "Director of Human Relations." It is a certain sign that the new role of the community has been recognized by the creation of positions indicating that someone is now being charged with a specific responsibility for leadership in that area.

A representative of the new positions at the central office level is found in an advertisement of the City School District of New York for an "Executive Director for Community School District Relations" at a minimum salary of $35,000 per year. The position is in the cabinet of the Chancellor of the City School District (*New York Times* 8/6/72).

At the district level there is also a need for a person to serve in the new role of relating schools and community. This is evidenced by an advertisement placed by Community School Board School District Number 5 of New York City. The board is seeking to employ an Executive Assistant who has a research background knowledge of the New York City Board of Education school system and diversified experience with community problems and their resolution; hours flexible, including evening work; salary: $15,000 (*New York Times* 7/23/72).

At the local school level, the professionals have attempted to relate to the community in different ways. Sometimes a specialist in community relations is added to the building faculty. Often teachers or team leaders are given special training to improve relations with the community (see, for example, Doll 1971 or Saxe 1971). Always the task was and is difficult. The roles are still far from defined.

NO PROTOTYPE MODEL FOR CITIZEN PARTICIPATION

In his review of various plans to involve citizens with their schools in better ways, Luvern Cunningham points out that there are several promising new mechanisms for improving citizen participation in school affairs. He recommends that:

> New forms of citizen participation should be encouraged to promote educational accountability to the public.
>
> Communities find new approaches to leadership development, especially for education.
>
> School systems establish and refine new links to other sources of strength within their communities.
>
> Existing structures for citizen participation be strengthened.
>
> Leadership and sanctioning agencies should encourage citizen participation in school affairs. [1971, pp. 168-175]

In discussing the first of his five recommendations listed above, Cunningham states succinctly the import of this discussion:

> There must be recognition on the part of school people that schools are not their private preserves or sacred trusts. Citizens on the other hand should acknowledge that schools are staffed by dedicated persons, each trying to do his job well. [Ibid., p. 170]

Essential Elements of Community Participation Plans

In describing the imperatives that must be part of a "viable decentralization and/or community control format," Cunningham considers that the format must:

Be responsive to the participation impulse.
Lead to improved education.
Meet the equality of opportunity mandate.
Accommodate lay professional antagonisms.
Be feasible financially.
Be achievable politically. [Ibid., pp. 191-198]

Regardless of how these imperatives are represented in a model for community participation, there will be no one ideal form. Like Cunningham we must "recognize and acknowledge the variation that exists in our country and avoid the belief that one pattern of decentralization or educational government is best" (ibid., p. 199).

That we have no ideal pattern to offer should not be surprising. Much of our concern today is about how to reform an ideal model that no longer fits the circumstances but is so well institutionalized that it is highly resistant to our best efforts to improve it.

After viewing the "alarming signs . . . that public school systems [especially in large cities] face serious challenges to their continued existence," the Council of Big City Boards of Education (1969) issued eleven specific guidelines for its member boards.

1. The board of education must assume leadership in any plan to involve citizens at the local level in educational planning.
2. The board must be constantly in contact with the community and transmit the concerns of the community to the professional staff of the schools.
3. The board must hold administrators and teachers accountable for the relevancy and effectiveness of the school program.
4. Community involvement must begin at the neighborhood level with the principal a key figure in the process.
5. In planning for community involvement, community organizations, teachers, city government representatives, students, parents, and any other concerned group, must be brought into the discussion and decision making.
6. Community involvement does not necessarily mean breaking up the school district into separate entities.
7. Community involvement should be regarded as a process rather than merely a matter of arrangements. Adequate safeguards must be included, however, to assure a means by which concerns may be expressed by citizens at a level lower than the central board.
8. School boards must spell out with certainty what they mean by community involvement—with clearly defined goals—and carefully delineated powers for local groups.
9. Local involvement must assure that due process will be observed in making changes, and capricious and arbitrary actions avoided.

10. Experimental projects must be clearly defined as such and all concerned parties must agree to a "hands off" attitude for the duration of the experiment.
11. Provision must be made for periodic review of arrangements involving local people so that the process may remain dynamic and self-renewing. [P. 4]

SUMMARY

This chapter has described the development of alternative arrangements to the typical, centralized model for relating schools to their communities. The arrangements of decentralization and community control were examined in detail. Although no ideal solution was presented, the nature of the trend toward more involved citizen participation was documented. Problems attending the transition in form from centralization to something else were noted. Despite the many problems, we conclude that the need to provide for citizen involvement demands serious and prompt attention. Some principles and guidelines are offered as being helpful regardless of the specific situation involved. We examine other strategies of citizen participation in the next chapter.

SUGGESTED ACTIVITIES

1. Ask several different people to give you their conception of the proper role of the citizen in relation to his local public school. Be sure that you include a parent and a teacher in your sample. It should be interesting to compare also the answers of a professor of "hard" science (chemistry, physics, astronomy) with those of a professor of "soft" science (history, political science, psychology). Predict in advance what each respondent will say. What assumptions make it possible for you to make these predictions?

2. Try to find out what the official policy of your school district is concerning the role of a citizen of a community in regard to his neighborhood school. So that you may avoid confusing your informants, make your query quite specific. For example, find out about the school's probable response to a concerned citizen (not a school parent) who wishes to attempt to persuade someone in charge to adopt an all-year school plan; a working mother who seeks to have the school accept responsibility for her first-grade

child thirty minutes before the prescribed opening time; a Viet Nam veteran who wishes to work with educators to plan a social studies treatment that does not glorify war and violence.

Analyze the reasons for the difficulty you will probably have in finding the answer to your question.

Compare the answers you received from persons in different roles or in the same role in the educational system. What difference does it make if they agree or disagree?

How does the policy that you discover work in action? Has there been a recent case in point? How was it handled? Does it verify the policy verbalized by those whom you queried?

3. Prepare a plan to create a community council for your school. On what basis will representatives be sought? How will they be chosen? What authority will the council have? When will they meet? Will they be paid expenses, honoraria?

4. Prepare a job description for a community coordinator and list the qualifications and duties.

5. Make an argument to replace an Anglo principal with a Chicano principal for a school in a predominantly Chicano neighborhood. Competence and commitment are not in question.

   Now make a similar argument to replace a Chicano in a predominantly Anglo neighborhood with an Anglo principal.

   In which case was your argument more persuasive? Why was there a difference? Is one case an instance of prejudice because of the implied disadvantaged status of a minority? Are there any differences in principle? Ideally should the ethnic status of an administrator be a factor in making assignments? Politically should it be a factor?

   If you were the decision maker, how would you resolve the cases?

SUGGESTED READINGS

Carter, Barbara. *Pickets, Parents, and Power.* New York: Citation Press, 1971.

Fantini, Mario, and Gittell, Marilyn. *Decentralization: Achieving Reform.* New York: Praeger, 1973.

Gittell, Marilyn, and Hollander, Edward T. *Six Urban School Districts.* New York: Frederick A. Praeger, 1968.

Janowitz, Morris. *Institution Building in Urban Education.* Chicago: University of Chicago Press, 1971.

Katz, Michael B. (ed.) *School Reform: Past and Present.* Boston: Little Brown, 1971.

Levin, Henry M. (ed.) *Community Control of Schools.* Washington, D.C.: The Brookings Institution, 1970.

Lutz, Frank W. (ed.) *Toward Improved Urban Education.* Worthington, Ohio: Charles A. Jones, 1970.

Ornstein, Allan C. *Metropolitan Schools: Administrative Decentralization vs. Community Control.* Metuchen, N.J.: Scarecrow Press, 1974.

Pharis, William; Robison, Lloyd E.; and Walden, John C. *Decision Making and Schools for the 70's.* Washington, D.C.: National Education Association, 1970.

Resnik, Henry S. *Turning on the System.* New York: Pantheon Books, 1970.

Wasserman, Miriam. *The School Fix.* New York: Outerbridge and Dienstfrey, 1970.

REFERENCES

Alinsky, Saul. "Organizing Low-Income Neighborhoods for Political Action." In *Urban School Administration,* edited by Troy McKelvey and Austin Swanson, pp. 37-49. Beverly Hills, Ca.: Sage, 1969.

Askew, Reubin O'D. "Can the States Recapture the Initiative?" *Compact* 7, no. 4 (September/October 1973): 22.

Brown, Roscoe C., Jr. "Decentralization of New York City Schools." Paper read to the American Educational Research Association, New Orleans, 27 February 1973.

Buder, Leonard. "Aftermath of a Bold Experiment." *New York Times,* 2 August 1970.

———. "Community Boards: Turmoil Over Local Control." *New York Times,* 3 December 1972.

Carter, Barbara. *Pickets, Parents and Power: The Story Behind the New York Teachers Strike.* New York: Citation Press, 1971.

Council of Big City Boards of Education. *The Movement Toward Greater Community Involvement in Educational Decision-Making.* Washington, D.C.: National School Boards Association, 1969.

Cunningham, Luvern F. *Governing Schools: New Approaches to Old Issues.* Columbus, Ohio: Charles E. Merrill, 1971.

Degnan, Walter. "Remarks on Decentralization." Speech for pre-convention meeting of DESP Large City Principals Associations, Las Vegas, Nevada, 14 April 1969.

Doll, Russell. "The Sociological Monkey on the Team Leader's Back." In *Perspectives on the Role of the Teacher Corps Team Leader*, edited by Richard W. Saxe, pp. 18-34. Project 452 272, B.E.P.D., 1971.

Fantini, Mario, and Gittell, Marilyn. *Decentralization: Achieving Reform.* New York: Praeger, 1973.

Farber, M. A. "Four Plan to Quit District 3 Board." *New York Times*, 9 May 1971.

Greer, Colin. *Cobweb Attitudes.* New York: Teachers College Press, 1970.

Gurule, Kay, and Ortega, Joe. "L.A. Decentralization with Problems." *Inequality in Education* 15 (November 1973): 43-44.

Halverson, Jerry F. "L.A. Decentralization with Promise." *Inequality in Education* 15 (November 1973): 39-43.

Justus, Hope. "Bakalis Drafts a Bombshell." *Chicago Tribune*, 21 July 1972.

Levin, Henry M., ed. *Community Control of Schools.* Washington, D.C.: Brookings Institution, 1970.

Newsletter American Educational Studies Association 3 (April 1972). "Underground Periodicals for Educators."

Ornstein, Allan. "Research on Decentralization." *Phi Delta Kappan* 54, no. 9 (May 1973): 610-614.

———. "Mr. Watson Distorts and Misinterprets." *Phi Delta Kappan* 55, no. 3 (November 1973): 200.

Roberts, Steven V. "Race: The Third Party in the School Crisis." *New York Times*, 22 September 1968.

Saxe, Richard W., ed. *Perspectives on the Role of the Teacher Corps Team Leader.* Project 452 272, B.E.P.D., 1971.

Time, 3 September 1973, p. 70. "The Boat Rocker."

Wasserman, Miriam. *The School Fix NYC USA.* New York: Outerbridge and Dienstfrey, 1970.

Watson, Bernard C. "Decentralization, Metropolitanism, and Deplorization: A Response to Allan Ornstein." *Phi Delta Kappan* 55, no. 3 (November 1973): 198-200.

chapter eleven

On Citizen Participation

> One who thinks about the relation of the school to the community which supports it will soon come upon questions of public policy which it would take an Einsteinian grasp of the calculus of felicity to answer.
>
> Willard Waller
> *The Sociology of Teaching*

In this final chapter we continue the examination of citizen participation introduced by the discussion of decentralization and community control. We begin with a consideration of additional ways of increasing citizen participation. This is followed by a return to the dilemma introduced in the beginning chapters—a need to find some balance between the organizational and professional aspects of education and the political and individual requirements for participation.

INCREASING CITIZEN PARTICIPATION

The reader will have long since identified an assumption implied in all preceding chapters: that increased citizen participation in education is desirable. Practices that put people and communities at a distance or in the position of adversaries have been disparaged. Practices that open the schools, lessen the distance between educators and communities, and support cooperative relationships have been approved.

The ideological and political basis for this assumption is well known. From this perspective, we can support increased citizen participation in education whether or not it can be established that the increase in citizen participation is accompanied by an increase in student achievement. Although we hold this position, we recognize that it is not persuasive to educators in general nor to the organizations that represent groups of teachers, administrators, and even boards of education.

What is lacking to secure the support of the professionals is empirical evidence, reliable data, to support the argument that citizen participation results in educational as well as political gains (see Ornstein 1973). These data are not at hand and, moreover, it will probably not be possible to collect and analyze them by present research methods and technology. There are suggestions that bringing the school and community closer together will permit educational improvements, but they are merely suggestions (see, for example, Scribner and O'Shea 1974). The correspondence between participation and improved student achievement is far from clear. It would be unpolitic as well as untrue for anyone to promise educational gains as a result of decentralization, community control, or increased citizen participation of any kind.

From the perspective of gains in student achievement, citizen participation is certainly not a panacea. It may even be irrelevant. Despite this admission, we shall next consider additional means of encouraging citizen participation. Our rationale has been stated before. Participation is part of the democratic ideology. It is needed to legitimate the schools. It makes new resources available to the schools. These considerations permit us to view participation as an end in itself while we await data to determine if it can be proven to be a means to facilitate student achievement.

LEVELS OF PARTICIPATION

A good way to begin a consideration of citizen participation is with Arnstein's "Ladder of Citizen Participation." (This source can be found in several places: Arnstein 1971; Arnstein 1966.) Arnstein describes eight levels of participation ranging from no participation to complete citizen control. In table 11-1 we attempt to apply Arnstein's classifications to some types of citizen participation in education.

TABLE 11-1 ARNSTEIN'S LADDER OF CITIZEN PARTICIPATION AND SCHOOL POLICY FORMATION

Participation Level	Educational Equivalent
Citizen Control	Free schools, complete community control
Delegated Power	Community control of specific areas (e.g., personnel)
Partnership	Joint Policy Boards (The Woodlawn Experimental Project)
Placation	Citizens on board of control (places usually allocated to representatives of groups on either community or central board of education)
Consultation	Local community hearings, surveys, needs assessment
Informing	Public relations practices, media, bulletins, letters
Therapy	Parent educational programs. Recruitment of local leaders by paraprofessional salaries and socialization to educator norms.
Manipulation	Token advisory committees dominated by professionals or friends

Terms at the top of the table describe degrees of citizen power—citizen control, delegated power, and partnership. The central three levels describe degrees of token representation—placation, consultation, and informing. The lowest terms describe arrangements that permit no participation at all for citizens.

The educational equivalents that we provide as illustrations of Arnstein's levels need not always be limited to the level at which they appear in table 11-1. The Woodlawn Experimental Project was identified as a "partnership" because community representatives shared power on a board with representatives of the schools. (Originally there were three partners: schools, community, and the University of Chicago. The University later released its places on the board to the community.) The recruitment of influential members of the community by giving them paraprofessional status was included as an example of therapy because that is one possible tactic open to educators. We do not imply that all paraprofessionals have been so recruited or even that the schools are seeking to do so. The example is the best we could conceive to show the meaning of *therapy* as a treatment of the citizen so as to cure him of wrong-headedness, that is, opposition to the policies of the educators. It also needs to be emphasized that the placement of a practice at a lower level is not an assessment of the usefulness of that practice. For example, needs assessment can be an example of token participation if that is the extent of citizen participation. When used in conjunction with other levels of citizen participation, needs assessment becomes a valuable, necessary practice in school-community relations. Table 11-1 refers only to the formal arrangements for participation.

Arnstein's typology was adapted by Cibulka and used in a study (1974) of district and school citizen advisory committees in Chicago between 1965 and 1970. Cibulka found the councils changing from consultation to informing to placation. When the pressure by the boards and the communities shifted to include their specifying how policy should be developed, the formal participation of citizens increased. Cibulka reasoned that this shift gave the boards more information enabling them to hold administrators accountable for more formal participation. More importantly for our understanding of the phenomena of participation, Cibulka's study demonstrated that at no point was a high level of formal participation accomplished.

FORMS OF PARTICIPATION

Another excellent review of the characteristics of the usual types of citizen participation is *Citizen Organizations* by Yin et al. (1973). This is the report of a RAND Corporation study that "examines the possibilities for developing a viable and permanent institutional structure for citizen participation in government decision making, in the context of the programs of the Department of Health, Education, and Welfare" (p. v). The study was not aimed at *social* reform but at *administrative* reform to link citizen participation with the securing of specific services.

Participation Without Power

First the RAND study considered five forms of citizen participation that did not fulfill the study's criterion of giving power to citizens: volunteering, employment of paraprofessionals, grievance procedures, citizen surveys, and citizen evaluations. These forms should not be dropped from consideration because they can be used in conjunction with other modes of citizen participation.

As we mentioned in chapter 7, it is common to use volunteers in schools. However, the report notes that "volunteers are usually not asked for and do not offer opinions about how programs should be organized, and they have at most little authority in the administration of routine activities" (ibid., p. 15). There are benefits for schools and for the volunteers in programs using volunteers but, used *alone,* volunteers do not bring power to citizens.

Paraprofessionals, especially in large numbers, may generate some small influence for citizens. Like volunteers, paraprofessionals may be effective in strengthening another form of participation that is capable of giving power to citizens.

Grievance procedures have the potential to reduce dissatisfaction and alienation for the complaining persons. Such procedures alone are not expected to increase the power of citizens. The usual routes for grievances are, first, to the school or agency involved, then to a representative (alderman, state legislator, congressman) or to the courts.

Citizen polls were considered in chapter 6. It is possible that polls may collect individual opinions resulting in a broader more powerful assessment than is possible by individuals acting alone. However, if no action need follow the poll, no power is changed. In any event polls are not likely to bring about important increases in citizen power over policies or practices in education. For polls to be important, educators must be convinced of the legitimacy of citizen views.

We have not discussed citizen evaluations—special program reviews conducted by teams dominated by citizens. In education, the closest thing to this has long been the survey. In evaluating schools, there are difficult technical issues that have tended to require professional assistance. There seems little interest in replacing professional surveyors by citizen-evaluators. If this mode of participation becomes an important tactic in changing power relations, it will probably be a result of the employment of professionals known to be of a certain persuasion to conduct the survey. We have all seen surveys whose goals of either firing or whitewashing the superintendent have been only partially concealed.

We turn next to a form of citizen participation that does seem to have the potential of enhancing citizen power: the citizen organization of boards and committees.

Participation that Enhances Power

Boards and committees can be classified by the level of authority that devolves to citizens. A governing board, at one extreme, determines policies, selects (and dismisses or rejects) personnel, approves budgets, and evaluates the quality of the service (education) provided. An advisory committee, at the other extreme, may serve only as a forum for the project staff to tell citizens about their program. Between these poles are committees of limited authority that have one or two limited responsibilities. The most important distinction is, however, between boards and committees (ibid., p. 25).

Studies of boards and committees support the conclusion that these forms of participation have an impact on the conduct of local public activities and services (ibid., p. 31). Nevertheless, participation on boards or committees is not likely to increase generalized trust in government. Moreover, bystanders—citizens who are not on boards or committees—are not likely to increase their trust because they can observe other citizens participating in government programs (ibid., p. 35).

The positive finding for participation was in the sense of having some effect on government actions: "a higher level of political participation is consistently associated with an increased sense of efficacy" (ibid., p. 36). This effect was not necessarily found in regard to participation in local school associations. Yin et al. conclude that "political participation generally is related to a general sense of political efficacy, but participation in local organizations may be related only to a sense of efficacy in regard to the specific program or activity" (ibid., p. 39).

When we consider parent participation in PTAs, we find Jencks reporting (1972, pp. 89-90) a conclusion that parent participation in an advisory form of citizen participation (the PTA) may also be linked to program effectiveness. This finding, drawn from the Coleman Report (Coleman et al. 1966), is one of the few arguments based on research for participation. In his own massive report, we find Jencks arguing for central financing, "both as a means of equalizing expenditures and as a way of making local schools somewhat more responsive to groups they have traditionally ignored" (Jencks et al. 1972, p. 258).

Despite the reported association of participation and student achievement, it is premature to make this claim. There are obvious and serious research questions to be raised about the meaning of the positive association between PTAs and children's learning. At this time, it is better to make the case that "an innovation like community control, for example, is not merely to be measured narrowly in terms of cognitive effects, but in the broadest sense of what it means to gain control over some part of one's life" (Grannis 1973, p. 9). That was the major focus of the RAND study. In summary, the RAND studies concluded that citizen participation increased citizen influence without hurting program effectiveness. Boards were found to be more powerful than committees. The participation cannot guarantee an improvement in the level of political alienation in society. The essence of the report is found in the recommendations. The study team recommended that "citizen-dominated boards have the following principal characteristics:

> Citizen-members are elected.
>
> Other citizen and community organizations are represented.
>
> Resources sufficient to support a staff reporting directly to the board are provided.
>
> The formal authority possessed by such boards includes at least the powers to influence substantially their program's budget and to investigate the complaints of citizens. [Yin et al. 1973, pp. 78-79]

Participation for Individual Problems

The preceding discussions have concentrated on involving citizens as a class. Conceivably, in the best of all possible worlds attention to the group needs would concurrently remove irritants to individuals. Since this is not a perfect world, educators will need to devise procedures for receiving and dealing with particular, personal problems of one or only a few citizens whether or not new forms of participation are adopted for the public in general.

The enlightened adversary tactic. This parent-centered approach implicitly assumes an adversary relationship between parents and educators. The orientation is conveyed clearly in an early section of Ellen Lurie's book, *How to Change the Schools: A Parent's Action Handbook on How to Fight the System:*

> My book is not the least bit intellectual; it is neither objective nor dispassionate. It is specific about the things I, and many of my fellow parents,

> hate most about the school system. And it suggests very tangible things other parents can do to try to change things. [1970, p. 8]

Lurie alerts her readers to abuses committed by schools and furnishes what is, in effect, a manual of tactics to battle "the real enemy: the school system" (ibid., p. 266). Educators should read Lurie carefully—not to protect themselves against attack, but to gain a new perspective on their activities.

In most cases, Ms. Lurie's charges are well founded. If educators find that their own schools feature some of the deplorable practices she castigates, they would be well advised to take the lead in making changes—not to beat critics to the punch, but because it is the sensible, humane action required by the situation.

In the same genre as Lurie's *Handbook* is *The Third Side of the Desk* by Hannah S. Hess (1973). This is another guide for parents and has the subtitle "How To Change the Schools." It is based on the case history of P.S. 84 in New York. Hess deals as much with curriculum and teaching methods as with confrontation tactics. Her goal is a more humane, child-supportive education regardless of the governance model that exists in the system: "to me, community control is only a tool to get good education. It is not an end in itself" (ibid., p. 271). If they cannot read the entire book, educators will certainly wish to study the "Screening Committee Questions" used to select a prospective principal (ibid., p. 260).

A more legalistic approach is taken by Freedom Through Equality, Inc., which assumes that, through existing rules and regulations, parents can make the schools respond. The slogan is: "Know Your Rights. See That Your Children Get the Education They Deserve" (1972, p. 1). The chapter headings of the publication, *A Handbook for Parents: Make the Public Schools Work for You,* suggest the scope of advice.

How to Assert Your Rights
How Your Child Can and Cannot Be Disciplined
What Schools and Classes Should Your Child Attend
Make Sure Educators Know You
School Records
Transportation
What There Is To Learn at School
Assistance Available to Needy Children

Title I Programs

Overcrowding and School Redistricting

Parent Groups and Community Organizations

Parents are advised that principals should be their first and strongest pressure point.

> Principals are free to make many important decisions without going through the school board. They are close to teachers and students. They are responsible for knowing what is happening in their school and must be able to account for it to the school board. But you should not let them forget that their first duty is to the children in the school. [Ibid.]

After reviewing a handbook such as this, educators may well wish to prepare one themselves if there is none available. One way to respond to the demand for accountability is to delineate guidelines of reciprocal responsibility similar to those set down in *A Handbook for Parents.*

Ombudsmen. The ombudsman concept became popular in government at all levels and in universities during the late 1960s (Rowat 1968, p. xii). It was not introduced into public school education until much later. In November 1973 the Seattle, Washington, schools reported that there were then only two major school systems (Seattle and Montgomery County, Maryland) that had ombudsmen (p. 12).

The term is appearing more frequently in educational publications. The Wichita, Kansas, schools now have an ombudsman who "is a neutral independent person who helps citizens with complaints about, suggestions for, or questions concerning the school system. In short, the Ombudsman's job is to be of service to you when you do not know where to turn for help" (brochure, n.d.). The ombudsman in Wichita was employed through a federal grant to the League of Women Voters. He reports to an advisory committee of parents, students, and representatives of community agencies and minority groups.

It is generally intended that the ombudsman should investigate individual complaints. Typically he has little actual authority to implement his recommendations. When an ombudsman is used in education, it would seem most helpful to have an analysis of the type and frequency of citizen complaints. The "Guidelines for the Office of the Ombudsman" in Seattle require that "the Ombudsman shall present a quarterly report of his work to the Superintendent and the Board. The report will preserve appropriate confidentiality of personnel for whom the Ombudsman has provided service" (Bottomly 1973).

The ombudsman concept has been extended to high schools in Cincinnati where eight students in each high school are being trained in communications, mediation, rumor control, conflict management, student rights, and problem analysis by the National Conference of Christians and Jews (NCCJ). The ombudsmen have an office, complete with phone and confidential files. They receive credit or a minimum wage for their work (*The BASA Adminovator* 1974, p. 1). The NCCJ is preparing a brochure that will describe the program; it may be obtained from their office (Mary Coyle, student intern, NCCJ, 1974: personal communication).

Ombudsman programs have met with modest success so far in education. In Dayton, Ohio, the work of the ombudsman increased confidence in local government, schools included. However, awareness of the existence and role of the ombudsman was "greatest among white respondents and those at higher education and income levels" (Public Opinion Center 1973).

It seems unlikely that the ombudsman can play an important part in increasing citizen participation in school affairs. The office does serve a temporary function as a kind of safety valve or as a symbol of concern for the individual citizen. In actual practice, most complaints are unfounded. Nevertheless the existence of the vehicle to register the complaint—valid or not—serves a useful role.

TACTICS OF PARTICIPATION

We have not attempted in this chapter to offer specific suggestions to educators seeking to bring about more and better citizen participation in educational policy formation. This is a deliberate omission due to our position that what is good practice in one situation may not work at all in another place. We are supported in this opinion by the reports of veterans of citizen-participation committees. When refusing to provide a list of do's and don'ts based on what they had learned, they commented:

> the truth is that such a list would really not help you. It might in fact be harmful, because each city is different; each state is different. . . . What works best in Philadelphia might be disastrous strategy in Nashville. [Arnstein 1972]

Despite the need to avoid citing cure-alls, some specific practices must be identified to serve as examples—not prototypes—of ways of providing for citizen participation. Much has been written about school-community advisory committees (see Kolodny 1970; Crockett 1971; Oakland Public Schools 1971; *Ohio School Boards Association Journal* 1972; Murphy n.d.; and New Jersey State Department of Education n.d.). However, it will be more efficient to draw primarily on one source for purposes of providing one pattern of practices. The source selected is Dale Mann's book, *A Principal's Handbook for Shared Control in Urban Community Schools* (1973).

Mann maintains that shared control has three characteristics:

1. the regular opportunity for community participation in a comprehensive range of policy matter;
2. the inclusion of all relevant points of view; and
3. the probability that the community's participation will have an effect on school policy. [Ibid., p. 5]

Mann takes up three different ways of selecting members for school-related groups: appointment, election, and a combination of appointment and election. He does not recommend appointment except for the unusual situation of selecting an ad hoc group to plan a better method of selection. He believes that appointed groups—no matter who does the appointing—will not be perceived as representative groups.

Elections are the preferred method of selecting citizen members for the committee or board. Any adult residing in the school district would be eligible to vote and all would be eligible to run for election except persons employed by the school. Proper notice of the election should be made well in advance by different media (for example, announcements, leaflets, telephone). Candidates should be nominated by petitions requiring only a few signatures and all should run at large except in some high school districts where such an arrangement would leave some areas unrepresented (ibid., pp. 18-20).

Elections should be held at the school during a time that is convenient for most people. Mann suggests the night of the school Open House. He would have the election held over a thirty-six-hour period to make it easier for voters to get to the polling place. Ballots would be secret and available in all relevant languages. Proof of residence (no minimum time limit) would be required and voters sign a list before they vote. A prompt, *public* counting of ballots is important. Candidates getting the most votes are elected (ibid., p. 21).

Combined election and appointment has the potential of insuring broad representation. For example, half the seats on a committee could be assigned to community organizations. The organizations could then elect or appoint their representatives according to their own policies. The other seats on the committee would be filled by an election of candidates at large as described above. The potential flaw in the combined election and appointment procedure is that it is possible that the organizations could double their influence by working to secure the election of additional members of their group. Clearly, the methods used to select members of the committee have great influence on the sort of committee resulting from the process (ibid., p. 23).

Authority of School-Community Groups

Mann begins his discussion of the activities of school-community groups with the assumption that neither total professional control nor total community control is possible. Principals in cooperation with the school-community group should consider five factors that help determine the role of the group:

> The interests and abilities of the neighborhood group itself.
>
> Other possible factors (teachers' unions, the central board, community action groups, and so on).
>
> Legal restraints (federal, state, and local laws, regulations, guidelines, contracts, and so on).
>
> The estimated effects of the involvement on achieving the school's goals.
>
> The availability of the means and opportunity to influence decisions. [Ibid., p. 28]

Areas of concern to school-community groups include curriculum policy, budget policy, personnel, and student concerns. The involvement of the school-community group should be at the policy level, not at the level of day-to-day operating decisions. The extent of involvement is developmental and it varies from one area to another. Intensity and scope of involvement in any one issue is a matter for continuing, mutual resolution. If no compromise can be arranged, the principal may have to invoke his legal authority to prevail. This resort to legal authority should be avoided whenever possible because it can have serious and debilitating consequences on school-community relations.

Organization of the School-Community Group
An odd-numbered group of between nine and fifteen members is suggested. The creation and distribution of clear bylaws can help prevent misunderstandings. Meetings should be planned on a schedule related to the timing of school decisions. The agenda should be conspicuously posted and circulated before meetings. With rare exceptions, all meetings should be public.

Mann calls attention to the need to provide information and training to both community and school faculty. Staff anxiety can be lessened when teachers participate in the public planning of the involvement procedures. Citizen representatives need orientations to school policy as well as practice in working together to arrive at group decisions. Finally, it would be especially helpful if the school-community group could meet with early success. This requires attention to a local issue of real importance but of manageable proportions rather than a major reform in educational practice. When the group achieves a success, it should be commended and publicized by the principal (ibid., p. 53).

NEED FOR BALANCE

To this point we have been examining ways of increasing citizen participation in school activities. Reasons for this emphasis have been reiterated in several places throughout the book. An additional reason is that, in general, throughout the entire nation, citizens do not have adequate access or influence to affect educational policies and practices.

Although the prevailing condition justifies the stress on increasing participation, it is necessary to acknowledge that, obviously, this is not universally true. There are certainly situations where school-community relations are ideal. There are also certainly situations where there is too much citizen participation in school activities! For this reason, it is necessary to consider the problem of securing and retaining an appropriate balance between community participation and professional autonomy.

An excellent theoretical conceptualization of the need for balance in the relationship between schools and communities was provided by Eugene Litwak and Henry J. Meyer. They identified at least three points of view among educators concerning the importance of the community in meeting school objectives: "closed door," "open door," and "balanced" (Litwak and Meyer 1974, pp. 4-6).

The "closed door" point of view holds that community involvement is extraneous and possibly harmful to the education of the students. This is the bureaucratic position widely held in European school systems. A community relations program for those who believe in this way would attempt to keep a maximum distance between schools and communities. Educators of this belief would reason that parents and others (including aides and volunteers) could only interfere with the effectiveness of the professionals.

"Open door" advocates believe that schools are only one of many educational institutions affecting students. Moreover, they assume that motivation for learning arises from the everyday, out-of-school lives of students. This is the position once ascribed to "progressive educators" and now held by many who favor a liberal, pupil-centered education. Community relations for these educators would lessen the distance between school and community and encourage closer contact.

The "balanced" position recognizes some merit in both of the other positions. Educators of the "balanced" persuasion acknowledge that sometimes schools and communities are so close that professional performance suffers and sometimes they are so far apart that they may be working against each other. These educators believe that there is an optimal social distance between the extremes of intimacy and isolation. Community relations for these educators would be designed to achieve an optimum balance. In a community of immigrants who fear and distrust the school, the need would be to close the distance between school and the community. In "Pill Hill," where a majority of professional, affluent parents intervene too often and too closely in school affairs, the need would be to increase the distance. In a community with both kinds of parents, the need would be to decrease and increase distance at the same time according to the group concerned—immigrants or professionals. The "balanced" position assumes that cooperation between expert professionals and others in the community is necessary.

Linking Mechanisms for Schools

Maintaining the appropriate balance is largely a function of linking mechanisms. These mechanisms may or may not be viewed by the schools as deliberate community relations tactics. Litwak and Meyer identify eight practices that seem to relate schools to their communities. The linking mechanisms are: detached worker, opinion leader, settlement house, auxiliary voluntary association, common messenger, mass media, formal authority, and delegated function (ibid., pp. 16-18).

Detached worker. The detached worker is a professional person sent to the community to develop a more trusting relationship. Some school-community coordinators serve in this manner. School nurses, social workers, and parent partners represent this approach. Teachers and principals who visit the homes of their students may be operating to the same effect as detached workers.

Opinion leader. In this linking mechanism, the educator uses the influence of the natural leaders of the community. It is hoped that gaining the support of the key leader will cause him to deliver the support of his group. Some bond issue or millage campaign strategies rely heavily on this approach.

Settlement House. This mechanism provides facilities and professional staff in the community. The staff can influence parents and others to support school objectives and to lessen the social distance. Community school programs and, to some extent, lighted schoolhouse programs are examples of this tactic.

Auxiliary voluntary agency. This linking mechanism brings together educators and members of the community. The familiar PTA or mothers club are good examples of auxiliary voluntary agencies. Usually the officers of the voluntary agency are not educators.

Common messenger. In this mechanism, persons who are members of both the community and the school are used as messengers. They can communicate both ways. Examples are students, paid aides, volunteers, and members of local boards or committees.

Mass media. This mechanism includes the typical media described in chapter 9 on public relations: bulletins, newspapers, radio, television, posters, and so on.

Formal authority. This is the authority of law or tradition that requires members of the community to conform to school requirements. Principals have this kind of authority. Attendance officers may also use delegated formal authority.

Delegated function. This mechanism delegates a responsibility to another organization that, in turn, links itself to the school community. The other organization may be a social agency or a medical agency.

The selection of which linking mechanisms to use is based on the goals of the school (to increase or decrease social distance) and principles of communication. (These principles are: initiative, intensity, focused expertise, and scope. Since their definitions are not essential to the development of the argument, they are not explained here. Any communications principles could be used. But, see Litwak and Meyer [1974], pp. 19-25.) Table 11-2 gives an overview of the utility

TABLE 11-2 COMPARATIVE USEFULNESS OF LINKING MECHANISMS USED BY SCHOOLS

Linking Mechanism	Estimated usefulness to:	
	close social distance	create or maintain social distance
Detached worker	Very high	Very low
Opinion leader	Potentially moderate	Very low
Settlement house	High, potentially very high when community is friendly	Very low
Voluntary association	Moderate, potentially very high when community is friendly	Moderate
Common messenger	Low	High
Mass media	Low	High
Formal authority	Very low	Very high

of the eight linking mechanisms for two major positions on school-community relations. It is adapted and abridged from Litwak and Meyer, who included the third position, "balanced," which is omitted from table 11-2. To generate the missing data on "balanced" school-community relations, readers need only restate the information provided in the other two columns. For example, the linking mechanism of detached worker is *very high* for closing social distance and *very low* for creating or increasing social distance. The missing "balanced" column would read: "very high when distance is to be decreased (for example, when the community is hostile); very low when distance is to be increased (for example, when the community is too involved)" (ibid., p. 27).

There are, of course, other linking mechanisms used by schools. It should also be evident that linking mechanisms—as we noted for public relations practices—cannot make a difference if the substance of the educational program in the schools is inadequate or not congruent with community goals.

Linking Mechanisms for Communities

Although most of our readers are more concerned with the use of linking mechanisms from the educator's perspective, the reciprocal nature of school-community relations requires attention to linking mechanisms by which the community attempts to influence the school. Some of the mechanisms are similar but there are important differences. Among the linking mechanisms available to the community are: advocate bureaucracy, strategic influencers, voluntary associations, mass media, ad hoc demonstrations, sustained collective action, common messenger, and individual ad hoc contact (ibid., pp. 35-40).

Advocate bureaucracy. The community may seek to use one bureaucracy to change another. Sometimes pressure groups (discussed in chapter 4) serve this purpose. The intervention of the ACLU on behalf of the rights of married students to participate in extracurricular activities and of the NAACP to remove racial bias from curriculum materials are examples of advocate bureaucracies. Law firms who bring suits against school systems and even newspaper "action lines" that investigate citizen complaints are also examples.

Strategic influencers. This mechanism consists of using the support of an important, powerful person on behalf of the community objective. The influential person may be within the school system or outside it. Securing the support of the governor for a decentralization plan is an easy example. Persuading the curriculum director or an assistant superintendent of the need to revise certain materials is going "over the head" of the principal to bring additional influence to bear on a community objective.

Voluntary associations. We have noted the role of the PTA as a possible school-community linking mechanism. Clearly, it can, and does, work both ways, school to community and community to school. Independent "Save Our Schools" types of organizations are other examples of voluntary associations acting to accomplish community goals.

Mass media. The media are not available on a regular basis but can be used to add to the impact of demonstrations or meetings or by creating newsworthy events. The tactic of serving as an information source to a sympathetic reporter is well known to more affluent, suburban critics of the schools. Reporters rely on such sources and are willing to cooperate and protect the identity of the news source if this should be necessary. Often the best access to mass media may be through an advocate bureaucracy, as discussed above.

Ad hoc demonstrations. This approach is often used in conjunction with the mass media to gain additional support for a community objective. Picketing, boycotts, marches, sit-ins are all examples of demonstrations. It is difficult, even for the initiators, to control the outcomes of demonstrations.

Sustained collective action. This mechanism resembles demonstrations, but is really a more sustained collective action against the school or school system to be changed. In addition to publicizing the community cause, this approach may cause economic damage—the loss of state aid due to sustained student boycotts. A strong organization is needed to support the strikes, boycotts, and other tactics characteristic of sustained collective action.

Common messenger. As mentioned above in the discussion of school linking mechanisms, a common messenger belongs to both the school and the community group. Some common messengers are employees, ranging from teachers (high powered) to crossing guards (low powered). Volunteers, board members, and students are all common messengers. An innovative use of common messengers is found in the Palo Alto, California, School-Community Input Team (SCIT). The SCITs, used to augment educational planning, are made up of citizens, parents, staff, and students (see Palo Alto Unified School District 1973).

Individual ad hoc contact. This mechanism refers to all of the individual parent contacts to complain, get information, inform schools, or for any other purpose. It has been discussed to a large extent in a section above, "Participation for Individual Problems."

An analysis of the community-initiated linking mechanisms by principles of communication helps determine which ones are most appropriate in a particular set of circumstances. Although examples of this analysis are supplied by Litwak and Meyer, readers are cautioned that, "with our present state of knowledge, the development of a community program to affect school-community relations will involve complex assessments, value judgments, and much trial and error" (1974, p. 50).

Although the balance theory is untested, it has much to offer educators seeking a rationale to support their school-community relations activities. The logic is compelling even though we may never be able to design a study that will provide a sound empirical base. Many subjective analyses can be made by educators. Certainly, at least in the area of school-community relations, we will never know anything if knowing comes only from the controlled research models of psychologists and statisticians. Educators, especially school administrators, will need to employ other ways of knowing (see March 1973, pp. 49-54).

IMPORTANT DEVELOPMENTS

It is, with apologies to Dickens, both the best of times and the worst of times to study citizen participation in education.* It is the best of times because of the unprecedented attention being given to the role of citizens and their schools at all levels of governance (see, for example, Guthrie and Skene 1974). It is the worst of times because the course of events is uncertain, the outcomes are in doubt, the search for consensus is still underway. Some of our colleagues are seeking to discover better ways of involving citizens in the educational institutions much as they are presently structured (Milwid, Scott, and Canizales n.d.). Others are gathering data about the participation of citizens in one or another of the departures from conventional educational institutions (see, for example, Lucco and Mosher 1974; Porter and Porter, forthcoming). The issues of decentralization or community control are unresolved and the larger issue of the survival of local influence or growth of centralization is perceived differently. (Fantini and Weinstein [1968, p. 60] predict an increase in local

---

* From *A Tale of Two Cities* (1859). The entire quotation seems as though Dickens were writing about education in the United States in the mid-seventies. "It was the best of times, it was the worst of times, it was the age of wisdom, it was the age of foolishness, it was the epoch of incredulity, it was the season of Light, it was the season of Darkness, it was the spring of hope, it was the winter of despair."

community control; Guthrie and Skene [1974] predict an erosion in local control and more centralization.) It is difficult and frustrating to close a study of school and community interaction in such an indeterminate situation. Perhaps, that is, however, the most certain conclusion possible today: school-community relationships are in a state of change.

NCSPS to NCCE

Since chapter 4 on pressure groups was completed, one of the groups surveyed has changed in name and function. What was the National Committee for the Support of Public Schools (NCSPS) is now the National Committee for Citizens in Education (NCCE). What was a Washington-based centralized genteel lobbying organization has become "an action-oriented public interest organization . . . to build a broad-based constituency for education; press for educational reforms and . . . help citizens to act on future alternatives" (Bowen and Marburger to Carey, 12 April 1974). The NCCE has launched a series of six open public hearings to secure testimony from teachers, educators, administrators, citizens, and experts on:

> Who controls public education.
> Who should control public education.
> What are or should be the roles of citizens in public education.
> How the system is changing.
> The desirability of change; what are the factors causing and governing these changes. [*NCCE Report* February/March 1974, p. 1]

Witnesses at the first hearing (held in Minneapolis) included superintendents, board members, state representatives, the State Commissioner, President of the State Board, Director of the State Department of Human Rights, Minneapolis Federation of Teachers, City of Minneapolis Education Association, President of the S.E. Community Education Council, Alternative Schools Parent Council Advisory members, Indian Community Concerns, President of the Minneapolis Research Institute, Citizens for Integrated Education, and a representative of an accountability project (*NCCE Report* April 1974, p. 3). The reports and recommendations of these meetings may be influential documents in themselves.

Institute for Responsive Education

The Institute for Responsive Education, headed by Don Davies, who was formerly Deputy Commissioner of the United States Office of

Education, is attempting to discover alternative forms of citizen participation at the same time as it works with agencies and individuals seeking improved tactics (*Education Summary* 3 August 1973, p. 3). According to Davies,

> the aim should not be unilateral, absolute power for citizens, but rather a more equitable sharing of power among the professionals, the elected or appointed central school board, and the consumer (parents, citizens, and students). Increased power for the citizens in the governance of the schools will help to create more effective, responsive educational institutions. [*Citizen Action in Education* Winter 1974, p. 1]

Davies is already able to deal directly to the problem of making schools more responsive. First, he maintains that citizens need expert, staff help. The job cannot be done entirely by volunteers. Second, Davies believes that real influence needs to be based on an alliance that crosses racial, ethnic, and class lines. Moreover, an effective group, to be taken seriously, must have staying power. The alliance or group should deal with the *substance* of education as well as the more apparent administrative and organizational issues (i.e., what is taught as well as the district boundaries or bus schedule). Davies's advice at this stage is important for citizens who seek the cooperation of educators: "the citizen educators should be devoted to *changing* the system, *not* destroying it" (*Education Summary*, loc. cit.).

Davies sees the Institute for Responsive Education as "one of a burgeoning number of efforts and enterprises with similar goals—to develop more effective, responsive educational institutions and to increase the average citizen's influence over the forces that affect his or her life" (*Citizen Action in Education* Winter 1974, p. 10). The Six Year Program of the Institute is:

> To identify and assess alternative models for effective citizen participation in educational decision making; to increase citizen interest and voluntary activity in the schools.
>
> To assist local groups by providing leadership training, consultant help, information, and materials.
>
> To increase the understanding of and support by citizens, parents, and educators for citizen participation in decision making.
>
> To encourage better utilization of corporate resources for school reform.
>
> To conduct informational activities—conferences, seminars, publications—and to help create a network of communications and mutual assistance among local citizens groups. [Institute for Responsive Education n.d.]

Kettering Foundation Projects

The Charles F. Kettering Foundation is supporting modest research projects that are intended, to quote the 1973 annual report, to "offer citizens and their institutions new techniques for constructive interaction as a way of making communities and 'governments' more effective in responding to their collective and individual interests" (p. 20). Like Davies, the foundation is not seeking increased citizen involvement per se, "but rather the development of new strategies, institutions, and techniques that can enable citizens to be more effective when and as they choose to be involved" (ibid., p. 21).

The Kettering Foundation is planning a communication network of "citizen involvement program leaders around the nation to stimulate an active exchange of information and ideas" (*New Ways* Summer 1973, p. 8). Kettering sponsors ombudsman programs and opinion polls. The report of the Kettering conference on school-community relations is essential reading for school administrators (Institute for the Development of Educational Activities 1973; see also *New Ways* Spring 1972, p. 8).

"The Responsiveness of Public Schools to Their Clientele Program"

The "Responsiveness" program is directed by L. Harmon Ziegler in the University of Oregon Center for the Advanced Study of Educational Administration (CASEA). Ziegler and his colleagues in CASEA are concerned that "there is a lag of at least four or five years between a change in citizen demands and the response of school districts to those demands" (*R & D Perspectives* Spring 1973, pp. 3-5). Their early studies looked at the way schools responded, to whom they responded, the kinds of influence observed, how influence was used, how decisions were made and the results of these processes. Based on these studies they generated 14,700 propositions describing various conditions under which they would consider school systems responsive. From the 14,700 propositions, they drew 75 of the most practical to present a view of conditions favorable for successful reforms (*Center* 1974, p. 9).

Based on the data secured in the early studies, the CASEA project group developed four models of decision-making structures: hierarchical, bargaining, polyarchical, and market oriented. The models include information about the costs and benefits of each for communities.

Hierarchical model. In this model, decision making is controlled by the leader through a typical, bureaucratic chain of command structure. The leader at the top of the scalar chain controls most of the decision resources. He cannot be overruled or ousted by voting or other negative expressions of subordinates. Even this most authoritative, centralized of the models would be considered responsive if it were the system preferred by the community. Otherwise, it would not be considered responsive.

The polyarchical model. In this model, resources are controlled by several leaders (for example, the superintendent, teachers' organization, PTA). The amount of decision-making resources controlled by any one party varies from issue to issue, making continual negotiations necessary.

The market oriented model. In this model, each school contracts independently for teachers and services. Even the superintendent is considered an auxiliary service.

The bargaining model. In this system each group (PTA, board, superintendent, and so on) negotiates with the others and with the concerned subpublic or factions in the community. The CASEA staff do not endorse this or any of the models but they perceive it as giving the public more ways of making its demands known. The notion is not to replace one model with another but to improve models.

Ziegler and his associates plan to test each of the models in actual practice. One basic source of data will be a demand response log that will detail the actions and reactions of all concerned when a demand is made. The logs will be kept by two research associates in each participating district. Other information will be secured at meetings and, it is hoped, in the offices of individual school administrators (ibid., p. 10).

The CASEA study is an ambitious attempt to provide an empirical basis for advocates of citizen participation. Certainly, experimental controls are lacking. Nevertheless, the observations of the approximations of the prototype models should be a rich source of urgently needed comparative data.

Other models and research studies of citizen participation in school activities are being reported in the educational literature (see, especially, Zelman and Grainer 1974; Pilo 1974; O'Shea 1973 and

1974; Boyd and Seldin 1974). These are all of importance to educators. It is, however, not yet possible to undertake a comprehensive "state of the art" review of progress in this area. Many programs are in the first stages of development. Few data of importance are obtainable at this early stage in the design and observation of new strategies for citizen involvement.

Finally, it needs to be repeated from time to time that improving citizen participation is but one aspect of a complex problem facing citizens and educators. We have maintained throughout these pages that bringing the people and their schools together needs to be accomplished. I trust that no one will accuse us of promising that accomplishing this—reuniting people and schools—will be a sufficient cause for all sorts of improvement. Would it were that simple! Neither have we implied that the task of involving citizens more importantly in the affairs of their schools will be an easy or even a rewarding one—merely that it is necessary.

SUMMARY

This chapter has been a review of ways of increasing and improving citizen participation in education. Different kinds of participation were presented in a kind of ladder of increasing levels of citizen involvement. Boards were found to be more powerful modes of participation than committees. Some kinds of participation such as volunteer service were said to be without increased power for the participant. Some of the more practical guidelines for individuals seeking to influence schools were considered. One manual designed to give specific help to educators seeking to establish school advisory committees was reviewed in some detail.

The need for a balance between citizen participation and professional autonomy was acknowledged and appropriate practices to increase or decrease the distance between schools and communities were evaluated. Finally, important new developments designed to improve citizen involvement were reviewed.

SUGGESTED ACTIVITIES

1. Investigate the degree of citizen participation in school policies at a local or subdistrict level. Place the school or subdistrict participation arrangement on Arnstein's Ladder of Citizen Participation. Explain why you believe your placement is correct.

2. Three benefits are said to come from parent involvement:

   Parents are able to complement the work of educators by becoming informed by their involvement.

   Education will be reformed by the presence of external observers. Educators will become more accountable. Parents may suggest changes.

   Citizens will enjoy the democratic right of participation.

   Make a list of the kinds of evidence you would seek to determine whether these intended benefits were being achieved. Then make a similar list of the major "costs" of parent involvement (for example, some loss of professional autonomy). Then note the kinds of evidence you would seek to determine whether these costs were being incurred.

3. Try to discover the best known, most vigorous critic of the schools in your district. Ask several educators for nominations. When you have identified the critic, analyze his tactics. Compare them with those advised by Lurie in *How to Change the Schools* or to Hess's suggestions in *The Third Side of the Desk.*

4. Identify a school that would be considered "closed door" using Litwak and Meyer's concept of balance in citizen participation. Make a list of all the linking mechanisms used by the school. Do the same for a school that would be considered "open door." Compare the lists of linking mechanisms.

5. Identify a school or a school district that has groups of clients that are:

   Too distant from the school in terms of social climate, and

   Too close, too involved in school activities.

   Try to discover if the school discriminates between the two groups in their community relations practices.

SUGGESTED READINGS

Brown, David S. "The Management of Advisory Committees: An Assignment for the 70's." *Public Administration Review* 22, no. 4 (July/August 1972): 334-342.

Campbell, Clyde. "School-Community Councils." *The Community School and Its Administration* 11, no. 6 (February 1973).

Caputo, David A. "The Citizen Component of Policy Evaluation." *Policy Studies Journal* 2, no. 2 (Winter 1973): 92-97.

Cronin, Joseph M. *The Control of Urban Schools.* New York: The Free Press, 1973. Chapters 8 and 9.

"Curriculum Essays on Citizens, Politics and Administration in Urban Neighborhoods." *Public Administration Review* 32, special issue (October 1972). Entire issue, especially pp. 670-786.

Davies, Don. *Citizen Participation in Education: Annotated Bibliography.* New Haven, Connecticut: Institute for Responsive Education, 1974.

Davies, Don. "The Emerging Third Force in Education." *Inequality in Education* no. 15 (November 1973): 5-12. This entire issue deals with citizen participation.

Denoyer, Richard, and Melancon, Donald. "School Community Development: Kankakee Style." *Illinois Journal of Education* 64, no. 4 (Fourth Quarter 1973-74): 9-11.

Fagan, Dorothy F. "Community Participation in Decision-Making." *Educational Horizons* 52, no. 1 (Fall 1973): 10-13.

Mann, Dale. "Political Representation and Urban School Advisory Councils." *Teachers College Record* 75, no. 3 (February 1974): 279-309.

Nystrand, Raphael O. "Community Action Programs and School Decision Making." *Administrators Notebook* 15, no. 8 (April 1967).

Ornstein, Allan C. *Race and Politics in School/Community Relations.* Pacific Palisades, Ca.: Goodyear Publishers, 1974.

Peterson, Paul E. "Community Representation and the 'Free Rider.' " *Administrator's Notebook* 22, no. 8 (April 1974).

Piele, Philip K. "School-Community Relations." *R & D Perspectives* (Spring 1969): 4-6.

Ravitch, Diane. *The Great School Wars.* New York: Basic Books, 1974.

Safran, Daniel. *Evaluating Parent Involvement,* Issue Paper No. 1, Center for the Study of Parent Involvement, 2544 Etna Street, Berkeley, California 94704, January 1974.

"Symposium on Neighborhoods and Citizen Involvement." *Public Administration Review* 32, no. 3 (May/June 1972). Entire issue.

Thompson, James D. *Organizations in Action.* New York: McGraw-Hill, 1967.

Weeres, Joseph B. "School-Community Conflict in a Large Urban School System." *Administrator's Notebook* 19, no. 9 (May 1971).

REFERENCES

Arnstein, Sherry R. "Eight Rungs on the Ladder of Citizen Participation." In *Citizen Participation: Effecting Community Change,* edited by Edgar S. Cahn and Barry A. Passett. New York: Praeger, 1971.

———. "Maximum Feasible Manipulation." *Public Administration Review* 32, special issue (September 1972): 377-390.

———. "A Ladder of Citizen Participation." *Journal of the American Institute of Planners* 35 (July 1966): 216-224.

BASA Adminovator 1, no. 1 (January 1974): 1. "Focusing on an Experiment in Ombudsmanry."

Bottomly, Forbes. "Memo to Board of Directors, Seattle Public Schools." 27 June 1973.

Bowen, Charles (acting chairman), and Marburger, Carl L. (senior associate), National Committee for Citizens in Education. Letter to Ms. Sarah Carey, chairperson, Commission on Educational Governance, 12 April 1974.

Boyd, William L., and Seldin, Florence. "Desegregation and Decentralization: The Politics of Education in Rochester, New York." Paper read at the American Educational Research Association convention, Chicago, 19 April 1974.

Center 1, no. 1 (1974): 9. "Four Models of School Responsiveness."

Cibulka, James G. "Measuring Formal Citizenship in Educational Programs." *Division Generator* 4, no. 2 (March 1974): 4-12.

Citizen Action in Education 1, no. 1 (Winter 1974): 1. "Searching for a 'Third Force': Can We Put the Public Back into Public Education?"

Coleman, James S., et al. *Equality of Educational Opportunity.* Washington, D.C.: United States Government Printing Office, 1966.

Crockett, Gloria. "Committee's Proposal for Citizen Involvement." Wichita Public Schools, 16 June 1971.

Education Summary, 3 August 1973, p. 3. "Hang in There, Citizen-Educators—Help Is on the Way."

Fantini, Mario, and Weinstein, Gerald. *Making Urban Schools Work.* New York: Holt, Rinehart and Winston, 1968.

Grannis, Joseph. "*Inequality* by Christopher Jencks: Four Critical Reactions." *IRCD Bulletin* 9, no. 1 (January 1973): 9.

Guthrie, James B., and Skene, Paula H. "Local Control Gives Way." *Compact* 8, no. 2 (March/April 1974): 17-21.

Handbook for Parents: Make the Public Schools Work for You. Milwaukee: Freedom Through Equality, Inc., 1972.

Hess, Hannah S. *The Third Side of the Desk.* New York: Scribner's, 1973.

Institute for Development of Educational Activities. *Better School-Community Relations.* Dayton, Ohio, 1973.

Institute for Responsive Education. "A Program to Study and Assist the Process of Citizen Participation in Educational Decision Making." Brochure. New Haven, Conn., n.d.

Jencks, Christopher, et al. *Inequality: A Reassessment of the Effect of Family and Schooling in America.* New York: Basic Books, 1972.

Jencks, Christopher. "The Coleman Report and Conventional Wisdom." In *On Equality of Educational Opportunity,* edited by Frederick Mosteller and Daniel Moynihan. New York: Vintage Books, 1972.

Kolodny, Jules. "Decentralizing an Urban School District." *New York University Education Quarterly* 1, no. 2 (Winter 1972): 17-22.

Litwak, Eugene, and Meyer, Henry J. *School, Family and Neighborhood: The Theory and Practice of School-Community Relations.* New York: Columbia University Press, 1974.

Lucco, Robert J., and Mosher, Edith K. "Decentralization Consensus or Confusion: Defining Citizen Participation in School Policy Formation." Paper read at the American Education Research Association conference, 15-19 April 1974.

Lurie, Ellen. *How to Change the Schools: A Parent's Action Handbook on How to Fight the System.* New York: Random House, 1970.

Mann, Dale. *A Principal's Handbook for Shared Control in Urban Community Schools.* New York: Columbia University, Teachers College, 1973.

March, James G. "Analytical Skills and the University Training of Educational Administrators." Seventh Annual Walter D. Cocking Memorial Lecture given at the National Conference of Professors of Educational Administration, Bellingham, Washington, 16 August 1973.

Milwid, Beth; Scott, Bob; and Canizales, Alma. *Access to the Schools.* San Francisco: The Service Center for Public Education, n.d.

Murphy, Jerome T. "Bureaucratic Politics and Poverty Politics." *Inequality in Education* 6 (n.d.).

New Jersey State Department of Education. *Planning Parent-Implemented Programs.* Trenton, n.d.

NCCE Report 1, no. 2 (February/March 1974): 1. "Commission on Educational Governance to Open Hearings in April."

______ 1, no. 3 (April 1974): 3. "Commission on Educational Governance, First Hearing Minneapolis."

New Ways (Spring 1972): 8. "School-Community Relations."

______ (Summer 1973): 8. "Citizen Involvement."

Oakland (California) Public Schools. "A Master Plan Citizens Committee for the Oakland Public Schools." 20 January 1971.

Ohio School Boards Association Journal 16, no. 10 (October 1972): 19-20. " 'Planned' Is Key Word in Community Involvement."

Ornstein, Allan. "Research on Decentralization." *Phi Delta Kappan* 54, no. 9 (May 1973): 610-614.

O'Shea, David. "Theoretical Perspectives on School District Decentralization." Paper read at the American Educational Research Association convention, Chicago, 15-19 April 1974.

______. "Theoretical Perspectives on School District Decentralization." *Division Generator* 4, no. 1 (December 1973): 11-20.

Palo Alto Unified School District. "The School/Community Input Team as a Social Invention." Palo Alto, Ca., 1973.

Pilo, Marvin R. "Sequential and Organizational Models of School Decentralization: New York City and Detroit." Paper read at the American Educational Research Association convention, Chicago, 19 April 1974.

Porter, David O., and Porter, Teddie Wood. "Searching for Models of Community Influence in Schools: A Theoretical Model and a Study for Independent Schools."

Public Opinion Center. "Public Awareness of the Ombudsman." Press release. Dayton, Ohio, 11 September 1973.

R & D Perspectives (Spring 1973): 3-5. "Four Models of School Responsiveness."

Rowat, D. C., ed. *The Ombudsman: Citizen's Defender.* Toronto: University of Toronto Press, 1968.

Scribner, Jay D., and O'Shea, David. "Political Developments in Urban School Districts." In *Uses of the Sociology of Education: The Seventy-Third Yearbook of the National Society for the Study of Education,* edited by C. Wayne Gordon. Chicago: University of Chicago, 1974.

Seattle Schools. "What's an Ombudsman?—Man in the Middle." Report to Parents, November 1973.

Wichita Public Schools. "School Ombudsman." Brochure, n.d.

Yin, Robert K.; Lucas, William A.; Szanton, Peter L.; and Spindler, J. Andrew. *Citizen Organizations: Increasing Client Control over Services.* Santa Monica, Ca.: RAND Corporation, 1973.

Zelman, Susan and Grainer, Marc. "An Evaluation of Citizen Participation in an Urban School." Paper read at the American Educational Research Association Convention, Chicago, 18 April 1974.

index of authors

index of subjects

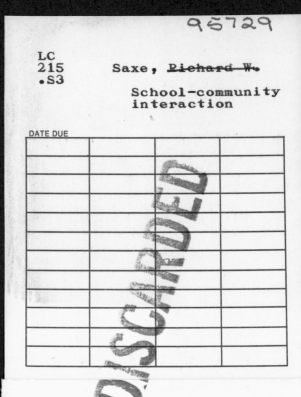